Agency and Responsibility

Essays on the Metaphysics of Freedom

EDITED BY

LAURA WADDELL EKSTROM

THE COLLEGE OF WILLIAM AND MARY

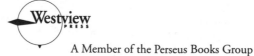

A Member of the Perseus Books Group

Copyright © 2001 by Westview Press, A Member of the Perseus Books Group

Published in 2001 in the United States of America by Westview Press, 5500 Central Avenue, Boulder, Colorado 80301–2877, and in the United Kingdom by Westview Press, 12 Hid's Copse Road, Cumnor Hill, Oxford OX2 9JJ

Find us on the World Wide Web at www.westviewpress.com

Library of Congress Cataloging-in-Publication Data
    Agency and responsibility : essay on the metaphysics of freedom /
edited by Laura Waddell Ekstrom
        p.   cm.
    Includes bibliographical references.
    ISBN 0-8133-6624-0 (pbk. : alk. paper)
    1. Free will and determinism.   2. Metaphysics.   I. Ekstrom, Laura Waddell.

BJ1461 .A32   2000
123'.5—dc21
                                                                00-043329

The paper used in this publication meets the requirements of the American National Standard for Permanence of Paper for Printed Library Materials Z39.48–1984.

10   9   8   7   6   5   4   3   2   1

Contents

v

PART III
FREE WILL AND MORAL RESPONSIBILITY

Introduction

LAURA WADDELL EKSTROM

Concerns over free will and responsibility arise most readily in reaction to particularly bizarre and devastating manifestations of human agency. Consider the following, a selection of the countless examples that might be drawn from recent news accounts. Eric Harris and Dylan Klebold plan and execute a shooting rampage at Colorado's Columbine High School, murdering and wounding fellow students and then killing themselves. A young Virginian man babysitting a friend's infant daughter shakes the crying child in frustration and, since that fails to stop her screaming, submerges her in a tub of scalding water, causing injuries from which she eventually dies. A prison inmate in New Hampshire, in fear of the new millennium, sews together his eyes and lips with a needle and dental floss.

Deep puzzlement over such cases begins from the recognition that these events do not merely happen. Rather, like all human actions, ranging from the heroic to the horrific, they are *done* or performed. Acts of generosity and massacre alike, loving care and child abuse, self-nourishment and self-abasement, have behind them human agency—all are undertaken and directed by human selves. Reflection on this fact helps to make plain why the problem of understanding such behaviors is so difficult. In part it is because the various strategies for understanding these behaviors affect our self-image—or more precisely, because they bring to the fore the fact that our self-image is itself inchoate and perhaps internally inconsistent.

I. Competing Pictures of Agency

Two "pictures" of human agency vie for our allegiance. According to one of them, every individual develops by way of psychological, social, and biological processes, beginning at the moment of conception, when genetic

1

material of the biological mother and father combine to form a unique structure. According to information encoded in this complex of genes, the organism grows in size and complexity from an embryo to a fetus to an infant exhibiting particular physical and psychological traits. Through the expression of the genetic material, and depending on the type and frequency of physical nourishment and touch, the degree of emotional attachment to primary caregivers, and the character of other social interactions, the individual's various systems—endocrine, respiratory, neurological, immune, and so on—develop as they do. The precise neuronal pathways in the brain that grow at an explosive rate in the early years form in response to genetic information and experiences, and they continue to grow and die off in subsequent years through experience and disuse. In short, a complex interaction of genetic and environmental factors (including, among others, traumas, accomplishments, level of poverty or affluence in the home, and quality of nutrition) continues through time to shape an individual's character. Just as a certain flower has the particular features that it does as a result of the properties of the material comprising its bulb and events in its development, so, too, do events determine just who each human being becomes.

According to this first story, behavior is the outward expression of character, and character is the psychological expression of genetically and environmentally produced neurophysiological constitution. In fact, each person is really nothing but a "bag of chemicals": flesh and bones, certainly, but these merely encase and support the more important, intricately fine-tuned array of electrical and chemical signals. Discoveries in the fields of genetics, neuroscience, and psychology continue to increase our ability to explain and predict individuals' beliefs and actions. Human beings, then, are not all that different from molecules—more complex, but just as predictable, since their behavior is as subsumable as that of molecules under natural laws. We are merely biological machines. Call this the scientific or *external* picture of human agency.

The preceding story contrasts with the following one. How I act is up to me, and how you act is up to you. Individuals make their lives; they choose their destinies. In fact, there is no such thing as destiny, in that there is no one particular dramatic or ending point toward which any human life inevitably leads, and no one is pushed along any single course of life by the interaction of genetic blueprint and environment. Rather, to a large extent each of us constructs the person we are by way of our choices concerning what values, preferences, and habits to adopt. Although one might have been raised in a state in which the population votes largely Republican, for instance, one can choose to become a Democrat, and, furthermore, making this choice need not be the necessary outcome of one's formative experiences and genetic endowment.

Early in life, according to this story, each of us began to form preferences: you would rather have had the red ball than the blue one; I liked dancing better than sports. It did not then seem to us that we were forced by anything to prefer one option over the other. We decided what we liked, and we let others know what we preferred. As our intellectual, physical, and emotional capabilities developed, our range of options expanded, and we became better at deliberating over our choices, recognizing more considerations as relevant. As in youth, in adult life it often seems to us that a variety of alternatives are available for what might happen next and that it is up to us to select among them. In other words, the commonsensical view of the future may be depicted as an array of forking paths. Not always, but often, such as when selecting the candidate for whom to vote, choosing how to spend a Saturday afternoon, deciding how to open a lecture, it seems that there are forking paths in front of me: it seems that, given exactly what has come before, the future might unfold in one way and it might unfold in another, depending on my choice. I am, in ordinary circumstances, aware of no force or agent compelling me to choose as I do. In fact, I have evidence that there is no invasive control of my life insofar as my actions follow on my decisions and my decisions follow on my deliberations—which are, it seems to me, directed by me.

According to the second picture of human agency, then, who we are is settled in part by how we freely choose to be, and what we do is not the necessary outcome of natural laws and of the past. There is some *indeterminism* in the construction of the self and hence in the course that our lives take, since the course of our lives is, to some extent, self-directed. This picture of human agency is assumed when we adopt the practical deliberative point of view. It is the way we seem to be subjectively. Call it the *internal* story of human agency.[1]

In one picture of human agency, then, the self is an inevitable product of genetics and environment, and every action is the deterministic outcome of the past and of natural laws. But in the other, who we are is largely a matter of self-creation; we are able to rise above or step outside of environmental influences and choose our actions in a way that is undetermined by what has come before. Because the internal story so easily recommends itself, we ordinarily take ourselves and others to have control over action and, in the absence of any recognized responsibility-undermining condition (such as blameless ignorance, severe psychosis, or coercion), to be morally responsible for what we do. But, of course, a global threat to agent control and hence to responsibility lies implicit in the external story. What to do in the face of these two pictures is deeply perplexing. The essays in this volume address in various ways the tension in our self-image and shed light on a number of issues generated by it. In the remainder of this introduction, I discuss these issues and say something about what remains to be done.

II. Reconciliation Strategies

One reconciliation strategy might be to describe the competing pictures of agency as views from different *standpoints* and suppose them reconciled by pointing out that they are equally true stories, simply told from different perspectives.[2] Despite its initial appeal, this strategy faces an obvious objection from the law of noncontradiction. In the external story, every human action is fully determined by past events and natural laws, and there is never more than one physically possible future. But in the internal story, agents are at least sometimes in the position of facing multiple available pathways into the future, such that which pathway becomes actual is up to their undetermined choice. The standpoint strategy, then, seems only an attempt to legitimate belief in contradictory claims.

One might respond to this objection by claiming that, despite appearances, the two standpoints do not make claims that are in genuine conflict.[3] Suppose we understand practical reasoning as reasoning the purpose of which is to determine the will, to answer the question of what one should do. And suppose we understand theoretical reasoning as reasoning the purpose of which is to describe and explain the world insofar as this can be done without engaging in practical reasoning. Theoretical reason is silent on the question of what we have most reason to do—and thus the claims of practical reason "do not appear" from a theoretical point of view.[4] The claims of theoretical reason are therefore not in conflict with practical claims. Furthermore, one might argue that no theoretical claim could imply that practical reason is impossible or pointless and that, whereas from the theoretical standpoint we have no reason to apply the concepts of freedom and moral responsibility to human actions, we do have reason to regard ourselves and others as free from the practical standpoint.

It is hard to see how this is more than just an expression of the problem. From one perspective we appear to be this way, and from another perspective we appear to be another way; and each perspective is a legitimate one to take. Or, from the theoretical standpoint it is inappropriate to consider our acts free and something for which we are morally responsible; but from the practical standpoint it is appropriate to understand them in this way. The question, "Which *is* it? Are we free in and morally responsible for performing some of our acts or not?" is likely to seem to the standpoint theorist to have missed the point entirely, but it is a question that anyone uncomfortable with the notion of true-from-a-perspective has difficulty shaking off. Consider a particular action of mine. Was this action causally determined by the past and natural laws, or was it not? The response that from one standpoint (the theoretical one) the act was causally determined by the laws and the past (and from this standpoint there is no justified claim that I was free in and am morally responsible for performing the act), whereas from another standpoint (the practical one) the act was undetermined and I was free in performing it, does not help in answering my question. It does not help to answer my question because the act either was determined or was not determined by the past and natural laws. Either at the moment of action there was one physically possible future *or* there was some physical indeterminism allowing the future to develop in any one of multiple ways.

An alternative reconciliation strategy is to say, not that the external and the internal stories are each true *from a certain standpoint,* but rather that the external story *is* true and the internal story is compatible with it, provided we expunge an aspect of the internal story, as I have characterized it, for its inaccuracy. According to the doctrine of causal determinism, there is at every moment exactly one physically possible future. According to the internal picture of agency, I said, we each sometimes, when deciding what to do, find ourselves facing a variety of alternatives for the future, such that which alternative becomes the actual course of events is up to us and is not determined by past events and natural laws. It is this understanding of agent control over action as requiring the falsity of determinism that is the incorrect element of the internal story, according to the traditional Humean compatibilist. A careful analysis of the notion of agent control over action, this reconciliationist alleges, will show that an account perfectly compatible with the external story and hence compatible with causal determinism is sufficient for grounding agents' moral responsibility.

Now if it could be shown that the culprit in generating our (apparently) internally inconsistent self-image is a certain ill-formed notion of agent control, then this would be a welcome result, enabling us to achieve a coherent self-understanding. Many contemporary philosophers, in fact, have been charmed by this compatibilist strategy. Ayer, Frankfurt, Lehrer, Watson, Fischer, and Wolf, among others, have set out detailed accounts of freely performed action (or of action sufficiently under the control of the agent that he may be legitimately held morally responsible for it) that are compatible with the action's being the deterministic outcome of the past and natural laws.

These various accounts of the power or ability central to free agency—such as being able to act as one wishes, unconstrained by threat or strong habit of obedience or psychologically constraining condition such as kleptomania,[5] or being able to act on one's second-order volitions,[6] or being able to act on one's values,[7] or being able to act from an appreciation of the True and the Good[8]—certainly depict valuable assets. But whether any of the accounts is sufficient to the task of characterizing free will remains controversial. Since the accounts are supposed to be attainable on the assumption of causal determinism, when we ask in any case whether the agent could have had a different motivation for action, we are given only the disappointing answer that he could have, in that he *would* have *if* the natural laws and the past had been different from what they actually were. But since the laws and the past were not different but were just as they were, the agent at the moment of decision could not, it seems, have possessed the *ability* to decide or desire or judge any differently than the way he did, as this would amount to an ability to do something such that the proposition that he did it entails the abrogation of a natural law or the falsification of a proposition concerning the past. This is why so many incompatibilist philosophers have taken the position voiced by Elizabeth Anscombe in the following passage:

> Ever since Kant, it has been a familiar claim among philosophers, that one can believe in both physical determinism and "ethical" freedom. The reconciliations have always seemed to me to be either so much gobbledegook, or to make the alleged freedom of action quite unreal. My actions are mostly physical movements; if these physical movements are physically predetermined by processes which I do not control, then my freedom is perfectly illusory. The truth of physical indeterminism is thus indispensable if we are to make anything of the claim to freedom.[9]

Anscombe's position on this question nonetheless remains strenuously contested. Controversy in recent literature has centered on various developments of a certain argument, sometimes called the consequence argument, which may be expressed, roughly, as follows: Since it is not up to me what happened in the distant past, and it is not up to me what the laws of nature are, if my current actions are the consequences of the past and laws, then my current actions are likewise not up to me. Consider one development of that argument.

III. The Metaphysics of Free Will

The language of logic allows us to present the argument with precision. Let '$A_{S,t}\ P$' represent 'S is at t able to bring it about that P is the case' and let '$A_{S,t}\ (\neg P)$' represent 'S is at t able to prevent its being the case that P.' Now consider some true proposition P. The notion of its being *beyond the control of S* at t that P is the case, may be defined as follows:

$$B_{S,t}\ P \equiv P \text{ and } \neg A_{S,t}\ (\neg P)$$

Consider the following inference rule:

Transfer Rule T: If $B_{S,t}\ P$ and $B_{S,t}\ (P \supset Q)$, then $B_{S,t}\ Q$

If some event or state of affairs is completely out of one's control, and it is beyond one's control that a second event or state of affairs is a consequence of the first, then, it seems highly reasonable to believe, the second event or state of affairs is also beyond one's control. For instance, let S represent *you* and let t be *noon today*. Let P represent: Glenn murdered Rita's husband at eleven fifty-nine this morning. Let Q represent: Rita is now a widow. If it is at noon today beyond your control that Glenn murdered Rita's husband at eleven fifty-nine this morning, and it is at noon today beyond your control that (if Glenn murdered Rita's husband at eleven fifty-nine this morning, then Rita is now a widow), then it is at noon today beyond your control that Rita is now a widow.

The following argument for incompatibilism—call it the Beyond Control Argument—uses Transfer Rule T. Let '*P*' stand for the proposition expressing the state of the universe at a past moment, t_0, before the existence of human beings. Let '*L*' stand for the conjunction of all the laws of nature. Let '*A*' stand for the proposition that agent S performs a certain act at time t. The symbol '$\Box$' represents "broadly logical necessity," so that the term '$\Box P$' is to be read *it is logically necessary that P*. Suppose that determinism is true. Then:

1. $\Box((P\&L) \supset A)$
2. $B_{S,t}\, P$
3. $B_{S,t}\, L$
4. $B_{S,t}\, (P\&L)$
5. $B_{S,t}\, ((P\&L) \supset A)$
6. $B_{S,t}\, A$

In addition to Rule T, the Beyond Control Argument relies on the following highly plausible inference rules, the first in arriving at premise 5 from premise 1, the second in deriving premise 4 from premises 2 and 3:

Inference Rule A: If $\Box P$, then $B_{S,t}\, P$

Inference Rule C:[10] If $B_{S,t}\, P$ and $B_{S,t}\, Q$, then $B_{S,t}\, (P\&Q)$

The first premise of the argument expresses the idea that if determinism is true, then our acts are the consequences of the laws of nature and events in the remote past. The second, third, and fourth premises set out precisely the idea that it is not up to us what went on before we were born, and neither is it up to us what the laws of nature are. Rule A, premise 5, and Rule T then show the reasoning leading to the conclusion of the consequence argument, namely, that the consequences of the past and laws (including our present acts) are not up to us. Hence if the thesis of causal determinism is true, then what we do is beyond our control and so our actions are not freely done.

The Beyond Control Argument is one of a family of related arguments for incompatibilism. In "The Incompatibility of Free Will and Determinism," Peter van Inwagen sets out a widely discussed version of the incompatibilist argument, construing free will as the ability to render certain propositions false. Since one cannot render false the conjunction of all the laws of nature (L), and one cannot render false a proposition (P1) expressing the entire state of the world at a moment in the very distant past, and on the assumption of determinism, P1 and L together entail the proposition that one performs a certain act at a particular time, van Inwagen argues, if determinism is true, then one cannot do otherwise than act as one does at that particular time. Hence free will and determinism are incompatible.

But does the argument falter in trading on an ambiguity? In "Are We Free to Break the Laws?" David Lewis argues that it does, since there is no single construal of the phrase "can render false" on which all premises of van Inwagen's argument are true. One might be *able* to render a proposition false (or to violate a law of nature) in either a strong sense or a weak sense. One is able to render a proposition P false in the *strong* sense just in case one can do something such that, if one did it, then P would be falsified by one's act itself or by an event caused by that act. By contrast, one is able to render a proposition false in the *weak* sense just in case one is able to do something such that, if one did it, the proposition would have been falsified somehow or another, but not necessarily by one's own act or by an event caused by one's act. It is, indeed, irrational to suppose that a free determined agent has the ability in the strong sense to render false a proposition concerning the past or to break a law of nature. Yet the compatibilist need not attribute such an incredible power to the free determined agent, Lewis argues. The free determined agent's ability to do otherwise is only a harmless *counterfactual* power over the natural laws (or the past); and thus the incompatibilist conclusion is blocked.

But it is debatable whether the distinction between the strong and weak senses of ability to render false a proposition can be used to undermine the incompatibilist conclusion. John Martin Fischer, in "A New Compatibilism," rejects Lewis's response to van Inwagen, appealing to both the present strict fixity of the past and the present strict fixity of the natural laws. Fischer explores a different response instead: "new compatibilism," reliant on a combination of the view that there is no single, unique actual world (termed *index possibilism*) and the view that all truths are world indexed (and there is a complete catalog of such indexed truths at each time and in each possible world). A new compatibilist asserts that a free determined agent's ability to do otherwise does not entail an ability to act such that the past would be different from what it actually was, since the past, conceived as the complete catalog of world-indexed truths, *does not change* in going from world to world. Fischer argues that new compatibilism nonetheless has highly implausible consequences.

IV. Self-Direction, Identification, and Indeterminism: Accounts of Free Action

This dispute has refined our understanding of the metaphysical issues pertinent to free agency. But it does not settle the matter of what sort of account of freedom answers to our considered judgments concerning the power we want or have reason to want. Incompatibilist arguments assume that free action requires the categorical and not conditionally analyzed ability to do otherwise.[11] Compatibilists, however, have denied this assumption. They suggest that free will is not rightly understood as the ability to do otherwise given the actual past and natural laws but rather as the ability to perform *self-directed* acts, acts uncompelled by an external agent and instead done on one's own.

The nature of the self and what it is to *identify* oneself with a course of action are hence pressing issues. In his influential paper, "Freedom of the Will and the Concept of a Person," Harry Frankfurt observes that persons are able to step back from their desires to pursue certain courses of action (first-level desires) and ask themselves whether or not they desire to have the desires they have. Frankfurt characterizes the self in terms of second-order volitions, or desires for certain first-level desires to lead one to act. He then analyzes free action as the ability to act as one wants at the first and higher levels of desire. Frankfurt's discussion illuminates the self-reflective capacities of persons. But his hierarchical analysis fails to resolve both a problematic regress of desires and the problem of externally imposed higher-level wants. Why should the identity of the self be constituted by higher-level desires, when Frankfurt imposes no strictures on how they were formed?

In response to such problems, Gary Watson proposes in his remarkable paper "Free Agency" that an agent acts freely in acting on values, which Watson characterizes as "those principles and ends which he—in a cool and non-self-deceptive moment—articulates as definitive of the good, fulfilling, and defensible life."[12] One might wonder whether this account is "too rationalistic," as Watson later believes,[13] and whether it falls prey to the problem of the external manipulation of one's evaluative judgments. Nevertheless, the exchange focuses our attention in a fruitful way on capacities central to free agency: to reflect on one's motivations in light of what one finds worthy of pursuit, to identify with certain of those motivations, and to express one's real self in action. These topics are explored with insight by Michael Bratman in "Identification, Decision, and Treating as a Reason." Bratman discusses recent developments in Frankfurt's views and contributes a novel proposal concerning the problem of identification.

But can any amount of reflective evaluation or psychic harmony be sufficient for making one free? Certainly the categorical ability to do, desire, or decide otherwise in the circumstances as a requirement for full agential control does have powerful intuitive support. Nonetheless, incompatibilists themselves face formidable—some say insurmountable—difficulties in formulating an account of free will incorporating indeterminism. Consider the recent remarks of John Dupre:

> It has sometimes been suggested that the arrival of quantum mechanics should immediately have solved the problem of free will and determinism. It was proposed, perhaps more often by scientists than by philosophers, that the brain would need only to be fitted with a device for amplifying indeterministic quantum phenomena.... Acts of free will could then be those that were initiated by such indeterministic nudges.... But this whole idea is hopeless ... despite the initial worries about determinism, indeterminism makes the conception of freedom of the will even less tenable.[14]

The challenge is to show exactly how physical indeterminism, whether at the micro- or the macro-level, might *enable* rather than subvert our power for acting freely. According to a familiar line of objection, insofar as an event is undetermined by prior events, it is entirely random or arbitrary, certainly not controlled. Incompatibilists must provide a positive and plausible account of the nature of a free act.

In "Human Freedom and the Self," Roderick Chisholm suggests that this problem is resolved by supposing that some events are caused not by other events but rather by the agent himself. According to Chisholm's agent-causal theory, free agents have the ability to be "unmoved movers," the initiators of causal chains who are not themselves causally determined to act. Chisholm wishes to explain free action in terms of the primitive notion of causation by an agent, but this merely replaces one set of puzzles with another. So I argue in "Indeterminist Free Action." Drawing on Elizabeth Anscombe's argument for a divorce between the notions of causation and determination, I suggest an account of free action appealing to indeterministic causation among events and not appealing to agent-causation as a primitive notion. A free act results from uncoercively and indeterministically formed preference, understood in a particular way. In "Responsibility, Luck, and Chance: Reflections on Free Will and Indeterminism," Robert Kane cleverly defends a similar causal-indeterminist view, working in particular to address the problem of luck raised against such indeterminist accounts.

Reviewing these competing accounts of free action in succession presents an opportunity to locate and render more precise our pretheoretically inchoate self-image. In which account do we best recognize ourselves and find the fewest theoretical difficulties?

V. Responsibility, Alternative Possibilities, and Frankfurt-type Scenarios

The right answer to this question depends on what we use the concept of free will *for*—what values it is supposed to secure for us. Human dignity is one proposal; creativity, authenticity, and even genuine romantic love are others. But the central source of interest in free will, as I alluded to at the beginning of this chapter, is its connection with moral responsibility. How ought we to respond to the actions of Klebold and Harris at Columbine High School, to the child abuser, and to the self-mutilating inmate: with disgust and horror, to be sure, but tinged with moral reprobation or with clinical objectivity and compassion? More generally, what conditions must an individual meet for him or her to be legitimately blamed or praised for an event?

Our ordinary practices of praise and blame, along with the accompanying institutions of punishment and reward, display sensitivity to considerations of agent control. But how much control and what sort of control are not made precise by any univocal set of intuitive judgments. Traditionally, philosophers have connected moral responsibility with alternative possibilities, suggesting the fitness of an incompatibilist analysis of the requisite type of free will. Several influential recent works, however, have in different ways called into question this traditional association.

In his seminal essay, "Freedom and Resentment," Peter Strawson develops an expressive account of moral responsibility according to which the primary function of our practices of praise and blame is to express or give vent to natural human reactive attitudes, such as anger, resentment, gratitude, and moral indignation. In Strawson's view, the natural and unrenounceable character of such attitudes provides them with justification—they need not be grounded in what Strawson sees as the "obscure and panicky metaphysics" of a libertarian account of free will. But both the claim to unrenounceability and the sufficiency of the expressive account for directing appropriate change in existing practices of praise and blame have been subjected to critical scrutiny.[15]

Susan Wolf challenges the traditional connection between responsibility and alternative possibilities from a different direction in defending what she calls "The Reason View" of moral responsibility. On Wolf's account, morally responsible action is action from an appreciation of the True and the Good or, in other words, action done for right reasons. Wolf's view generates an interesting "asymmetry thesis," according to which, when one does the right act for the right reasons, one need not have had the ability to do otherwise at the time in order to be praiseworthy; yet, when one does the wrong act, one is blameworthy only if one did have the ability to do otherwise at the time one performed the act. The requirement that an agent have the ability to do otherwise to be blameworthy is consistent, Wolf believes, with physical determinism but is inconsistent with the truth of "psychological determinism."[16] The fairness of blaming bad-acting agents whose acts are physically determined and the coherency of praising agents who cannot do otherwise than act in accordance with the True and the Good are controversial.

Some philosophers take the issue of an alternative-possibilities condition for responsibility to have been already put to rest by a certain type of scenario, originally made famous in a paper by Harry Frankfurt.[17] In "Frankfurt-type" scenarios, the subject of much contemporary discussion, the agent performs his act on his own, yet he cannot do otherwise. He cannot do otherwise because a counterfactual intervener waits in the wings: a neurosurgeon who has, unknown to the agent, implanted a device by which she can monitor and control the agent's behavior, or a mind-reader, or some other nefarious agent who *would have* made the agent do exactly what he did, *were* he to be about to do otherwise. Since the counterfactual intervener never in fact intervenes, but only monitors the agent's activity, the alleged intuition is that the agent acts responsibly, although he could not have done otherwise.

"Libertarianism and Frankfurt's Attack on the Principle of Alternative Possibilities," by David Widerker, and "Rescuing Frankfurt-Style Cases," by Alfred Mele and David Robb, are instances of provocative recent work on this issue. It is Widerker's view that Frankfurt-type cases fail to overturn the principle according to which a person must have been able to do otherwise in order to be morally responsible for his or her act. Mele and Robb reconstruct a Frankfurt-type scenario so as not to beg any questions against the incompatibilist and so as not to rely on the existence of any *sign* by which a counterfactual intervener may tell what the agent is going to do. The more sophisticated case, they argue, demonstrates Frankfurt's original point against the principle of alternative possibilities. The exchange raises the question of what sort of principle is correct, if any, concerning the relation between responsibility and alternative possibilities.

Advances in the recent philosophical literature on free will and moral responsibility have sharpened our understanding of the pivotal issues. If after reading the best of what contemporary philosophy has to offer on the subject we find ourselves still struggling for an appropriate response to the puzzling human behavior we encounter, this indicates that further work is in order. Either we need to be shown how two seemingly contradictory pictures of human agency can be reconciled and convinced that we haven't *lost* anything in the reconciliation, or we must be given clearer direction on how to tell which of the two stories to reject.

Notes

I am grateful to George Harris for comments on this essay.

1. Compare Thomas Nagel, "Moral Luck," in *Free Will*, ed. Gary Watson (Oxford: Oxford University Press, 1982), pp. 174–186. Nagel despairs of finding a way to reconcile the competing views of human agents: "I believe that in a sense the problem has no solution, because something in the idea of agency is incompatible with actions being events, or people being things. But as the external determinants of what someone has done are gradually exposed, in their effect on consequences, character, and choice itself, it becomes gradually clear that actions *are* events and people things" (p. 184).

2. Labeling the two pictures the "external" and the "internal" stories may seem to recommend this analysis.

3. In a recent book, *Freedom and Responsibility* (Princeton: Princeton University Press, 1998), Hilary Bok develops an argument along these lines. I do not suppose myself to have done justice to Bok's complex and carefully developed argument, nor do I suppose that she would have no response to my objections.

4. Bok, 1998, p. 74.

5. A. J. Ayer, *Philosophical Essays* (London: Macmillan, 1954), pp. 271–284.

6. Harry Frankfurt, "Freedom of the Will and the Concept of a Person," *Journal of Philosophy* 68, 1971, pp. 5–20. (Reprinted in this volume.)

7. Gary Watson, "Free Agency," *Journal of Philosophy* 72, 1975, pp. 205–220. (Reprinted in this volume.)

8. Susan Wolf, *Freedom Within Reason* (New York: Oxford University Press, 1990), chapter 4. (Reprinted in this volume.)

9. Elizabeth Anscombe, "Causality and Determination," p. 146 in her *Metaphysics and the Philosophy of Mind: The Collected Papers of Elizabeth Anscombe*, University of Minnesota Press. (Reprinted in this volume.)

10. In fact, given that Rule C is derivable from Rule A and Rule T, the argument most basically relies on two inference principles. Proof: 1. $Bs,t\ P$. 2. $Bs,t\ Q$. 3. $\Box[P \supset (Q \supset (P\&Q))]$ 4. $Bs,t\ [P \supset (Q \supset (P\&Q))]$ (from 3 and Rule A) 5. $Bs,t\ [Q \supset (P\&Q)]$ (from 1,4, and Rule T) 6. $Bs,t\ (P\&Q)$. Thomas McKay and David Johnson, in "A Reconsideration of an Argument Against Compatibilism," *Philosophical Topics* 24, 1996, p. 115, present a structurally identical proof of a rule much like C ("the principle of agglomeration") using a somewhat different operator, van Inwagen's 'Np'.

11. For discussion of the conditional analysis of ability, see J. L. Austin, "Ifs and Cans," in his *Philosophical Papers* (Oxford: Oxford University Press, 1961); Peter van Inwagen, *An Essay on Free Will* (Oxford: Clarendon Press, 1983), pp. 114–126; and Laura Waddell Ekstrom, *Free Will* (Boulder: Westview Press, 2000), pp. 58–62.

12. Gary Watson, "Free Agency," p. 105 in *Free Will,* ed. Gary Watson (Oxford: Oxford University Press), 1982. (Reprinted in this volume.)

13. Gary Watson, "Free Action and Free Will," *Mind* 46, 1987, p. 150.

14. John Dupre, "The Solution to the Problem of Freedom of the Will," *Philosophical Perspectives* 10, 1996, p. 385.

15. See Galen Strawson, "On 'Freedom and Resentment'," reprinted in *Perspectives on Moral Responsibility,* ed. John Martin Fischer and Mark Ravizza (Ithaca: Cornell University Press, 1993), pp. 67–100; Fischer, *The Metaphysics of Free Will* (Cambridge, MA: Blackwell, Aristotelian Society series, vol. 14, 1994), pp. 211–213; Ekstrom, *Free Will,* pp. 146–153.

16. Susan Wolf, *Freedom Within Reason,* chapter 5.

17. Harry Frankfurt, "Alternate Possibilities and Moral Responsibility," *Journal of Philosophy* 66, 1969, pp. 829–839.

Part I

The Metaphysical Issues: Free Will and Causal Determinism

1

The Incompatibility of Free Will and Determinism

PETER VAN INWAGEN

In this paper I shall define a thesis I shall call 'determinism', and argue that it is incompatible with the thesis that we are able to act otherwise than we do (i.e., is incompatible with 'free will'). Other theses, some of them very different from what I shall call 'determinism', have at least an equal right to this name, and, therefore, I do not claim to show that *every* thesis that could be called 'determinism' without historical impropriety is incompatible with free will. I shall, however, assume without argument that what I call 'determinism' is legitimately so called.

In Part I, I shall explain what I mean by 'determinism'. In Part II, I shall make some remarks about 'can'. In Part III, I shall argue that free will and determinism are incompatible. In Part IV, I shall examine some possible objections to the argument of Part III. I shall not attempt to establish the truth or falsity of determinism, or the existence or nonexistence of free will.

I

In defining 'determinism', I shall take for granted the notion of a proposition (that is, of a non-linguistic bearer of truth-value), together with certain

From *Philosophical Studies* 27 (1975): 185–199. Copyright 1975 by Kluwer Academic Publishers. Reprinted with kind permission from the author and Kluwer Academic Publishers.

allied notions such as denial, conjunction, and entailment. Nothing in this paper will depend on the special features of any particular account of propositions. The reader may think of them as functions from possible worlds to truth-values or in any other way he likes, provided they have their usual features. (E.g., they are either true or false; the conjunction of a true and a false proposition is a false proposition; they obey the law of contraposition with respect to entailment.)

Our definition of 'determinism' will also involve the notion of 'the state of the entire physical world' (hereinafter, 'the state of the world') at an instant. I shall leave this notion largely unexplained, since the argument of this paper is very nearly independent of its content. Provided the following two conditions are met, the reader may flesh out 'the state of the world' in any way he likes:

(i) Our concept of 'state' must be such that, given that the world is in a certain state at a certain time, nothing follows *logically* about its states at other times. For example, we must not choose a concept of 'state' that would allow as part of a description of the momentary state of the world, the clause, '... and, at t, the world is such that Jones's left hand will be raised 10 seconds later than t.'

(ii) If there is some observable change in the way things are (e.g., if a white cloth becomes blue, a warm liquid cold, or if a man raises his hand), this change must entail some change in the state of the world. That is, our concept of 'state' must not be so theoretical, so divorced from what is observably true, that it be possible for the world to be in the *same* state at t_1 and t_2, although (for example) Jones's hand is raised at t_1 and not at t_2.

We may now define 'determinism'. We shall apply this term to the conjunction of these two theses:

(a)   For every instant of time, there is a proposition that expresses the state of the world at that instant.

(b)   If A and B are any propositions that express the state of the world at some instants, then the conjunction of A with the laws of physics entails B.

By a proposition that expresses the state of the world at time t, I mean a true proposition that asserts of some state that, at t, the world is in that state. The reason for our first restriction on the content of 'state' should now be evident: if it were not for this restriction, 'the state of the world' could be defined in such a way that determinism was trivially true. We could, without this restriction, build sufficient information about the past and future into each proposition that expresses the state of the world at an instant, that, for every pair of such propositions, each *by itself entails* the other. And in that case, determinism would be a mere tautology, a thesis equally applicable to every conceivable state of affairs.

This amounts to saying that the 'laws of physics' clause on our definition does some work: whether determinism is true depends in the character of the laws of physics. For example, if all physical laws were vague propositions like 'In every nuclear reaction, momentum is *pretty nearly* conserved', or 'Force is *approximately* equal to mass times acceleration', then determinism would be false.

This raises the question, What is a law of physics? First, a terminological point. I do not mean the application of this term to be restricted to those laws that belong to physics in the narrowest sense of the word. I am using 'law of physics' in the way some philosophers use 'law of nature'. Thus, a law about chemical valences is a law of physics in my sense, even if chemistry is not ultimately 'reducible' to physics. I will not use the term 'law of nature' because, conceivably, *psychological* laws, including laws (if such there be) about the voluntary behavior—of rational agents, might be included under this term.[1] Rational agents are, after all, in some sense part of 'Nature'. Since I do not think that everything I shall say about laws of physics is true of such 'voluntaristic laws', I should not want to use, instead of 'laws of physics', some term like 'laws of nature' that might legitimately be applied to voluntaristic laws. Thus, for all that is said in this paper, it may be that some version of determinism based on voluntaristic laws is compatible with free will.[2] Let us, then, understand by 'law of physics' a law of nature that is not about the voluntary behavior of rational agents.

But this does not tell us what 'laws of nature' are. There would probably be fairly general agreement that a proposition cannot be a law of nature unless it is true and contingent, and that no proposition is a law of nature if it entails the existence of some concrete individual, such as Caesar or the earth. But the proposition that there is no solid gold sphere 20 feet in diameter (probably) satisfies these conditions, though it is certainly not a law of nature.

It is also claimed sometimes that a law of nature must 'support its counterfactuals'. There is no doubt something to this. Consider, however, the proposition, 'Dogs die if exposed to virus V'. The claim that this proposition supports its counterfactuals is, I think, equivalent to the claim that 'Every dog is such that if it were exposed to virus V, it would die' is *true*. Let us suppose that this latter proposition *is* true, the quantification being understood as being over all dogs, past, present, and future. Its truth, it seems to me, is quite consistent with its being the case that dog-breeders *could* (but will not) institute a program of selective breeding that *would* produce a sort of dog that is immune to virus V. But if dog-breeders could do this, then clearly 'Dogs die if exposed to virus V' is not a law of nature, since in that case the truth of the corresponding universally quantified counterfactual depends upon an accidental circumstance: if dog-breeders were to institute a certain program of selective breeding they are quite capable of instituting, then 'Every dog is such that if it were exposed to virus V, it would die' would be false. Thus a proposition may 'support its counterfactuals' and yet not be a law of nature.

I do not think that any philosopher has succeeded in giving a (nontrivial) set of individually necessary and jointly sufficient conditions for a proposition's being a law of nature or of physics. *I* certainly do not know of any such set. Fortunately, for the purposes of this paper we need not know how to analyze the concept 'law of physics'. I shall, in Part III, argue that certain statements containing 'law of physics' are analytic. But this can be done in the absence of a satisfactory analysis of 'law of physics'. In fact, it would hardly be possible for one to *provide* an analysis of some concept if one had no preanalytic convictions about what statements involving that concept are analytic.

For example, we do not have to have a satisfactory analysis of memory to know that 'No one can remember future events' is analytic. And if someone devised an analysis of memory according to which it was possible to remember future events, then, however attractive the analysis was in other respects, it would have to be rejected. The analyticity of 'No one can remember future events' is one of the *data* that anyone who investigates the concept of memory must take account of. Similarly, the claims I shall make on behalf of the concept of physical law seem to me to be basic and evident enough to be data that an analysis of this concept must take account of: any analysis on which these claims did not 'come out true' would be for that very reason defective.

II

It seems to be generally agreed that the concept of free will should be understood in terms of the *power* or *ability* of agents to act otherwise than they in fact do. To deny that men have free will is to assert that what a man *does* do and what he *can* do coincide. And almost all philosophers[3] agree that a necessary condition for holding an agent responsible for an act is believing that that agent *could have* refrained from performing that act.[4] There is, however, considerably less agreement as to how 'can' (in the relevant sense) should be analyzed. This is one of the most difficult questions in philosophy. It is certainly a question to which I do not know any nontrivial answer. But, as I said I should do in the case of 'law of physics', I shall make certain conceptual claims about 'can' (in the 'power' or 'ability' sense) in the absence of any analysis. Any suggested analysis of 'can' that does not support these claims will either be neutral with respect to them, in which case it will be incomplete, since it will not settle all conceptual questions about 'can', or it will be inconsistent with them, in which case the arguments I shall present in support of these claims will, in effect, be arguments that the analysis fails. In Part IV, I shall expand on this point as it applies to one particular analysis of 'can', the well-known 'conditional' analysis.

I shall say no more than this about the meaning of 'can'. I shall, however, introduce an idiom that will be useful in talking about ability and inability in complicated cases. Without this idiom, the statement of our argument would be rather unwieldy. We shall sometimes make claims about an agent's abilities by using sentences of the form:

S can render [could have rendered] ... false.

where '...' may be replaced by names of propositions.[5] Our ordinary claims about ability can easily be translated into this idiom. For example, we translate:

He could have reached Chicago by midnight.

as

He could have rendered the proposition that he did not reach Chicago by midnight false.

and, of course, the translation from the special idiom to the ordinary idiom is easy enough in such simple cases. If we were interested only in everyday ascriptions of ability, the new idiom would be useless. Using it, however, we may make ascriptions of ability that it would be very difficult to make in the ordinary idiom. Consider, for example, the last true proposition asserted by Plato. (Let us assume that this description is, as logicians say, 'proper'.) One claim that we might make about Aristotle is that he could have rendered this proposition false. Now, presumably, we have no way of discovering *what* proposition the last true proposition asserted by Plato was. Still, the claim about Aristotle would seem to be either true or false. To discover its truth-value, we should have to discover under what conditions the last true proposition asserted by Plato (i.e., that proposition having as one of its accidental properties, the property of being the last true proposition asserted by Plato) would be false, and then discover whether it was within Aristotle's power to produce these conditions. For example, suppose that if Aristotle had lived in Athens from the time of Plato's death till the time of his own death, then the last true proposition asserted by

Plato (whatever it was) would be false. Then, if Aristotle could have lived (i.e., if he had it within his power to live) in Athens throughout this period, he could have rendered the last true proposition asserted by Plato false. On the other hand, if the last true proposition asserted by Plato is the proposition that the planets do not move in perfect circles, then Aristotle could not have rendered the last true proposition asserted by Plato false, since it was not within his power to produce any set of conditions sufficient for the falsity of this proposition.[6]

It is obvious that the proposition expressed by 'Aristotle could have rendered the last true proposition asserted by Plato false', is a proposition that we should be hard put to express without using the idiom of rendering propositions false, or, at least, without using some very similar idiom. We shall find this new idiom very useful in discussing the relation between free will (a thesis about abilities) and determinism (a thesis about certain propositions).

III

I shall now imagine a case in which a certain man, after due deliberation, refrained from performing a certain contemplated act. I shall then argue that, if determinism is true, then that man *could not have* performed that act. Because this argument will not depend on any features peculiar to our imagined case, the incompatibility of free will and determinism *in general* will be established, since, as will be evident, a parallel argument could easily be constructed for the case of any agent and any unperformed act.

Here is the case. Let us suppose there was once a judge who had only to raise his right hand at a certain time, T, to prevent the execution of a sentence of death upon a certain criminal, such a hand-raising being the sign, according to the conventions of the judge's country, of a granting of special clemency. Let us further suppose that the judge—call him 'J'—refrained from raising his hand at that time, and that this inaction resulted in the criminal's being put to death. We may also suppose that the judge was unbound, uninjured, and free from paralysis; that he decided not to raise his hand at T only after a period of calm, rational, and relevant deliberation; that he had not been subjected to any 'pressure' to decide one way or the other about the criminal's death; that he was not under the influence of drugs, hypnosis, or anything of that sort; and finally, that there was no element in his deliberations that would have been of any special interest to a student of abnormal psychology.

Now the argument. In this argument, which I shall refer to as the 'main argument', I shall use 'T_0' to denote some instant of time earlier than J's birth, 'P_0' to denote the proposition that expresses the state of the world at

T_0, 'P' to denote the proposition that expresses the state of the world at T, and 'L' to denote the conjunction into a single proposition of all laws of physics. (I shall regard L itself as a law of physics, on the reasonable assumption that if A and B are laws of physics, then the conjunction of A and B is a law of physics.) The argument consists of seven statements, the seventh of which follows from the first six:

(1)   If determinism is true, then the conjunction of P_0 and L entails P.

(2)   If J had raised his hand at T, then P would be false.

(3)   If (2) is true, then if J could have raised his hand at T, J could have rendered P false.[7]

(4)   If J could have rendered P false, and if the conjunction of P_0 and L entails P, then J could have rendered the conjunction of P_0 and L false.

(5)   If J could have rendered the conjunction of P_0 and L false, then J could have rendered L false.

(6) J could not have rendered L false.

Thus,

(7)   If determinism is true, J could not have raised his hand at T.

That (7) follows from (1) through (6) can easily be established by truth-functional logic. Note that all conditionals in the argument except for (2) are truth-functional. For purposes of establishing the *validity* of this argument, (2) may be regarded as a simple sentence. Let us examine the premises individually.

(1) This premise follows from the definition of determinism.

(2) If J had raised his hand at T, then the world would have been in a different state at T from the state it was in fact in. (See our second condition on the content of 'the state of the world'.) And, therefore, if J had raised his hand at T, some contrary of P would express the state of the world at T. It should be emphasized that 'P' does not *mean* 'the proposition that expresses the state of the world at T'. Rather, 'P' *denotes* the proposition that expresses the state of the world at T. In Kripke's terminology, 'P' is being used as a *rigid designator*, while 'the proposition that expresses the state of the world at T' is perforce non-rigid.[8]

(3) Since J's hand being raised at T would have been sufficient for the falsity of P, there is, if J could have raised his hand, at least one condition sufficient for the falsity of P that J could have produced.

(4) This premise may be defended as an instance of the following general principle:

If S can render R false, and if Q entails R, then S can render Q false.

This principle seems to be analytic. For if Q entails R, then the denial of R entails the denial of Q. Thus, any condition sufficient for the falsity of R is also sufficient for the falsity of Q. Therefore, if there is some condition that S can produce that is sufficient for the falsity of R, there is some condition (that same condition) that S can produce that is sufficient for the falsity of Q.

(5) This premise may be defended as an instance of the following general principle, which I take to be analytic:

If Q is a true proposition that concerns only states of affairs that obtained before S's birth, and if S can render the conjunction of Q and R false, then S can render R false.

Consider, for example, the propositions expressed by

The Spanish Armada was defeated in 1588.

and

Peter van Inwagen never visits Alaska.

The conjunction of these two propositions is quite possibly true. At any rate, let us assume it is true. Given that it is true, it seems quite clear that I can render it false if and only if I can visit Alaska. If, for some reason, it is not within my power ever to visit Alaska, then I *cannot* render it false. This is a quite trivial assertion, and the general principle (above) of which it is an instance is hardly less trivial. And it seems incontestable that premise (5) is also an instance of this principle.

(6) I shall argue that if anyone *can* (i.e., has it within his power to) render some proposition false, then that proposition is not a law of physics. This I regard as a conceptual truth, one of the data that must be taken account of by anyone who wishes to give an analysis of 'can' or 'law'. It is this connection between these two concepts, I think, that is at the root of the incompatibility of free will and determinism.

In order to see this connection, let us suppose that both of the following are true:

(A) Nothing ever travels faster than light.
(B) Jones, a physicist, can construct a particle accelerator that would cause protons to travel at twice the speed of light.

It follows from (A) that Jones will never exercise the power that (B) ascribes to him. But whatever the reason for Jones's failure to act on his ability to render (A) false, it is clear that (A) and (B) are consistent, and that (B) entails that (A) is not a law of physics. For given that (B) is true, then Jones is able to conduct an experiment that would falsify (A); and surely it is a feature of any proposition that is a physical law that no one *can* conduct an experiment that would show it to be false.

Of course, most propositions that look initially as if they might be physical laws, but which are later decided to be nonlaws, are rejected because of experiments that are actually performed. But this is not essential. In order to see this, let us elaborate the example we have been considering. Let us suppose that Jones's ability to render (A) false derives from the fact that he has discovered a mathematically rigorous proof that under certain conditions C, realizable in the laboratory, protons would travel faster than light. And let us suppose that this proof proceeds from premises so obviously true that all competent physicists accept his conclusion without reservation. But suppose that conditions C never obtain in nature, and that actually to produce them in the laboratory would require such an expenditure of resources that Jones and his colleagues decide not to carry out the experiment. And suppose that, as a result, conditions C are never realized and nothing ever travels faster than light. It is evident that if all this were true, we should have to say that (A), while *true,* is not a law of physics. (Though, of course, 'Nothing ever travels faster than light except under conditions C' might be a law.)

The laboratories and resources that figure in this example are not essential to its point. If Jones *could* render some proposition false by performing *any* act he does not in fact perform, even such a simple act as raising his hand at a certain time, this would be sufficient to show that that proposition is not law of physics.

This completes my defense of the premises of the main argument. In the final part of this paper, I shall examine objections to this argument suggested by the attempts of various philosophers to establish the compatibility of free will and determinism.

IV

The most useful thing a philosopher who thinks that the main argument does not prove its point could do would be to try to show that some premise of the argument is false or incoherent, or that the argument begs some important question, or contains a term that is used equivocally, or something of that sort. In short, he should get down to cases. Some philosophers, however, might continue to hold that free will and determinism, in the sense of Part I, are compatible, but decline to try to point out a mistake in the argument. For (such a philosopher might argue) we have, in everyday life, *criteria* for determining whether an agent could have acted otherwise than he did, and these criteria determine the *meaning* of 'could have acted otherwise'; to know the meaning of this phrase is simply to know how to apply these criteria. And since these criteria make no mention of determinism, anyone who thinks that free will and determinism are incompatible is simply confused.[9]

As regards the argument of Part III (this philosopher might continue), this argument is very complex, and this complexity must simply serve to hide some error, since its conclusion is absurd. We must treat this argument like the infamous 'proof' that zero equals one: It may be amusing and even instructive to find the hidden error (if one has nothing better to do), but it would be a waste of time to take seriously any suggestion that it is sound.

Now I suppose we do have 'criteria', in some sense of this overused word, for the application of 'could have done otherwise', and I will grant that knowing the criteria for the application of a term can plausibly be identified with knowing its meaning. Whether the criteria for applying 'could have done otherwise' can (as at least one philosopher has supposed[10]) be taught by simple ostension is another question. However this may be, the 'criteria' argument is simply invalid. To see this, let us examine a simpler argument that makes the same mistake.

Consider the doctrine of 'predestinarianism'. Predestinarians hold (i) that if an act is foreseen it is not free, and (ii) that all acts are foreseen by God. (I do not claim that anyone has ever held this doctrine in precisely this form.) Now suppose we were to argue that predestinarianism must be compatible with free will, since our criteria for applying 'could have done otherwise' make no reference to predestinarianism. Obviously this argument would be invalid, since predestinarianism is incompatible with free will. And the only difference I can see between this argument and the 'criteria' argument for the compatibility of free will and determinism is that predestinarianism, unlike determinism, is *obviously* incompatible with free will. But, of course, theses may be incompatible with one another even if this incompatibility is not obvious. Even if determinism cannot, like predestinarianism, be seen to be incompatible with free will on the basis of a simple formal inference, there is, nonetheless, a conceptual connection between the two theses (as we showed in our defense of premise (6)). The argument of Part III is intended to draw out the implications of this connection. There may well be a mistake in the argument, but I do not see why anyone should think that the very idea of such an argument is misconceived.

It has also been argued that free will *entails* determinism, and, being itself a consistent thesis, is *a fortiori* compatible with determinism. The argument, put briefly, is this. To say of some person on some particular occasion that he acted freely is obviously to say at least that he acted on that occasion. Suppose, however, that we see someone's arm rise and it later turns out that there was *no cause whatsoever* for his arm's rising. Surely we should have to say that *he* did not really raise his arm at all. Rather, his arm's rising was a mere chance happening, that, like a muscular twitch, had nothing to do with *him*, beyond the fact that it happened to involve a part of his body. A necessary condition for this person's really having raised his hand is that *he* caused his hand to rise. And surely '*he* caused' means '*his* character, desires, and beliefs caused'.[11]

I think that there is a great deal of confusion in this argument, but to expose this confusion would require a lengthy discussion of many fine points in the theory of agency. I shall only point out that if this argument is supposed to refute the conclusion of Part III, it is an *ignoratio elenchi*. For I did not conclude that free will is incompatible with the thesis that every event has a cause, but rather with determinism as defined in Part I. And the denial of this thesis does not entail that there are uncaused events.

Of course, one might try to construct a similar but relevant argument for the falsity of the conclusion of Part III. But, so far as I can see, the plausibility of such an argument would depend on the plausibility of supposing that if the present movements of one's body are not completely determined by physical law and the state of the world before one's birth, then these present movements are not one's own doing, but, rather, mere random happenings. And I do not see the least shred of plausibility in this supposition.

I shall finally consider the popular 'conditional analysis' argument for the compatibility of free will and determinism. According to the advocates of this argument—let us call them 'conditionalists'—what statements of the form:

(8)   *S* could have done *X*

mean is:

(9)   If *S* had chosen to do *X*, *S* would have done *X*.[12]

For example, 'Smith could have saved the drowning child' means, 'If Smith had chosen to save the drowning child, Smith would have saved the drowning child.' Thus even if determinism is true (the conditionalists argue), it is possible that Smith did not save but *could have* saved the drowning child, since the conjunction of determinism with 'Smith did not save the child' does not entail the falsity of 'If Smith had chosen to save the child, Smith would have saved the child'.

Most of the controversy about this argument centers around the question whether (9) is a correct analysis of (8). I shall not enter into the debate about whether this analysis is correct. I shall instead question the relevance of this debate to the argument of Part III. For it is not clear that the main argument would be unsound if the conditional analysis *were* correct. Clearly the argument is *valid* whether or not (8) and (9) mean the same. But suppose the premises of the main argument were rewritten so that every clause they contain that is of form (8) is replaced by the corresponding clause of form (9)—should we then see that any of these premises is false? Let us try this with premise (6), which seems, *prima facie,* to be the crucial premise of the argument. We have:

(6a) It is not the case that if *J* had chosen to render *L* false, *J* would have rendered *L* false.

Now (6a) certainly seems true: If someone chooses to render false some proposition *R,* and if *R* is a law of physics, then surely he will fail. This little argument for (6a) *seems* obviously sound. But we cannot overlook the possibility that someone might discover a mistake in it and, perhaps, even construct a convincing argument that (6a) is false. Let us, therefore, assume for the sake of argument that (6a) is demonstrably false. What would this show? I submit that it would show that (6a) does not mean the same as (6), since (6) is, as I have argued, *true.*

The same dilemma confronts the conditionalist if he attempts to show, on the basis of the conditional analysis, that any of the other premises of the argument is false. Consider the argument got by replacing every clause of form (8) in the main argument with the corresponding clause of form (9). If all the premises of this new argument are true, the main argument is, according to the conditionalist's own theory, sound. If, on the other hand, any of the premises of the new argument is false, then (*I* would maintain) this premise is a counterexample to the conditional analysis. I should not be begging the question against the conditionalist in maintaining this, since I have given arguments for the truth of each of the premises of the main argument, and nowhere in these arguments do I assume that the conditional analysis is wrong.

Of course, any or all of my arguments in defense of the premises of the main argument may contain some mistake. But unless the conditionalist could point to some such mistake, he would not accomplish much by showing that some statement he *claimed* was equivalent to one of its premises was false.[13]

Notes

1. For example, 'If a human being is not made to feel ashamed of lying before his twelfth birthday, then he will lie whenever he believes it to be to his advantage.'

2. In 'The Compatibility of Free Will and Determinism', *The Philosophical Review* (1962), J. V. Canfield argues convincingly for a position that we might represent in this terminology as the thesis that a determinism based on voluntaristic laws could be compatible with free will.

3. See, however, Harry Frankfurt, 'Alternate Possibilities and Moral Responsibility', *The Journal of Philosophy* (1969).

4. Actually, the matter is rather more complicated than this, since we may hold a man responsible for an act we believe he could not have refrained from, provided we are prepared to hold him responsible for his being unable to refrain.

5. In all the cases we shall consider, '...' will be replaced by names of *true* propositions. For the sake of logical completeness, we may stipulate that any sentence formed by replacing '...' with the name of a *false* proposition is trivially true. Thus, 'Kant could have rendered the proposition that 7 + 5 = 13 false' is trivially true.

6. Richard Taylor has argued (most explicitly in 'Time, Truth and Ability' by 'Diodorus Cronus', *Analysis* (1965)) that every true proposition is such that, necessarily, no one is able to render it false. On my view, this thesis is mistaken, and Taylor's arguments for it can be shown to be unsound. I shall not, however, argue for this here. I shall argue in Part III that we are unable to render *certain sorts of* true proposition false, but my arguments will depend on special features of these sorts of proposition. I shall, for example, argue that no one can render false a law of physics; but I shall not argue that this is the case because laws of physics are *true*, but because of other features that they possess.

7. 'J could have raised his hand at T' is ambiguous. It might mean either (roughly) 'J possessed, at T, the ability to raise his hand', or 'J possessed the ability to bring it about that his hand rose at T'. If J was unparalyzed at T but paralyzed at all earlier instants, then the latter of those would be false, though the former might be true. I mean 'J could have raised his hand at T' in the latter sense.

8. See Saul Kripke, 'Identity and Necessity', in *Identity and Individuation* (ed. by Milton K. Munitz), New York (1971).

9. Cf. Antony Flew, 'Divine Omniscience and Human Freedom', *New Essays in Philosophical Theology* (ed. by Antony Flew and Alasdair MacIntyre), London (1955), pp. 149–151 in particular.

10. Flew, *loc. cit.*

11. Cf. R. E. Hobart, 'Free Will as Involving Determination and Inconceiveable Without It', *Mind* (1934); A. J. Ayer, 'Freedom and Necessity', in his collected *Philosophical Essays*, New York (1954); P. H. Nowell-Smith, 'Freewill and Moral Responsibility', *Mind* (1948); J. J. C. Smart, 'Free Will, Praise, and Blame', *Mind* (1961).

12. Many other verbs besides 'choose' figure in various philosophers' conditional analyses of ability. E.g., 'wish', 'want', 'will', 'try', 'set oneself'. Much of the important contemporary work on this analysis, by G. E. Moore, P. H. Nowell-Smith, J. L. Austin, Keith Lehrer, Roderick Chisholm, and others, is collected in *The Nature of Human Action* (ed. by Myles Brand), Glenview, Ill. (1970). See also 'Fatalism and Determinism', by Wilfrid Sellars, in *Freedom and Determinism* (ed. by Keith Lehrer) New York (1966), pp.141–174.

13. For an argument in some respects similar to what I have called the 'main argument', see Carl Ginet's admirable article, 'Might We Have No Choice?' in Lehrer, *op. cit.*, pp. 87–104. Another argument similar to the main argument, which is (formally) much simpler than the main argument, but which is stated in language very different from that of traditional statements of the free-will problem, can be found in my "A Formal Approach to the Problem of Free Will and Determinism," *Theoria* (1974).

2

Are We Free to Break the Laws?

DAVID LEWIS

Soft determinism seems to have an incredible consequence. It seems to imply, given certain acceptable further premises, that sometimes we are able to act in such a way that the laws of nature are broken. But if we distinguish a strong and a weak version of this incredible consequence, I think we shall find that it is the strong version that is incredible and the weak version that is the consequence.

Soft determinism is the doctrine that sometimes one freely does what one is predetermined to do; and that in such a case one is able to act otherwise though past history and the laws of nature determine that one will not act otherwise.

Compatibilism is the doctrine that soft determinism may be true. A compatibilist might well doubt soft determinism because he doubts on physical grounds that we are ever predetermined to act as we do, or perhaps because he doubts on psychoanalytic grounds that we ever act freely. I myself am a compatibilist but no determinist, hence I am obliged to rebut some objections against soft determinism but not others. But for the sake of the argument, let me feign to uphold soft determinism, and indeed a particular instance thereof.

I have just put my hand down on my desk. That, let me claim, was a free but predetermined act. I was able to act otherwise, for instance to raise my

From *Theoria*, Vol. XLVII (1981): 113–121. Reprinted by permission of the author and *Theoria*.

hand. But there is a true historical proposition about the intrinsic state of the world long ago, and there is a true proposition *L* specifying the laws of nature that govern our world such that *H* and *L* jointly determine what I did. They jointly imply the proposition that I put my hand down. They jointly contradict the proposition that I raised my hand. Yet I was free; I was able to raise my hand. The way in which I was determined not to was not the sort of way that counts as inability.

What if I had raised my hand? Then at least one of three things would have been true. Contradictions would have been true together; or the historical proposition *H* would not have been true; or the law proposition *L* would not have been true. Which? Here we need auxiliary premises; but since I accept the premises my opponent requires to make his case, we may proceed. Of our three alternatives, we may dismiss the first; for if I had raised my hand, there would still have been no true contradictions. Likewise we may dismiss the second; for if I had raised my hand, the intrinsic state of the world long ago would have been no different.[1] That leaves the third alternative. If I had raised my hand, the law proposition *L* would not have been true. That follows by a principle of the logic of counterfactuals which is almost uncontroversial:[2] $A \,\square\!\!\rightarrow B \vee C \vee D, A \,\square\!\!\rightarrow -B, A \,\square\!\!\rightarrow -C, \therefore A \,\square\!\!\rightarrow D$.

If *L* had not been true, that implies that some law of nature would have been broken, for *L* is a specification of the laws. That is not to say that anything would have been both a law and broken—that is a contradiction in terms if, as I suppose, any genuine law is at least an absolutely unbroken regularity. Rather, if *L* had not been true, something that is in fact a law, and unbroken, would have been broken, and no law. It would at best have been an almost-law.

In short, as a (feigned) soft determinist, who accepts the requisite auxiliary premises and principle of counterfactual logic, I am committed to the consequence that if I had done what I was able to do—raise my hand—then some law would have been broken.

"That is to say," my opponent paraphrases, "you claim to be able to break the very laws of nature. And with so little effort! A marvelous power indeed! Can you also bend spoons?"

Dinstinguo. My opponent's paraphrase is not quite right. He has replaced the weak thesis that I accept with a stronger thesis that I join him in rejecting. The strong thesis is utterly incredible, but it is no part of soft determinism. The weak thesis is controversial, to be sure, but a soft determinist should not mind being committed to it. The two theses are as follows.

(Weak Thesis) I am able to do something such that, if I did it, a law would be broken.

(Strong Thesis) I am able to break a law.

To see the difference, consider not a marvelous ability to break a law but a commonplace ability to break a window. Perhaps I am able to throw a stone in a certain direction; and perhaps if I did, the stone would hit a certain window and the window would break. Then I am able to break a window. For starters: I am able to do something such that, if I did it, a window would be broken. But there is more to be said. I am able to do something such that, if I did it, my act would cause a window-breaking event.

Or consider a commonplace ability to break a promise. Perhaps I am able to throw a stone; and perhaps if I did, I would break my promise never to throw a stone. Then I am able to break a promise. For starters: I am able to do something such that, if I did it, a promise would be broken. But there is more to be said. I am able to do something such that, if I did it, my act would itself be a promise-breaking event.

Next, consider what really would be a marvelous ability to break a law—an ability I could not credibly claim. Suppose that I were able to throw a stone very, very hard. And suppose that if I did, the stone would fly faster than light, an event contrary to law. Then I really would be able to break a law. For starters: I would be able to do something such that, if I did it, a law would be broken. But there is more to be said. I would be able to do something such that, if I did it, my act would cause a law-breaking event.

Or suppose that I were able to throw a stone so hard that in the course of the throw my own hand would move faster than light. Then again I would be able to break a law, regardless of what my act might cause. For starters: I would be able to do something such that, if I did it, a law would be broken. But there is more to be said. I would be able to do something such that, if I did it, my act would itself be a law-breaking event.

If no act of mine either caused or was a window-, promise-, or law-breaking event, then I think it could not be true that I broke a window, a promise, or a law. Therefore I am able to break a window, a promise, or a law only if I am able to do something such that, if I did it, my act either would cause or would be a window-, promise-, or law-breaking event.

Maybe my opponent will contend that according to soft determinism, there is another way of being able to break a law. But I see no reason to grant this contention.

Now consider the disputed case. I am able to raise my hand, although it is predetermined that I will not. If I raised my hand, some law would be broken. I even grant that a law-breaking event would take place. (Here I use the present tense neutrally. I mean to imply nothing about when a law-breaking event would take place.) But is it so that my act of raising my hand would cause any lawbreaking event? Is it so that my act of raising my hand would itself be a law-breaking event? Is it so that any other act of mine would cause or would be a law-breaking event? If not, then my ability to raise my hand confers no marvelous ability to break a law, even though a law would be broken if I did it.[3]

Had I raised my hand, a law would have been broken beforehand. The course of events would have diverged from the actual course of events a little while before I raised my hand, and, at the point of divergence there would have been a law-breaking event—a divergence miracle, as I have called it ([4]). But this divergence miracle would not have been caused by my raising my hand. If anything, the causation would have been the other way around. Nor would the divergence miracle have been my act of raising my hand. That act was altogether absent from the actual course of events, so it cannot get under way until there is already some divergence. Nor would it have been caused by any other act of mine, earlier or later. Nor would it have been any other act of mine. Nor is there any reason to say that if I had raised my hand there would have been some other law-breaking event besides the divergence miracle; still less, that some other law-breaking event would have been caused by, or would have been, my act of raising my hand. To accommodate my hypothetical raising of my hand while holding fixed all that can and should be held fixed, it is necessary to suppose one divergence miracle, gratuitous to suppose any further law-breaking.

Thus I insist that I was able to raise my hand, and I acknowledge that a law would have been broken had I done so, but I deny that I am therefore able to break a law. To uphold my instance of soft determinism, I need not claim any incredible powers. To uphold the compatibilism that I actually believe, I need not claim that such powers are even possible.

I said that if I had raised my hand, the divergence miracle beforehand would not have been caused by my raising my hand. That seems right. But my opponent might argue *ad hominem* that according to my own analysis of causation ([3]), my raising my hand does turn out to cause the divergence miracle. The effect would precede the cause, but I do not object to that. We seem to have the right pattern of counterfactual dependence between distinct events: (1) if I had raised my hand, the divergence miracle would have occurred, but (2) if I had not raised my hand, it would not have occurred.

I reply that we do not have this required pattern, nor would we have had it if I had raised my hand. Therefore I am safe in denying that the miracle would have been caused by my act. We do not have the pattern because (1) is false. What is true is only that if I had raised my hand, then some or other divergence miracle would have occurred. There is no particular divergence miracle that definitely would have occurred, since the divergence might have happened in various ways.[4]

If I had raised my hand, (1) would have been true. But we still would not have had the right pattern, because in that case (2) would have been false. Consider a counterfactual situation in which a divergence miracle beforehand has allowed me to raise my hand. Is it so, from the standpoint of that situation, that if I had not raised my hand, the miracle would not have taken place? No; the miracle might have taken place, only to have its work undone straightway by a second miracle. (Even in this doubly counterfactual context, when I speak of a miracle I mean a violation of the actual laws.) What is true, at most, is that if I had not raised my hand, then the first miracle might not have taken place.

My incompatibilist opponent is a creature of fiction, but he has his prototypes in real life. He is modelled partly on Peter van Inwagen ([5], [6], [7]) and partly on myself when I first worried about van Inwagen's argument against compatibilism. He definitely is not van Inwagen; he does not choose his words so carefully. Still I think that for all his care, van Inwagen is in the same boat with my fictitious opponent.

Van Inwagen's argument runs as follows, near enough. (I recast it as a *reductio* against the instance of soft determinism that I feign to uphold.) I did not raise my hand; suppose for *reductio* that I could have raised my hand, although determinism is true. Then it follows, given four premises that I cannot question, that I could have rendered false the conjunction HL of a certain historical proposition H about the state of the world before my birth and a certain law proposition L. If so, then I could have rendered L false. (Premise 5.) But I could not have rendered L false. (Premise 6.) This refutes our supposition.

To this I reply that Premise 5 and Premise 6 are not both true. Which one is true depends on what van Inwagen means by "could have rendered false".

It does not matter what "could have rendered false" means in ordinary language; van Inwagen introduced the phrase as a term of art. It does not even matter what meaning van Inwagen gave it. What matters is whether we can give it any meaning that would meet his needs—any meaning that would make all his premises defensible without circularity. I shall consider two meanings. I think there is nothing in van Inwagen's text to suggest any third meaning that might work better than these two.[5]

First, a preliminary definition. Let us say that an event would falsify a proposition iff, necessarily, if that event occurs then that proposition is false. For instance, an event consisting of a stone's flying faster than light would falsify a law. So would an act of throwing in which my hand moves faster than light. So would a divergence miracle. But my act of throwing a stone would not itself falsify the proposition that the window in the line of fire remains intact; all that is true is that my act would cause another event that would falsify that proposition. My act of raising my hand would falsify any sufficiently inclusive conjunction of history and law. But it would not itself falsify any law—not if all the requisite lawbreaking were over and done with beforehand. All that is true is that my act would be preceded by another event—the divergence miracle—that would falsify a law.

Let us say that I could have rendered a proposition false in the weak sense iff I was able to do something such that, if I did it, the proposition would have been falsified (though not necessarily by my act, or by any event caused by my act). And let us say that I could have rendered a proposition false in the strong sense iff I was able to do something such that, if I did it, the proposition would have been falsified either by my act itself or by some event caused by my act.

The Weak Thesis, which as a soft determinist I accept, is the thesis that I could have rendered a law false in the weak sense. The Strong Thesis, which I reject, is the thesis that I could have rendered a law false in the strong sense.

The first part of van Inwagen's argument succeeds whichever sense we take. If I could have raised my hand despite the fact that determinism is true and I did not raise it, then indeed it is true both in the weak sense and in the strong sense that I could have rendered false the conjunction HL of history and law. But I could have rendered false the law proposition L in the weak sense, though I could not have rendered L false in the strong sense. So if we take the weak sense throughout the argument, then I deny Premise 6. If instead we take the strong sense, then I deny Premise 5.

Van Inwagen supports both premises by considering analogous cases. I think the supporting arguments fail because the cases produced are not analogous: they are cases in which the weak and strong senses do not diverge. In support of Premise 6, he invites us to reject the supposition that a physicist could render a law false by building and operating a machine that would accelerate protons to twice the speed of light. Reject that supposition by all means; but that does nothing to support Premise 6 taken in the weak sense, for the rejected supposition is that the physicist could render a law false in the strong sense. In support of Premise 5, he invites us to reject the supposition that a traveler could render false a conjunction of a historical proposition and a proposition about his future travels otherwise than by rendering false the nonhistorical conjunct. Reject that supposition by all means, but that does nothing to support Premise 5 taken in the strong sense. Given that one could render false, in the strong sense, a conjunction of historical and nonhistorical propositions (and given that, as in the cases under consideration, there is no question of rendering the historical conjunct false by means of time travel or the like), what follows? Does it follow that one could render the nonhistorical conjunct false in the strong sense? That is what would support Premise 5 in the strong sense. Or does it only follow, as I think, that one could render the nonhistorical conjunct false in at least the weak sense? The case of the traveler is useless in answering that question, since if the traveler could render the proposition about his future travels false in the weak sense, he could also render it false in the strong sense.

Notes

1. I argue for this in [4].

2. The inference is valid in any system that treats the conditional as a propositionally (or even sententially) indexed family of normal necessities, in the sense of Brian F. Chellas, ([l]).

3. Up to a point, my strategy here resembles that of Keith Lehrer ([2], p. 199). Lehrer grants a weak thesis: the agent could have done something such that, if he had done it, there would have been a difference in either laws or history. He rejects, as I would, the step from that to a stronger thesis: the agent could have brought about a difference in laws or history. So far, so good. But Lehrer's reason for rejecting the stronger thesis is one I cannot accept. His reason is this: it is false that if the agent had preferred that there be a difference in laws or history, there would have been a difference in laws or history. I say, first, that this conditional may not be false. Suppose the agent is predetermined to prefer that there be no difference; had he preferred otherwise, there would have been a difference. (Had anything been otherwise than it was predetermined to be, there would have been a difference in either laws or history.) And second, if this conditional is not false, that is not enough to make the stronger thesis true. There must be some other reason, different from the one Lehrer gives, why the stronger thesis is false.

4. Cf. [4], p. 463. At this point I am relying on contingent features of the world as we suppose it to be; as Allen Hazen has pointed out to me, we can imagine a world of discrete processes at which one divergent history in which I raise my hand clearly takes less of a miracle than any of its rivals. I think this matters little, since the task of compatibilism is to show how freedom and determinism might coexist at a world that might, for all we know, be ours.

5. Van Inwagen has indicated (personal communication, 1981) that he would adopt a third meaning for "could have rendered false", different from both of the meanings that I discuss here. His definition is roughly as follows: an agent could have rendered a proposition false iff he could have arranged things in a certain way, such that his doing so, plus the whole truth about the past, together strictly imply the falsehood of the proposition. On this definition, Premise 6 simply says that I could not have arranged things in any way such that I was predetermined not to arrange things in that way. It is uninstructive to learn that the soft determinist is committed to denying Premise 6 thus understood.

References

1 CHELLAS, B. F. "Basic conditional logic". *Journal of philosophical logic*, vol. 4 (1975), pp. 133–153.

2 LEHRER, K. "Preferences, conditionals and freedom". In Peter van Inwagen, ed., *Time and Cause*. Dordrecht: Reidel, 1980.

3 LEWIS, D. "Causation". *Journal of Philosophy*, vol. 70 (1973), pp. 556–567.
4 LEWIS, D. "Counterfactual dependence and time's arrow". *Noûs*, vol. 13 (1979), pp. 455–476.
5 VAN INWAGEN, P. "A formal approach to the problem of free will and determinism". *Theoria*, vol. 40 (1974), pp. 9–22.
6 VAN INWAGEN, P. "The incomparability of free will and determinism". *Philosophical Studies*, vol. 27 (1975), pp. 185–199.
7 VAN INWAGEN, P. "Reply to Narveson". *Philosophical Studies*, vol. 32 (1977), pp. 89–98.

3

A New Compatibilism

JOHN MARTIN FISCHER

I. Introduction

We typically think of ourselves as having more than one genuine alternative. When we make plans for the future, and deliberate about future courses of action, we presuppose that we have more than one option open to us. This is a deep, natural, and seemingly universal assumption. Additionally, insofar as we think of ourselves as moral agents—persons— we tend to assume that we can determine which path we will take among *various* paths that are genuinely open to us. It is natural to suppose that it is in virtue of *selecting* the path that we actually take (from among various open options) that we become accessible to moral praise or blame.

But there is a very plausible argument that appears to imply that we cannot be confident that we ever actually possess genuinely open alternative possibilities. That is, there is an argument that calls into question the idea that we have more than one path that is accessible to us. I shall begin by laying out a version of this argument and defending it (briefly) from certain criticisms. I believe the version I shall be presenting is a simple, natural, and potent version of the argument. I shall then develop a novel way of responding to the argument—a way of protecting our deep and natural view of ourselves as (at least sometimes) possessing alternative possibilities.

From *Philosophical Topics*, Vol. 24, no. 2 (1996): 49–66. Reprinted by permission of *Philosophical Topics*.

Finally, I shall be concerned to explain the considerable price of this response, despite its manifest appeal.

II. The Conditional Version of The Argument for Incompatibilism

I shall say that causal determinism is the doctrine that for any given time, a complete statement of the temporally nonrelational (or "hard") facts about that time, together with a complete statement of the laws of nature, entails every truth as to what happens after that time. Although contemporary science appears to imply that causal determinism is false, it might turn out that this doctrine is true. I would contend that we do not know that causal determinism is false. In part because of this fact, it is interesting to inquire as to what would be the case if indeed causal determinism were true.

I shall be presenting a version of an argument for the *incompatibility* of causal determinism and the possession of genuinely open alternative possibilities—freedom to do (or, say, choose) otherwise. In order to present this version of the argument, I need two ingredients (in addition to the definition of causal determinism). The first ingredient seeks to capture the common-sense, intuitive idea that the past is fixed and out of our control now. I shall give expression to this intuitive idea by employing a certain sort of conditional, which I shall call the "Principle of the Fixity of the Past":

(FP) For any action Y, agent S, and time T, if it is true that if S were to do Y at T, some (temporally nonrelational or "hard") fact about the past relative to T would not have been a fact, then S cannot do Y at T.

That is, if it is a necessary condition of an agent's performing some action at a time that the past (relative to that time) would have been different from what it actually was, then it follows that the agent *cannot* perform the action.

The second ingredient seeks to capture the common-sense, intuitive idea that the laws of nature are out of our control and thus constitute constraints on our abilities. The conditional which gives expression to this idea is the "Principle of the Fixity of the Laws":

(FL) For any action Y and agent S, if it is true that if S were to do Y, some natural law which actually obtains would not obtain, then S cannot do Y.

That is, if it is a necessary condition of an agent's performing an action that there be some violation of an actually obtaining natural law, then surely it follows that the agent *cannot* perform the action.

The Conditional Version of the Argument for Incompatibilism proceeds as follows.[1] Suppose, for the sake of the argument, that causal determinism is true. Also imagine that, as it happens, some ordinary agent, Jill, does something quite ordinary—she raises her hand at time T2. It follows that a statement describing the universe in the past (relative to T2), together with a statement of the laws of nature, entails that Jill raises her hand at T2.

Now one of the following conditionals must be true: (1) If Jill were to do otherwise than raise her hand at T2, then the universe would have been different in the past (relative to T2) than it actually was; (2) if Jill were to do otherwise at T2, then the natural laws would be different from what they actually are; or (3) if Jill were to do otherwise at T2, then either the universe would have been different in the past (relative to T2) than it actually was or the natural laws would be different from what they actually are. But given the Principle of the Fixity of the Past, (I) if (1) were true, then Jill cannot do otherwise than raise her hand at T2. And given the Principle of the Fixity of the Laws, (II) if (2) were true, then Jill cannot do otherwise than raise her hand at T2. And given the above (i.e., [I] and [II]) it is plausible to say that (III) if (3) were true, then Jill cannot do otherwise than raise her hand at T2. So (IV) Jill cannot do otherwise than raise her hand at T2.

The argument contains a subargument. That is, (I) and (II) are alleged to imply (III). Then it is claimed that (I), (II), and (III), together with the claim that the associated conditionals (1), (2), and (3) are jointly exhaustive, imply (IV). This is the Conditional Version of the Argument for Incompatibilism. It seems to me to be valid, and it seems to employ very plausible ingredients. (And, clearly, the argument's conclusion can be generalized to apply to all agents and times.) According to the conclusion of this argument, since we cannot be sure that causal determinism is false, we cannot be confident that we are ever free to do otherwise.

I am somewhat puzzled as to why the argument as presented above, has elicited such spirited objections (from certain quarters). For example, Peter van Inwagen has objected to the transition from (I) and (II) to (III), claiming that it involves a logical error; thus, he contends that the Conditional Version is "logically defective."[2] Indeed, van Inwagen has complained that, although I am aware of a logical barrier to deducing (III) from (I) and (II), I "attempt to do so anyway."[3] Ted Warfield has also rather strenuously objected to the Conditional Argument. He says, referring to my presentation of the Conditional Version in my book, *The Metaphysics of Free Will: An Essay on Control*:

Fischer admits, in a note, that his argument is invalid but says that nonetheless he "believe[s] that it is reasonable to accept its conclusion, given both its formal structure and the *content* of its premises." I can make no sense of this claim.[4]

I (and my coauthor) have sought fully to explain and defend the transition from (I) and (II) to (III), and thus, the Conditional Version of the Argument for Incompatibilism, elsewhere.[5] But it might be useful *very briefly* to reply to the objections here; this should help to clarify the argument. It is crucial to see that Warfield is *incorrect* in attributing to me the view that the Conditional Argument is invalid. Here is the note to which Warfield refers:

> I do not claim that the Conditional Version of the Argument for Incompatibilism is 'formally valid'; that is, I do not claim it instantiates some structure which is valid simply in virtue of its form. Rather, I believe that it is reasonable to accept its conclusion, given both its formal structure and the *content* of its premises.[6]

It is clear that I do *not* "admit" that the Conditional Version of the Argument is "invalid"; I merely say that it is not *formally valid*. But I do nevertheless contend that it is a valid argument in the following sense: given its form and also the content of its premises (and conclusion), one cannot accept the premises without accepting the conclusion (on pain of contradiction). More specifically, the relevant portion of the argument is the subargument from (I) and (II) to (III). My contention is that, given the form and content of (I), (II), and (III), it would be contradictory to fail to accept (III) if one were to accept (I) and (II).

I hope that the reader will find this at least plausible. When I consider (I), (II), and (III), I cannot see how (I) and (II) could be true but (III) false. And I have not seen, and cannot now imagine, any triad of sentences with *relevantly similar* form and content in which the analogue of (III) is false, whereas the analogues of (I) and (II) are true. Consider, for example, the following case. Suppose that Smith is now so disposed that one of three conditionals will be true of him when he goes into the voting booth some months from now: (1*) If Smith were to vote, he would vote for Clinton; (2*) if Smith were to vote, he would vote for Dole; (3*) if Smith were to vote, he would vote for either Dole or Clinton. Let us suppose that circumstances are such that these are the only three possibilities.

Now (I*) if (1*) were true, then Smith's voting would result in his voting for a candidate of one of the two major political parties in the United States. Similarly, (II*) if (2*) were true, then Smith's voting would result in his voting for a candidate of one of the two major political parties in the United States. And it seems to follow from (I*) and (II*) that (III*) if (3*) were true, then Smith's voting would result in his voting for a candidate of one of the two major political parties in the United States. Further, given (I*), (II*), and (III*), together with the claim that (1*), (2*), and (3*) exhaust the field of possibilities, it seems to me that it follows that (IV*) Smith's voting would result in his voting for a candidate of one of the two major political parties in the United States. I do not claim that this argument is "formally valid." Rather, I claim that it is valid in virtue of its form *together with the content of its premises (and conclusion)*. Further, I *cannot* see why the Conditional Version of the Argument for Incompatibilism is relevantly different.

Although, of course, I have not here offered a full defense of the Conditional Version of the Argument, I hope the above suffices to make it at least tolerably plausible. I should hasten to point out that there are (obviously) *other* versions of the Argument for Incompatibilsm—other ways of putting together the basic intuitions concerning the fixity of the past and natural laws to yield the incompatibilistic conclusion. Although I shall employ the Conditional Version in this paper (and it is thus useful to see its structure clearly), the points I shall be exploring in what follows do not *depend* in any way upon employing this particular version. If one does not like the Conditional Version, one could simply adapt the points I shall be developing to the other versions of the Argument for Incompatibilism.

III. What's a Compatibilist to Do?

Given that the Conditional Version of the Argument is valid, there seem to be only two moves open to the compatibilist. First, he may deny the Principle of the Fixity of the Past. Typically, a compatibilist who wishes to deny (FP) will distinguish between what he takes to be a plausible and an implausible view about the past's fixity. The plausible view has it that one does not have it in one's power to initiate backward-flowing causal chains which would issue in the past's being different from how it actually was. But it is *implausible,* according to this sort of compatibilist, to contend that (FP) is *also* true, i.e., that it is also true that one cannot have it in one's power to perform some action which is such that if one were to perform it, the past would have been different from the way it actually was.

The "Multiple-Pasts Compatibilist," then, argues that there is no obstacle to saying that agents are free so to act that certain features of the past would not have been features of the past.[7] Since this sort of compatibilist denies that the intuitive idea of the fixity of the past is robust enough to generate the pertinent premise in the incompatibilist's argument, I shall say that this sort of compatibilist denies that the fixity of the past is robust.

The other move open to a compatibilist is to deny that the intuitive idea of the fixity of the natural laws entails that Jill is not free at $T2$ so to act that some actually obtaining natural law would not have been a natural law. This sort of compatibilist argues that our uncontroversial intuitions about the fixity of natural laws are not sufficient to support the pertinent premise of the incompatibilist's argument.[8] I shall say then that the "Local-Miracle Compatibilist" denies that the fixity of the natural laws is robust.

But then the compatibilist is in an *extremely* uncomfortable position, because there is considerable intuitive pressure to say that the fixity of the past *is* robust and that the fixity of the natural laws *is* robust. That is to say, if it is indeed a necessary condition of Jill's refraining from raising her hand at $T2$ that the past (relative to $T2$) would have been different from what it actually was, then it really would seem that Jill is not free at $T2$ to refrain from raising her hand. And if it is a necessary condition of Jill's refraining from raising her hand at $T2$ that some natural law which actually obtains would not obtain, then it really would seem that Jill is not free at $T2$ to refrain from raising her hand. Whereas these intuitive judgments are not decisive, they certainly have a certain cogency. And given the incompatibilist's argument as developed above (the Conditional Version), it appears that the strategies just explored are the *only* moves open to the compatibilist; it seems that the compatibilist *must* deny the robustness of the fixity of the past or the robustness of the fixity of the natural laws. It seems, then, that in order to protect our common-sense view of ourselves as having more than one genuinely available path into the future, one would have to say something extremely implausible.

IV. A New Compatibilism

I now wish to explore a new sort of compatibilism. This novel approach seeks to deny the incompatibilist's conclusion *without* denying either the robustness of the fixity of the past or the robustness of the fixity of the natural laws (or the validity of the Conditional Version of the Argument for Incompatibilism). That such an approach is possible might seem highly dubious. If the Conditional Version is indeed valid, then how could one possibly avoid the conclusion without denying either the Principle of the Fixity of the Past or the Principle of the Fixity of the Laws? It might appear as if this would require magic, but I shall show that it is indeed possible. And, given the relatively implausible claims to which other sorts of compatibilist are committed, it is at least worthwhile to formulate and evaluate such an approach.

1. World-Indexation

The "New Compatibilism" starts with the claim that all statements about what happens (or obtains) must be world-indexed. That is, if W1 is the actual world and if C obtains at T1, then this should be expressed (for our purposes) by "C obtains at T1 in W1." On this view, there are no index-free statements about what happens (or obtains). Further, given that it is possible that some other condition C* have obtained at T1, there is presumably at least one world—call it W2—in which C* obtained at T1. So it seems that "C* obtains at T1 in W2" is true at T1 in W1—this is just another way of saying that it is true, in W1, that C* could have obtained at T1.

Presumably, there is a *complete catalogue* of world-indexed truths about what obtains at *T1*, two members of which are: "C obtains in *W1*," and "C* obtains in *W2*." This complete catalogue of world-indexed truths is composed of members all of which are true in *W1*. But note, further, that all of the members of this complete catalogue of world-indexed truths are *also* true in *all* possible worlds. The picture here is actually rather simple: at each point in time and in each possible world, there is a true set of statements about what obtains in all of the possible worlds. This corresponds to a true set of statements about actualities and possibilities (relative to each world).

The New Compatibilist relies upon the view that the appropriate way to look at the description of (for example) past states of the universe is in terms of the complete catalogue of world-indexed truths. Consider, again, Jill at *T2*. Suppose that causal determinism obtains and that Jill raises her hand at *T2*. Imagine, further, that although C obtained in the actual world, *W1*, at *T1*, it is true that if Jill were to refrain from raising her hand at *T2*, C* would have obtained (in the pertinent world, W2) at *T1*. So the complete catalogue of world-indexed truths at *T1* includes as members, "C obtains (at *T1*) in *W1*," "C* obtains (at *T1*) in *W2*," and so forth. And note that this complete catalogue of world-indexed truths *does not change from world to world*. That is, this complete catalogue of truths actually was true at *T1* and would have been true at *T1* had Jill refrained from raising her hand at *T2*. Thus, on this picture, Jill's being free at *T2* to refrain from raising her hand does not appear to require that Jill be free at *T2* so to act that the past would have been different from the way it actually was: the past—conceived in terms of the complete catalogue of world-indexed truths—stays the same as one goes from world to world. On this picture, the compatibilist—it appears—can fully endorse both the robust fixity of the natural laws *and* the robust fixity of the past.[9]

To see more clearly how the New Compatibilist's ploy works, recall the "Principle of the Fixity of the Past":

(FP)   For any action Y, agent S, and time T, if it is true that if S were to do Y at T, some (temporally nonrelational or "hard") fact about the past relative to T would not have been a fact, then S cannot do Y at T.

On the New Compatibilist's approach (which involves world-indexation), it is *not* the case that if Jill were to have refrained from raising her hand at T2, then some actually obtaining temporally genuine fact about T1 would not have been a fact: all of the (world-indexed) facts about T1 would have been just as they actually were. Thus, (FP) cannot be employed to show that Jill is not able to refrain from raising her hand at T2.

2. Indexical Possibilism

But the appearance may be misleading. Someone might object that, upon closer inspection, it turns out that the compatibilist just described *cannot* embrace the robust fixity of the past. This is because *something* about the past changes from world to world, despite the existence of an unchanging complete catalogue of world-indexed truths of the kind sketched above. More specifically, what changes is a fact (or, perhaps, the "truth-maker" for the statement) about *which world is the actual world*. So, if Jill raises her hand, the statement "*W1* is the actual world" is true at T1. But if Jill refrains, then the statement "*W2* is the actual world" is true at T1. If this is indeed the case, then (despite the initial appearance) the compatibilist *cannot* embrace the robust fixity of the past: Jill is *not* able so to act that *all* facts about the past would still obtain.

Of course, as stated above, the intuitive idea of the fixity of the past—and thus the Principle of the Fixity of the Past—applies only to temporally nonrelational (or "hard") facts about the past. It might be claimed that a fact such as "World *W1* is actual" is *not* such a fact; after all, if this fact obtains at T1, it entails all sorts of clearly nonrelational facts about the future relative to T1 (insofar as a possible world is complete with regard to the future).

For simplicity's sake, I shall continue to speak of such facts as "World *W1* is actual," but in certain contexts this sort of fact can be replaced by a fact such as "World-segment *W1 (T1)* is actual," where a world-segment that is indexed to a time is simply the segment of the world up to and including that time. So, in the example above, if Jill refrains from raising her hand at T2, then the statement "World-segment *W2 (T1)* is actual" would be true at T1. Thus, on this approach, the relevant facts are *not* temporally relational (or "soft") facts.[10]

I shall now explore a way of defending the New Compatibilism against the worry presented above (i.e., that the compatibilist cannot embrace the robust fixity of the past, since, for example, Jill is *not* able so to act that *all* the facts would remain the same). The problem arises from the view that the identity of *the actual world* changes, given Jill's behavior. But now a certain kind of metaphysician can respond that *there is no single, unique actual world.* Thus, the New Compatibilism conjoins the complete-catalogue picture with the metaphysical doctrine of "indexical possibilism." That is, it combines the contention that all the truths are world-indexed (the "complete-catalogue view") with the doctrine that there is no single, unique actual world ("indexical possibilism").

I cannot here give a detailed, careful explanation of the metaphysical issues pertaining to the distinction between actualism and possibilism.[11] But such a discussion is not necessary, given my purposes in this paper. I shall begin by briefly describing "possibilism," and then I shall seek to distinguish it from "actualism." The possibilist about possible worlds claims that all possible worlds are concrete objects. But there are two versions of possibilism: an absolutist version and an indexical version. Absolutist possibilism claims that there is a unique possible world that possesses the property of *actuality;* the other possible worlds, although concrete and in some sense existent, are not actual or "real." Indexical possibilism claims that all possible worlds are equally "actual" and equally "real." On the indexical view, each possible world is actual "relative to itself," but there is no nonrelative truth about which world is "the actual world."[12]

In contrast, actualism claims that possible worlds are abstract entities— propositions, states of affairs, properties, and so forth (depending on the particular version of actualism). The actualist claims that there is one actual world that "corresponds to" this concrete universe: on one version of actualism, the actual world is "the way this concrete universe is," whereas other possible worlds are "ways this universe might have been."

Actualism and absolutist possibilism share an *absolute* conception of actuality: there is a unique world that is *the* actual world. Indexical possibilism denies this claim; it argues for a certain sort of ontological parity. On this view, an inhabitant of W1 would be speaking truly if he said, "W1 is the actual world," but this statement must be understood as implicitly relativistic: he must be interpreted as saying that W1 is actual *relative to W1.* Of course, an inhabitant of W2 would equally be speaking the truth if he said, "W2 is the actual world," and so forth. (He should be interpreted as saying that W2 *is* actual *relative to W2,* and so forth.) According to indexical possibilism, there are no true, "nonrelative" actuality claims.

Now it should be evident that an indexical possibilist can defend the New Compatibilism against the objection based on the alleged changing character of one feature of the past—the identity of the actual world (or world-segment). The response is that there is no unique, nonrelative truth as to which world is the actual world. On this view, there *are*, of course, world-relativized truths as to which world is actual, but such claims generate no problem with regard to the fixity of the past: these world-relativized truths (such as, "World *W1* is the actual world relative to *W1*") are, of course, the *same* in all possible worlds.

Indexical possibilism is a highly controversial doctrine (to say the least). I do not intend to offer any arguments for this doctrine here. I simply point out that it is one available position on the nature of actuality which has been seriously defended—specifically, by David Lewis—despite its unintuitive initial impression. Note that Lewis certainly does not deny the apparent implausibility of indexical possibilism. Rather, he argues that it is worth paying the price of some intuitive implausibility in order to gain considerable theoretical advantages which cannot be got in other ways. He says:

> The incredulous stare is a gesture meant to say that modal realism [indexical possibilism] fails the test [of intuitive plausibility versus theoretical advantage]. That is a matter of judgment and, with respect, I disagree. I think it is entirely right and proper to count that [intuitive implausibility] as a serious cost. How serious is serious enough to be decisive? ... That is our central question, yet I don't see how anything can be said about it. *I* still think the price is right, high as it is. Modal realism ought to be accepted as true. The theoretical benefits are worth it. Provided, of course, that they cannot be had for less.[13]

Lewis's point is that if we reject indexical possibilism, then we are unable properly to understand and explain important and basic modal notions. So, if we accept indexical possibilism (together with the complete-catalogue view), we can both reap these theoretical benefits and block the incompatibilist's argument. That is, we can both explain other modal notions and preserve our fundamental, common-sense views about the modality of freedom.

Of course, the price of accepting indexical possibilism is high (in terms of unintuitive implications).[14] But it should be pointed out that abstractionist conceptions of possible worlds are *also* not without their own apparently unintuitive implications. For example, on the abstractionist picture, since possible worlds are abstract entities (such as properties or "ways this universe could be"), it follows that we do not live in the actual world—we are not parts of the actual world! (Rather, we live in this concrete universe, and the actual world is [say] a property of it—the way it is.) Thus, if one insists that the incompatibilist's argument cannot be blocked in the way suggested above (because of the New Compatibilist's commitment to indexical possibilism), then one may have to both give up considerable theoretical advantages and *also* say some very unintuitive things. The conclusion of this line of reasoning could be stated in the following somewhat flamboyant fashion: either we can say that we are free to do otherwise, even if causal determinism is true (in part on the basis of the acceptance of indexical possibilism), or we may have to say that we do not live in the actual world!

Above, I promised to show how it is *possible* to embrace compatibilism *without* denying that the past is fixed in a robust sense or that the natural laws are fixed in a robust sense or that the Conditional Version of the Argument for Incompatibilism is invalid. I believe I have done this. Such a compatibilism—the New Compatibilism—combines the complete-catalogue view with indexical possibilism.

3. God's Foreknowledge

It is interesting to note that a parallel "New Compatibilist" strategy seems to apply to the argument for the incompatibility of God's foreknowledge and human freedom to do otherwise.[15] On this approach, one insists on a certain picture of God's knowledge. That is, one insists that at every time in the past, God believed the complete catalogue of *world-indexed* truths about the future. So, for example, at *T1* God believes that Jill raises her hand at *T2* in *W1*, that John goes to the market at *T2* in *W1*, that Jill goes swimming at *T3* in *W1*, that John comes home at *T4* in *W1*, and so forth. Further, at *T1* God believes that Jill refrains from raising her hand at *T2* in *W2*, that John plays tennis instead of going to the market at *T2* in *W2*, and so forth. This corresponds to the idea that God knows not just what will actually happen but what *might* happen as well. (It *gives expression* to this idea in a particular way—employing the notion of world-indexed truths.) And, of course, the complete catalogue of world-indexed truths does not change from world to world. Thus, if one adopts the complete-catalogue view of God's beliefs and (as above) combines it with indexical possibilism, one can embrace compatibilism about God's foreknowledge and human freedom to do otherwise *without* denying the robustness of the fixity of the past or the claim that God's prior beliefs are (or involve) genuine, temporally nonrelational (or "hard") facts about the past.

Just as there is a parallel between the arguments for the incompatibility of causal determinism and freedom to do otherwise and God's foreknowledge and human freedom to do otherwise, the New Compatibilist strategies of response sketched above are parallel. But it might be thought that indexical possibilism is theologically highly implausible. After all, it is a traditional theological tenet that God chose our world from all of the possible worlds as *the* world which he would actualize. In Leibniz's picture, all of the possible worlds in some sense existed in God's mind, and then God chose to make this one *the actual world.* Elsewhere, I have argued that indexical possibilism is indeed theologically implausible, and thus its use by the theological compatibilist is rather dubious.[16] But I wish to point out here that such a worry clearly does not apply to the compatibilist position about *causal determinism* and freedom to do otherwise.

V. How Can Contingency Come from Necessity?

The New Compatibilist buys into two chief contentions: the world-indexation of all truths and indexical possibilism. But a consequence of the claim that all truths are world-indexed is that all truths are necessary! So, for example, consider the claim, "Condition C obtains at *T1* in *W1*." If this is true, it is true in all possible worlds, and thus *necessarily true*. Isn't it mysterious that saving a certain sort of contingency—freedom to do otherwise—requires making all truths necessary? And how could one be free to do otherwise if all truths, including those about how one actually behaves, are *necessarily true*?

Let us suppose, again, that Jill raises her hand at *T2*. The New Compatibilist must say that the truth describing her behavior is "Jill raises her hand at *T2* in world *W1*." But this truth is a necessary truth. How, then, can it be the case that Jill has it in her power to refrain from raising her hand at *T2*? Presumably, Jill's power to refrain from raising her hand at *T2* would involve the power to render false the true statement describing her behavior. But how could she render false a necessary truth?

The New Compatibilist, insofar as he is committed to the world-indexation of all truths, is committed to all truths being necessary truths. Thus, he must deny that Jill's power to refrain from raising her hand at *T2* would involve the power to render false the true statement describing her behavior. Rather, he must understand Jill's power in terms of *accessibility to other possible worlds*.[17] So Jill's having it in her power to refrain from raising her hand at *T2* is understood in terms of her "having access" to world *W2* (in which she refrains from raising her hand at *T2*).

The situation, then, is as follows. If Jill does in fact raise her hand at *T2* in *W1*, it is necessarily true that Jill raises her hand at *T2* in *W1*. That is, "Jill raises her hand at *T2* in *W1*" is true in all possible worlds. Similarly, it is necessarily true that Jill refrains from raising her hand at *T2* in *W2*: "Jill refrains from raising her hand at *T2* in *W2*" is true in all possible worlds. And, insofar as Jill has it in her power in *W1* to refrain from raising her hand at *T2*, it is the case that Jill has access (from *W1*) to *W2*.

For an indexical possibilist, individuals are "world-bound"—particular individuals exist in only one possible world. After all, if all possible worlds are equally concrete and real, how could the same individual exist in (or "at," in Lewis's preferred mode of speaking) more than one possible world? Given that individuals are world-bound, what does it mean to say that an individual (such as Jill) has "access" to a different possible world?

Although individuals are world-bound, on the indexical possibilist's picture, it is nevertheless true that individuals have "counterparts" in other possible worlds.[18] On this sort of approach, a given concrete individual is such that he *possibly* possesses some property just in case *his counterpart* does indeed have the property in some other possible world. So, similarly, an agent has the power in some possible world *W* to perform an action just in case his counterpart performs the action in some possible world suitably related to *W*.[19] Thus, an agent in *W* may have access to another possible world *W1*; the agent himself does not exist in *W1*, but his *counterpart* does. Access to other worlds is made possible, as it were, by the counterpart relation.

VI. The Price of the New Compatibilism

Despite its considerable attractions, the New Compatibilism is not without its drawbacks. Even if the New Compatibilist can make sense of attributions of freedom to do otherwise in his worlds of necessary truths, it is extremely implausible to contend that all truths are necessary truths. This "Spinozistic" contention constitutes a highly implausible "modal collapse."

The modal collapse issues from the New Compatibilist's insistence that all truths are world-indexed. But why need anyone accept the contention that all truths are world-indexed? Granted, some are, but why suppose all truths are world-indexed? So, for example, it can be granted that there is the truth, "Condition *C* obtains at *T1* in *W1*." But why isn't there *also* the truth, "Condition *C* obtains at *T1*?" This index-free truth is clearly a *different* truth from the world-indexed truth, because the index-free truth is *contingent*, whereas the world-indexed truth is *necessary*. And if the index-free truth obtains, then the New Compatibilism must be rejected, since there will indeed be truths about the past which differ from world to world.

Thus far I have simply presented the New Compatibilist as *claiming* (without argument) that all truths are world-indexed. I do not see how this claim could be established. One might try the following. Recall that we are, of course, assuming here (provisionally) the other ingredient in the New Compatibilism: indexical possibilism. On this view, all possible worlds are equally concrete and "real." It may then seem that there *cannot* be index-free truths.

To see this, ask yourself what the index-free truth could describe. Of course, if there were just one concrete universe (as on the absolutist conception of actuality), then an index-free truth would naturally be thought to describe some aspect or part of this universe. But, on the assumption of indexical possibilism, what could the index-free truth describe? It must, presumably, describe the situation in a particular possible world. After all, there are many equally concrete and real worlds; to say, for example, "Condition C obtains at T1" leaves out the crucial information about *which* of these worlds is being described. Thus, if one seriously adopts the assumption of indexical possibilism, it can seem that there simply could not be genuinely index-free truths; all apparently index-free truths must implicitly contain world-indexation.

Although I confess to finding these issues extremely difficult and obscure, I do not think the above argument is compelling. Note, again, that it has the extremely implausible result of rendering all truths *necessary truths*. And this, surely, is not David Lewis's intention in developing his indexical possibilism; nor does Lewis claim that this is indeed a consequence of his metaphysical views.

Return to the question of what an index-free truth—such as, "Condition C obtains at T"—describes (on the indexical possibilist picture). The answer, I think, is simple: it describes the situation in (say) W1. The point is that it does not follow from this (i.e., from the truths describing a particular world) that the world-indexation must be built into the truth itself. And given this fact, contingency is preserved: there are index-free statements, even under the assumption of indexical possibilism. And, of course, this is as it should be: an indexical possibilist, such as Lewis, would insist that merely adopting his metaphysical framework should *not* have the sort of "substantive" implication about modalities we have described above: the modal collapse. In other words, adopting his "metatheory" of modal statements should *not* in itself imply that all truths are necessary.[20]

I have rejected the New Compatibilist's assertion that *all* truths are (at the appropriate level of analysis) world-indexed. I imagine that a New Compatibilist might respond as follows. Suppose God (or anyone else) knows the complete catalogue of world-indexed truths about W1 at T1. What precisely is left out? What exactly does God not know? Intuitively, if God knows the complete catalogue of world-indexed truths about W1 at T1, then He knows everything there is to know about W1 at T1. And if this is so, then the complete catalogue of world-indexed truths about W1 at T1 includes all truths about W1 at T1—nothing is left out.

Against this I would claim that something most definitely *is* left out. Considering the world-indexed truth "C obtains at T1 in W1." What is left out is precisely the *contingent* truth in W1, "C obtains at T1." Now anyone who knows in W1 the world-indexed truth, "C obtains at T1 in W1," will *eo ipso* know in W1 the index-free truth, "C obtains at T1." So anyone who knows the complete catalogue of world-indexed truths will thereby know all the index-free truths. Hence, anyone who knows the complete catalogue of world-indexed truths will thereby know everything there is to know about the relevant world at the relevant time—nothing will have been left out. But this obviously does *not* show that the index-free statements are not distinct items of knowledge, without knowing which an individual would fail to know everything there is to know.

Put in slightly different words, knowing the relevant world-indexed truth implies knowing, in the mentioned world, the associated index-free truth.[21] This explains why knowing the total configuration of world-indexed truths implies knowing everything there is to know. But, of course, the explanation also shows that knowing the world-indexed statements *alone* (and apart from the index-free statements) would *not* exhaust the field of knowledge. What would be left out here, rather conspicuously, would be *everything contingently true in the world!* I think it does not overstate the matter to suggest that this is a rather large lacuna.[22]

VII. Conclusion: The Troubles with Compatibilism

The New Compatibilism is attractive in part because it is so natural to suppose that we do sometimes have alternative possibilities and so unpalatable to swallow the commitments of other sorts of compatibilism. But we have seen that, despite its considerable appeal, the New Compatibilism also comes with a steep price tag: one must not only accept the contentious doctrine of indexical possibilism, but, in addition, one must accept a doctrine (the complete-catalogue view) that issues in a modal collapse (in which all truths are necessary truths).

The proponents of all of the sorts of compatibilism mentioned above, then, are committed to some highly implausible things. The Multiple-Pasts Compatibilist must deny the Principle of the Fixity of the Past, and thus deny the robust fixity of the past. The Local-Miracle Compatibilist must deny the Principle of the Fixity of the Laws, and thus deny the robust fixity of the laws. And the New Compatibilist must embrace both indexical possibilism and the complete-catalogue view; thus he is (among other things) committed to a modal collapse.

Some philosophers have contended not only that the Conditional Version of the Argument for Incompatibilism is invalid but that all valid arguments for incompatibilism depend, either explicitly or implicitly, on a certain modal principle: the "Principle of the Transfer of Powerlessness." The Transfer Principle can be stated roughly as follows. If P obtains and one cannot render it false that P obtains, and if it is true that if P then Q, and one cannot render it false that if P then Q, then it follows that Q is true and that one cannot render it false that Q.

Although I disagree with the view that all good arguments for incompatibilism rely, at some level, on the Transfer Principle, let us assume, for the sake of the argument, that this is so. On this assumption, and given that one does *not* reject the robust fixity of the past or the natural laws, then one *must* reject the Transfer Principle in order to preserve compatibilism.[23] But the Transfer Principle is eminently plausible. Thus, this sort of compatibilism is also intuitively unattractive.

I have elsewhere contended that there is yet *another* version of the Argument for Incompatibilism which does not either explicitly or implicitly rely on the Transfer Principle. I have called this the Basic Version of the Argument for Incompatibilism. If I am correct—and this version does not depend on the Transfer Principle—then the only way to block this argument is to deny what I have called the "Basic Version" of the Principle of the Fixity of the Past (and the Natural Laws). This principle states that an agent has it in his power in world $W1$ to perform some action A at T only if it is possible for his performing A to be an extension of the past relative to T in $W1$, holding fixed the natural laws of $W1$. That is, the principle requires that in order for it to be within an agent's power in $W1$ to do A at T, there must be a possible world with the same past relative to T and the same laws as in $W1$ in which the agent does A at T. Insofar as this Basic Version seems to capture the intuitive notions of the fixity of the past and the natural laws rather elegantly, it would appear to be very implausible to reject it.

So *all* conceivable forms of compatibilism (about causal determinism and alternative possibilities) have considerable costs associated with them. Here, as elsewhere in philosophy, when one cleans up the mess in one place, it appears in another, just as in Dr. Seuss's *The Cat in the Hat Comes Back*. It is, then, a good thing that our moral responsibility and personhood do *not* depend on our having genuine alternative possibilities. In other words, it is a good thing that the doctrine of "semicompatibilism" is true: causal determinism is compatible with moral responsibility, even if causal determinism rules out freedom to do otherwise.[24]

Above, I contended that there are attractive features of, and also problems with, all the forms of compatibilism of which I can conceive. So one might think that, insofar as I am a semicompatibilist, I "sort of" believe that causal determinism is compatible with alternative possibilities or that I believe that causal determinism is "sort of" compatible with alternative possibilities. But, of course, these are not my views! Indeed, I need not take *any* stand on whether compatibilism (about causal determinism and alternative possibilities) is true, although I am strongly inclined to think that its costs outweigh its benefits. Where I take my stand is here: I believe that in assessing moral responsibility, one ought to *disregard* considerations pertaining to freedom to do otherwise (and, indeed, *any* sorts of alternative possibilities such as freedom to choose otherwise). Having separated moral responsibility from freedom to do (or choose) otherwise, I believe there are no *additional* reasons why causal determinism should be thought decisively to rule out moral responsibility.[25,26]

Notes

1. For this argument, see John Martin Fischer and Mark Ravizza, "When the Will Is Free," in James E. Tomberlin, ed., *Philosophical Perspectives VI: Ethics* (Atascadero, Calif.: Ridgeview Publishing Co., 1992), 427–28; and John Martin Fischer, *The Metaphysics of Free Will: An Essay on Control* (Cambridge, Mass.: Blackwell Publishers, 1994), 62–63.

2. Peter van Inwagen, "When the Will Is Not Free," *Philosophical* Studies 75 (1994): 95–113, esp. 98.

3. Ibid., 99.

4. Ted A. Warfield, review of *The Metaphysics of Free Will: An Essay on Control,* by John Martin Fischer, *Faith and Philosophy* 14 (1997): 261–65; the quotation appears on 263. (I am grateful to Warfield for kindly sending me a manuscript copy of this review.)

5. See John Martin Fischer and Mark Ravizza, "Free Will and the Modal Principle," *Philosophical Studies* 83 (1996): 213–30.

6. Fischer, op. cit., 228 n. 43.

7. For a discussion of this sort of strategy, see Fischer, op. cit., 78–86.

8. There is a discussion of this sort of compatibilism in Fischer, op. cit., 67–78.

9. Note that the New Compatibilist is in effect challenging the soundness of the Condition Version of the Argument for Incompatibilism (in virtue of challenging the premise that the three conditionals, [1], [2], and [3] exhaust the field).

10. For further discussion and clarification of the distinction between hard and soft facts, see the selection of papers in John Martin Fischer, ed., *God, Foreknowledge, and Freedom* (Stanford, Calif.: Stanford University Press, 1989); and Fischer, *The Metaphysics of Free Will,* 111–130.

11. The classic discussion is in David Lewis, *On the Plurality of Worlds* (Oxford: Blackwell Publishers, 1986).

12. David Lewis has argued forcefully for indexical possibilism in his "Anselm and Actuality," *Noûs* 4 (1970): 175–88; and *On the Plurality of Worlds.*

13. Lewis, *On the Plurality of Worlds,* 135.

14. It might be thought that one could avoid the unintuitive implications of indexical possibilism while still adopting an indexical analysis of "actual" and thus being able to protect the New Compatibilism. That is, one can separate the semantic thesis—that "actual" should be treated indexically—from some of the apparently extravagant metaphysical implications of Lewis's indexical possibilism (i.e., that all possible worlds are equally concrete and real). (I am indebted to Anthony Brueckner for reminding me of this point.) For indexical accounts of "actual," without Lewis's metaphysics, see, for example, David Kaplan, "Demonstratives" (manuscript, University of California, Los Angeles); Nathan U. Salmon. *Reference and Essence* (Princeton, N.J.: Princeton University Press, 1981), and "Existence," in James E. Tomberlin, ed., *Philosophical Perspectives I: Metaphysics* (Atascadero, Calif.: Ridgeview Publishing Co., 1987), 49–108, esp. 73–90.

On the indexical approach to "actual," no statement about which world is actual will be changing from world to world. But note that the intuitive idea of the fixity of the past can be formulated in such a way as to exhibit the inadequacy of the semantic approach (in the absence of Lewis's metaphysics) to protect the New Compatibilism. That is, one can give expression to the idea of the fixity of the past roughly as follows:

No agent has it in his power at a time T so to act that some feature of the single, concrete, real world would have been different from what it actually was. Now the freedom of an agent to do other than he actually does will run afoul of this condition, even given the semantic doctrine of the indexicality of actuality.

15. I developed—and evaluated—this strategy in John Martin Fischer, "Freedom and Actuality," in Thomas V. Morris, ed., *Divine and Human Action: Essays in the Metaphysics of Theism* (Ithaca, N.Y.: Cornell University Press, 1988), 236–54.

16. See ibid., esp. 251.

17. I am indebted, for this suggestion, to very helpful correspondence with Carl Ginet. Note that Peter van Inwagen employs talk of "access to other possible worlds" in his discussion of freedom in his *An Essay on Free Will* (Oxford: Clarendon Press, 1983), 83–93.

18. See David Lewis, "Counterpart Theory and Quantified Modal Logic," *Journal of Philosophy* 63 (1968): 113–26; "Counterparts of Persons and Their Bodies," *Journal of Philosophy* 68 (1971): 203–11; *Counterfactuals* (Cambridge, Mass.: Harvard University Press, 1973); and *On the Plurality of Worlds*.

19. There is considerable debate about what this "suitable relationship" must be. See, for example, Keith Lehrer, "'Can' in Theory and Practice: A Possible Worlds Analysis," in Myles Brand and Doug Walton. eds., *Action Theory: Proceedings of the Winnipeg Conference on Human Action* (Dordrecht: P. Reidel Publishing Co., 1976); Terence Horgan, "Lehrer on 'Could'-Statements," *Philosophical Studies* 32 (1977): 403–11; Terence Horgan, "'Could', Possible Worlds and Moral Responsibility," *Southern Journal of Philosophy* 17 (1979): 345–58; Robert Audi, "Avoidability and Possible Worlds," *Philosophical Studies* 33 (1978): 413–21; and John Martin Fischer, "Lehrer's New Move: 'Can' in Theory and Practice," *Theoria* 45 (1979): 49–62.

20. Above, I pointed out that one might think that there are two possibilities: either we are free to do otherwise (since we have adopted indexical possibilism conjoined with the complete-catalogue view) or we cannot properly make sense of certain basic modal notions (since we have given up indexical possibilism). Given the argument of this section, it seems plausible to pose a different dilemma: either we produce a modal collapse, and thus cannot preserve our ordinary thinking about modality, or we are not free to do otherwise (having given up the New Compatibilistic assumptions), and thus cannot serve our ordinary thinking about the modality of freedom.

For reasons I mention in the following section, I do not believe that this dilemma should lead us into despair. I *do* believe that we must give up some of our ordinary thinking about freedom (i.e., that we can be confident that we sometimes have genuinely available alternative possibilities). But I do *not* believe that this entails that we need to give up our confidence that we sometimes act freely (and exercise a certain sort of control), a freedom on the basis of which we can be held morally accountable.

21. Say that God does not exist in (all) possible worlds but somehow exists separately (and outside possible worlds). Then His knowing the complete catalogue of world-indexed truths would *not* imply His knowing the index-free truths. On this interpretation of God, His knowing the complete catalogue of world-indexed truths would not imply that He knows all there is to know: something would, most definitely, be missing (i.e., all the contingent truths).

22. It might be said that the world-indexed truths come with a kind of "excess baggage"—the index-free truths. Whereas the world-indexed truths are *immutable* (unchanging from possible world to possible world), the index-free truths are indeed mutable. The strategy here is to identify a set of truths that is different from (although closely related to) the set of world-indexed truths and to point out that these are indeed mutable (and thus capable of running afoul of the Principle of the Fixity of the Past).

Elsewhere I have pursued a similar (although slightly different) kind of strategy. I have argued that certain temporally relational or "soft" facts about times come with "excess baggage." That is, I have argued that in the case of certain soft facts, there are different (although closely related) facts which are temporally nonrelational (or "hard) and which must be falsified if the soft facts are to be falsified. It would follow that these soft facts, despite their softness, can run afoul of the Principle of the Fixity of the Past (in virtue of having hard baggage). See, for example, Fischer, *The Metaphysics of Free Will*, 111–30.

In both sorts of case, it is the "excess baggage" that causes the difficulty. In the first case (pertaining to world-indexed truths), the baggage is a related fact that is indeed mutable. In the latter sort of case (pertaining to certain sorts of soft facts), the baggage is a related fact that is indeed hard. In both sorts of case, an agent's doing otherwise would require *some change* in the hard facts about the past. The general strategy of analysis, then, is to identify some "related fact" which "piggybacks" in certain ways on the ostensibly unproblematic fact. In virtue of this related fact, an agent's doing otherwise would indeed run afoul of the Principle of the Fixity of the Past.

As is well known, J. L. Austin said, "In philosophy it is *can* that we seem to uncover, just when we had thought some problem settled, grinning residually up at us like the frog at the bottom of the beer mug" ("Ifs and Cans," in J. L. Austin, *Philosophical Papers* [Oxford: Clarendon Press, 1961], 153–80, esp. 179). My point is that in analyzing claims involving "can do otherwise," there are certain facts that constitute a seemingly ineradicable residuum: if an agent can do otherwise, he *must* "falsify" or "render false" these genuine facts about the past. These residual elements are my analogues to Austin's frog at the bottom of the beer mug. The grin is, perhaps, the grin of the incompatibilist!

23. Philosophers inclined toward this strategy are Michael Slote, "Selective Necessity and the Free-Will Problem," *Journal of Philosophy* 79 (1982): 5–24; and Daniel Dennett, *Elbow Room: The Varieties of Free Will Worth Wanting* (Cambridge, Mass.: MIT Press, 1984),148–49. For a critical discussion, see Fischer, *The Metaphysics of Free Will*, 29–44.

24. I defend semicompatibilism in Fischer, *The Metaphysics of Free Will*.

25. I do not deny that some will contend that there are indeed such reasons. I have considered some putative reasons of this sort in Fischer, *The Metaphysics of Free Will*. 147–54. For further discussion of this point, see Alfred Mele, "Soft Libertarianism and Frankfurt-Style Scenarios," *Philosophical Topics*, Vol. 24 (1996): 123–142.

26. Some of the ideas on which this paper is based originally appeared in "Freedom and Actuality." I have received considerable help from Carl Ginet, Anthony Brueckner, Chris Hill, Phillip Bricker, and Mark Ravizza.

4

Causality and Determination

ELIZABETH ANSCOMBE

I

It is often declared or evidently assumed that causality is some kind of necessary connection, or alternatively, that being caused is—nontrivially—instancing some exceptionless generalization saying that such an event always follows such antecedents. Or the two conceptions are combined.

Obviously there can be, and are, a lot of divergent views covered by this account. Any view that it covers nevertheless manifests one particular doctrine or assumption. Namely:

If an effect occurs in one case and a similar effect does not occur in an apparently similar case, there must be a relevant further difference.

Any radically different account of causation, then, by contrast with which all those diverse views will be as one, will deny this assumption. Such a radically opposing view can grant that often—though it is difficult to say generally when—the assumption of relevant difference is a sound principle of investigation. It may grant that there are necessitating causes, but will refuse to identify causation as such with necessitation. It can grant that there are situations in which, given the initial conditions and no interference, only one result will accord with the laws of nature; but it will not

Inaugural lecture. Copyright 1971 by Cambridge University Press. Reprinted with the permission of Cambridge University Press.

see general reason, in advance of discovery, to suppose that any given course of things has been so determined. So it may grant that in many cases difference of issue can rightly convince us of a relevant difference of circumstances; but it will deny that, quite generally, this *must* be so.

The first view is common to many philosophers of the past. It is also, usually but not always in a neo-Humeian form, the prevailing received opinion throughout the currently busy and productive philosophical schools of the English-speaking world, and also in some of the European and Latin American schools where philosophy is pursued in the same sort of way; nor is it confined to these schools. So firmly rooted is it that for many even outside pure philosophy, it routinely determines the meaning of "cause", when consciously used as a theoretical term: witness the terminology of the contrast between 'causal' and 'statistical' laws, which is drawn by writers on physics—writers, note, who would not conceive themselves to be addicts of any philosophic school when they use this language to express that contrast.

The truth of this conception is hardly debated. It is, indeed, a bit of *Weltanschauung:* it helps to form a cast of mind which is characteristic of our whole culture.

The association between causation and necessity is old; it occurs for example in Aristotle's *Metaphysics:* "When the agent and patient meet suitably to their powers, the one acts and the other is acted on OF NECESSITY." Only with 'rational powers' an extra feature is needed to determine the result: "What has a rational power [e.g. medical knowledge, which can kill or cure] OF NECESSITY does what it has the power to do and as it has the power, when it has the desire" (Book IX, Chapter V).

Overleaping the centuries, we find it an axiom in Spinoza, "Given a determinate cause, the effect follows OF NECESSITY, and without its cause, no effect follows" *(Ethics, Book I, Axiom III).* And in the English philosopher Hobbes:

> A cause simply, or an entire cause, is the aggregate of all the accidents both of the agents how many soever they be, and of the patients, put together; which when they are supposed to be present, IT CANNOT BE UNDERSTOOD BUT THAT THE EFFECT IS PRODUCED at the same instant; and if any of them be wanting, IT CANNOT BE UNDERSTOOD BUT THAT THE EFFECT IS NOT PRODUCED. *(Elements of Philosophy Concerning Body, Chapter IX)*

It was this last view, where the connection between cause and effect is evidently seen as *logical* connection of some sort, that was overthrown by Hume, the most influential of all philosophers on this subject in the English-speaking and allied schools. For he made us see that, given any particular cause—or 'total causal situation' for that matter—and its effect, there is not in general any contradiction in supposing the one to occur and the other not to occur. That is to say, we'd know what was being described—what it would be like for it to be true—if it were reported for example that a kettle of water was put, and kept, directly on a hot fire, but the water did not heat up.

Were it not for the preceding philosophers who had made causality out as some species of logical connection, one would wonder at this being called a discovery on Hume's part: for vulgar humanity has always been over-willing to believe in miracles and marvels and *lusus naturae*. Mankind at large saw no contradiction, where Hume worked so hard to show the philosophic world—the Republic of Letters—that there was none.

The discovery was thought to be great. But as touching the equation of causality with necessitation, Hume's thinking did nothing against this but curiously reinforced it. For he himself assumed that NECESSARY CONNECTION is an essential part of the idea of the relation of cause and effect *(Treatise of Human Nature, Book I, Part III, Sections II and VI)*, and he sought for its nature. He thought this could not be found in the situations, objects or events called "causes" and "effects", but was to be found in the human mind's being determined, by experience of CONSTANT CONJUNTION, to pass from the sensible impression or memory of one term of the relation to the convinced idea of the other. Thus to say that an event was caused was to say that its occurrence was an instance of some exceptionless generalization connecting such an event with such antecedents as it occurred in. The twist that Hume gave to the topic thus suggested a connection of the notion of causality with that of deterministic laws—i.e. laws such that always, given initial conditions and the laws, a unique result is determined.

The well-known philosophers who have lived after Hume may have aimed at following him and developing at least some of his ideas, or they may have put up a resistance; but in no case, so far as I know,[1] has the resistance called in question the equation of causality with necessitation.

Kant, roused by learning of Hume's discovery, laboured to establish causality as an *a priori* conception and argued that the objective time order consists "in that order of the manifold of appearance according to which, IN CONFORMITY WITH A RULE, the apprehension of that which happens follows upon the apprehension of that which precedes.... In conformity with such a rule there must be in that which precedes an event the condition of a rule according to which this event INVARIABLY and NECESSARILY follows" *(Critique of Pure Reason, Book II, Chapter II, Section III, Second Analogy)*. Thus Kant tried to give back to causality the character of a *justified* concept which Hume's considerations had taken away from it. Once again the connection between causation and necessity was reinforced. And this has been the general characteristic of those who have sought to oppose Hume's conception of causality. They have always tried to establish the necessitation that they saw in causality: either *a priori*, or somehow out of experience.

Since Mill it has been fairly common to explain causation one way or another in terms of 'necessary' and 'sufficient' conditions. Now "sufficient condition" is a term of art whose users may therefore lay down its meaning as they please. So they are in their rights to rule out the query: "May not the sufficient conditions of an event be present, and the event yet not take place?" For "sufficient condition" is so used that if the sufficient conditions for X are there, X occurs. But at the same time, the phrase cozens the understanding into not noticing an assumption. For "sufficient condition" sounds like: "enough". And one certainly *can* ask: "May there not be *enough* to have made something happen—and yet it not have happened?"

Russell wrote of the notion of cause, or at any rate of the 'law of causation' (and he seemed to feel the same way about 'cause' itself), that, like the British monarchy, it had been allowed to survive because it had been erroneously thought to do no harm. In a destructive essay of great brilliance he cast doubt on the notion of necessity involved, unless it is explained in terms of universality, and he argued that upon examination the concepts of determination and of invariable succession of like objects upon like turn out to be empty: they do not differentiate between any conceivable course of things and any other. Thus Russell too assumes that necessity or universality is what is in question, and it never occurs to him that there may be any other conception of causality ('The Notion of Cause', in *Mysticism and Logic*).

Now it's not difficult to show it prima facie wrong to associate the notion of cause with necessity or universality in this way. For, it being much easier to trace effects back to causes with certainty than to predict effects from causes, we often know a cause without knowing whether there is an exceptionless generalization of the kind envisaged, or whether there is a necessity.

For example, we have found certain diseases to be contagious. If, then, I have had one and only one contact with someone suffering from such a disease, and I get it myself, we suppose I got it from him. But what if, having had the contact, I ask a doctor whether I will get the disease? He will usually only be able to say, "I don't know—maybe you will, maybe not."

But, it is said, knowledge of causes here is partial; doctors seldom even know any of the conditions under which one invariably gets a disease, let alone all the sets of conditions. This comment betrays the assumption that there is such a thing to know. Suppose there is: still, the question whether there is does not have to be settled before we can know what we mean by speaking of the contact as cause of my getting the disease.

All the same, might it not be like this: knowledge of causes is possible without any satisfactory grasp of what is involved in causation? Compare the possibility of wanting clarification of 'valency' or 'long-run frequency', which yet have been handled by chemists and statisticians without such clarification; and valencies and long-run frequencies, whatever the right way of explaining them, have been known. Thus one of the familiar philosophic analyses of causality, or a new one in the same line, may be correct, though knowledge of it is not necessary for knowledge of causes.

There is something to observe here, that lies under our noses. It is little attended to, and yet still so obvious as to seem trite. It is this: causality consists in the derivativeness of an effect from its causes. This is the core, the common feature, of causality in its various kinds. Effects derive from, arise out of, come of, their causes. For example, everyone will grant that physical parenthood is a causal relation. Here the derivation is material, by fission. Now analysis in terms of necessity or universality does not tell us of this derivedness of the effect; rather it forgets about that. For the necessity will be that of laws of nature; through it *we* shall be able to derive knowledge of the effect from knowledge of the cause, or vice versa, but that does not show us the cause as source of the effect. Causation, then, is not to be identified with necessitation.

If *A* comes from *B*, this does not imply that every *A*-like thing comes from some *B*-like thing or set-up or that every *B*-like thing or set-up has an *A*-like thing coming from it; or that given *B*, *A* had to come from it, or that given *A*, there had to be *B* for it to come from. Any of these may be true, but if any is, that will be an additional fact, not comprised in *A*'s coming from *B*. If we take "coming from" in the sense of travel, this is perfectly evident.

"But that's because we can observe travel!" The influential Humeian argument at this point is that we can't similarly observe causality in the individual case (Ibid. Bk I, Pt III, Section II). So the reason why we connect what we call the cause and what we call the effect as we do must lie elsewhere. It must lie in the fact that the succession of the latter upon the former is of a kind regularly observed.

There are two things for me to say about this. First, as to the statement that we can never observe causality in the individual case. Someone who says this is just not going to count anything as 'observation of causality'. This often happens in philosophy; it is argued that 'all we find' is such-and-such, and it turns out that the arguer has excluded from his idea of 'finding' the sort of thing he says we don't 'find'. And when we consider what we are allowed to say we do 'find', we have the right to turn the tables on Hume, and say that neither do we perceive bodies, such as billiard balls, approaching one another. When we 'consider the matter with the utmost attention', we find only an impression of travel made by the successive positions of a round white patch in our visual fields ... etc. Now a 'Humeian' account of causality has to be given in terms of constant conjunction of physical things, events, etc., not of experiences of them. If, then, it must be allowed that we 'find' bodies in motion, for example, then what theory of perception can justly disallow the perception of a lot of causality? The truthful—though unhelpful—answer to the question: "How did we come by our primary knowledge of causality?" is that in learning to speak we learned the linguistic representation and application of a host of causal concepts. Very many of them were represented by transitive and other verbs of action used in reporting what is observed. Others—a good example is "infect"—form, not observation statements, but rather expressions of causal hypotheses. The word "cause" itself is highly general. How does someone show that he has the concept *cause?* We may wish to say: only by having such a word in his vocabulary. if so, then the manifest possession of the concept presupposes the mastery of much else in language. I mean: the word "cause" can be *added* to a language in which are already represented many causal concepts. A small selection: *scrape, push, wet, carry, eat, bum, knock over, keep off, squash, make* (e.g. noises, paper boats), *hurt.* But if we care to imagine languages in which no special causal concepts are represented, then no description of the use of a word in such languages will be able to present it as meaning *cause.* Nor will it even contain words for natural kinds of stuff, nor yet words equivalent to "body", "wind", or "fire". For learning to use special causal verbs is part and parcel of learning to apply the concepts answering to these and many other substantives. As surely as we learned to call people by name or to report from seeing it that the cat was on the table, we also learned to report from having observed it that someone drank up the milk or that the dog made a funny noise or that things were cut or broken by whatever we saw cut or break them.

(I will mention, only to set on one side, one of the roots of Hume's argument, the implicit appeal to Cartesian scepticism. He confidently challenges us to "produce some instance, wherein the efficacy is plainly discoverable to the mind, and its operations obvious to our consciousness or sensation" (ibid. Bk I, Pt III, Section XIV). Nothing easier: is cutting, is drinking, is purring not 'efficacy'? But it is true that the apparent perception of such things may be only apparent: we may be deceived by false appearances. Hume presumably wants us to 'produce an instance' in which *efficacy* is related to sensation as *red* is. It is true that we can't do that; it is not so related to sensation. He is also helped, in making his argument that we don't perceive 'efficacy', by his curious belief that "efficacy" means much the same thing as "necessary connection"! But as to the Cartesian-sceptical root of the argument, I will not delay upon it, as my present topic is not the philosophy of perception.)

Second, as to that instancing of a universal generalization, which was supposed to supply what could not be observed in the individual case, the causal relation, the needed examples are none too common. "Motion in one body in all past instances that have fallen under our observation, is follow'd upon impulse by motion in another": so Hume (Ibid. Bk II, Pt III,

Section I). But, as is always a danger in making large generalizations, he was thinking only of the cases where we do observe this—billiard balls against freestanding billiard balls in an ordinary situation; not billiard balls against stone walls. Neo-Humeians are more cautious. They realize that if you take a case of cause and effect, and relevantly describe the cause A and the effect B, and then construct a universal proposition, "Always, given an A, a B follows" you usually won't get anything true. You have got to describe the absence of circumstances in which an A would not cause a B. But the task of excluding all such circumstances can't be carried out. There is, I suppose, a vague association in people's minds between the universal propositions which would be examples of the required type of generalizations, and scientific laws. But there is no similarity.

Suppose we were to call propositions giving the properties of substances "laws of nature". Then there will be a law of nature running "The flash-point of such a substance is … ", and this will be important in explaining why striking matches usually causes them to light. This law of nature has not the form of a generalization running "Always, if a sample of such a substance is raised to such a temperature, it ignites"; nor is it equivalent to such a generalization, but rather to: "If a sample of such a substance is raised to such a temperature and doesn't ignite, there must be a cause of its not doing so." Leaving aside questions connected with the idea of a pure sample, the point here is that 'normal conditions' is quite properly a vague notion. That fact makes generalizations running "Always …" merely fraudulent in such cases; it will always be necessary for them to be hedged about with clauses referring to normal conditions; and we may not know in advance whether conditions are normal or not, or what to count as an abnormal condition. In exemplar analytical practice, I suspect, it will simply be a relevant condition in which the generalization, "Always if such and such, such and such happens … ", supplemented with a few obvious conditions that have occurred to the author, turns out to be untrue. Thus the conditional "If it doesn't ignite then there must be some cause" is the better gloss upon the original proposition, for it does not pretend to say specifically, or even disjunctively specifically, what *always* happens. It is probably these facts which make one hesitate to call propositions about the action of substances "laws of nature". The law of inertia, for example, would hardly be glossed: "If a body accelerates without any force acting on it, there must be some cause of its doing so." (Though I wonder what the author of *Principia* himself would have thought of that.) On the other hand just such 'laws' as that about a substance's flash-point are connected with the match's igniting because struck.

Returning to the medical example, medicine is of course not interested in the hopeless task of constructing lists of all the sets of conditions under each of which people always get a certain disease. It is interested in finding what that is special, if anything, is always the case when people get a particular disease; and, given such a cause or condition (or in any case), in finding circumstances in which people don't get the disease, or tend not to. This is connected with medicine's concern first, and last, with things as they happen in the messy and mixed up conditions of life: only between its first and its last concern can it look for what happens unaffected by uncontrolled and inconstant conditions.

II

Yet my argument lies always open to the charge of appealing to ignorance. I must therefore take a different sort of example.

Here is a ball lying on top of some others in a transparent vertical pipe. I know how it got there: it was forcibly ejected with many others out of a certain aperture into the enclosed space above a row of adjacent pipes. The point of the whole construction is to show how a totality of balls so ejected always build up in rough conformity to the same curve. But I am interested in this one ball. Between its ejection and its getting into this pipe, it kept hitting sides, edges, other balls. If I made a film of it I could run it off in slow motion and tell the impact which produced each stage of the journey. Now was the result necessary? We would probably all have said it was in the time when Newton's mechanics was undisputed for truth. It was the impression made on Hume and later philosophers by that mechanics, that gave them so strong a conviction of the iron necessity with which everything happens, the "absolute fate" by which "Every object is determined to a certain degree and direction of its motion" (A Treatise of Human Nature, Bk II, Pt III, Section I).

Yet no one could have deduced the resting place of the ball—because of the indeterminateness that you get even in the Newtonian mechanics, arising from the finite accuracy of measurements. From exact figures for positions, velocities, directions, spins and masses you might be able to calculate the result as accurately as you chose. But the minutest inexactitudes will multiply up factor by factor, so that in a short time your information is gone. Assuming a given margin of error in your initial figure, you could assign an associated probability to that ball's falling into each of the pipes. If you want the highest probability you assign to be really high, so that you can take it as practical certainty, it will be a problem to reckon how tiny the permitted margins of inaccuracy must be—analogous to the problem: how small a fraction of a grain of millet must I demand is put on the first square of the chess board, if after doubling up at every square I end up having to pay out only a pound of millet? It would be a figure of such smallness as to have no meaning as a figure for a margin of error.

However, so long as you believed the classical mechanics you might also think there could be no such thing as a figure for a difference that had no meaning. Then you would think that though it was not feasible for us to find the necessary path of the ball because our margins of error are too great, yet there *was* a necessary path, which could be assigned a sufficient probability for firm acceptance of it, by anyone (not one of us) capable of reducing his limits of accuracy in measurement to a sufficiently small compass. Admittedly, so small a compass that he'd be down among the submicroscopic particles and no longer concerned with the measurements, say, of the ball. And now we can say: with certain degrees of smallness we get to a region for which Newton's mechanics is no longer believed.

If the classical mechanics can be used to calculate a certain real result, we may give a sense to, and grant, the 'necessity' of the result, given the antecedents. Here, however, you can't use the mechanics to calculate the result, but at most to give yourself a belief in its necessity. For this to be reasonable the system has got to be acknowledged as true. Not, indeed, that that would be enough; but if so much were secured, then it would be worthwhile to discuss the metaphysics of absolute measures of continuous quantities.

The point needs some labouring precisely because 'the system does apply to such bodies'—that is, to moderately massive balls. After all, it's Newton we use to calculate Sputniks! "The system applies to these bodies" is true only in the sense and to the extent that it yields sufficient results of calculations about these bodies. It does not mean: in respect of these bodies the system is the truth, so that it just doesn't matter that we can't use it to calculate such a result in such a case. I am not saying that a deterministic system involves individual predictability: it evidently does not. But in default of predictability the determinedness declared by the deterministic system has got to be believed because the system itself is believed.

I conclude that we have no ground for calling the path of the ball determined—at least, until it has taken its path—but, it may be objected, is not each stage of its path determined, even though we cannot determine it? My argument has partly relied on loss of information through multiplicity of impacts. But from one impact to the next the path is surely determined, and so the whole path is so after all.

It sounds plausible to say: each stage is determined and so the whole is. But what does "determined" mean? The word is a curious one (with a curious history); in this sort of context it is often used as if it *meant* "caused". Or perhaps "caused" is used as if it meant "determined". But there is at any rate one important difference—a thing hasn't been caused until it has happened; but it may be determined before it happens.

(It is important here to distinguish between being *determined* and being *determinate*. In indeterministic physics there is an apparent failure of both. I am concerned only with the former.)

When we call a result determined we are implicitly relating it to an antecedent range of possibilities and saying that all but one of these is disallowed. What disallows them is not the result itself but something antecedent to the result. The antecedences may be logical or temporal or in the order of knowledge. Of the many—antecedent—possibilities, *now* only one is antecedently—possible.

Mathematical formulae and human decisions are limiting cases; the former because of the obscurity of the notion of antecedent possibilities, and the latter because decisions can be retrieved.

In a chessgame, the antecedent possibilities are, say, the powers of the pieces. By the rules, a certain position excludes all but one of the various moves that were in that sense antecedently possible. This is logical antecedence. The next move is determined.

In the zygote, sex and eye-colour are already determined. Here the antecedent possibilities are the possibilities for sex and eye-colour for a child; or more narrowly: for a child of these parents. Now, given the combination of this ovum and this spermatozoon, all but one of these antecedent possibilities is excluded.

It might be said that anything was determined once it had happened. There is now no possibility open: it *has* taken place! It was in this sense that Aristotle said that past and present were necessary. But this does not concern us: what interests us is *pre*-determination.

Then "each stage of the ball's path is determined" must mean "Upon any impact, there is only one path possible for the ball up to the next impact (and assuming no air currents, etc.)." But what ground could one have for believing this, if one does not believe in some system of which it is a consequence? Consider a steel ball dropping between two pins on a Galton board to hit the pin centred under the gap between them. That it should balance on this pin is not to be expected. It has two possibilities; to go to the right or to the left. If you have a system which forces this on you, you can say: "There has to be a determining factor; otherwise, like Buridan's ass, the ball must balance." But if you have not, then you should say that the ball may be undetermined until it does move to the right or the left. Here the ball had only two significant possibilities and was perhaps unpredetermined between them. This was because it cannot be called determined—no reasonable account can be given of insisting that it is so—within a small range of possibility, actualization within which will lead on to its falling either to the right or to the left. With our flying ball there will also be such a small range of possibility. The further consequences of the path it may take are not tied down to just two significant possibilities, as with one step down the Galton board: the range of further possibility gets wider as we consider the paths it may take. Otherwise, the two cases are similar.

We see that to give content to the idea of something's being determined, we have to have a set of possibilities, which something narrows down to one—before the event.

This accords well with our understanding of part of the dissatisfaction of some physicists with the quantum theory. They did not like the undeterminedness of individual quantum phenomena. Such a physicist might express himself by saying "I believe in causality!" He meant: I believe that the real physical laws and the initial conditions must entail uniqueness of result. Of course, within a range of co-ordinate and mutually exclusive identifiable possible results, only one happens: he means that the result that happens ought to be understood as the only one that was possible before it happened.

Must such a physicist be a 'determinist'? That is, must he believe that the whole universe is a system such that, if its total states at t and t' are thus and so, the laws of nature are such as then to allow only one possibility for its total state at any other time? No. He may not think that the idea of a total state of the universe at a time is one he can do anything with. He may even have no views on the uniqueness of possible results for whatever may be going on in any arbitrary volume of space. For "Our theory should be such that only the actual result was possible for that experiment" doesn't mean "Our theory should have excluded the experiment's being muffed or someone's throwing a boot, so that we didn't get the result", but rather: "Our theory should be such that only this result was possible as *the result of the experiment.*" He hates a theory, even if he has to put up with it for the time being, that essentially assigns only probability to a result, essentially allows of a range of possible results, never narrowed down to one until the event itself.

It must be admitted that such dissatisfied physicists very often have been determinists. Witness Schroedinger's account of the 'principle of causality': "The exact physical situation at *any* point P at a given moment t is unambiguously determined by the exact physical situation within a certain surrounding of P at any previous time, say $t - \tau$. If τ is large, that is if that previous time lies far back, it may be necessary to know the previous situation for a wide domain around P" *(Science and Humanism)*. Or Einstein's more modest version of a notorious earlier claim: if you knew all about the contents of a sphere of radius 186,000 miles, and knew the laws, you would be able to know for sure what would happen at the centre for the next second. Schroedinger says: *any* point P; and *a* means *any* sphere of that radius. So their view of causality was not that of my hypothetical physicist, who I said may not have views on the uniqueness of possible results for whatever may be going on in any arbitrary volume of space. My physicist restricts his demand for uniqueness of result to situations in which he has got certain processes going in isolation from inconstant external influences, or where they do not matter, as the weather on a planet does not matter for predicting its course round the sun.

The high success of Newton's astronomy was in one way an intellectual disaster: it produced an illusion from which we tend still to suffer. This illusion was created by the circumstance that Newton's mechanics *had a good model in the solar system*. For this gave the impression that we had here an ideal of scientific explanation; whereas the truth was, it was mere obligingness on the part of the solar system, by having had so peaceful a history in recorded time, to provide such a model. For suppose that some planet had at some time erupted with such violence that its shell was propelled rocket-like out of the solar system. Such an event would not have violated Newton's laws; on the contrary, it would have illustrated them. But also it would not have been calculable as the past and future motions of the planets are presently calculated on the assumption that they can be treated as the simple 'bodies' of his mechanics, with no relevant properties but mass, position and velocity and no forces mattering except gravity.

Let us pretend that Newton's laws were still to be accepted without qualification: no reserve in applying them in electrodynamics; no restriction to bodies travelling a good deal slower than light; and no quantum phenomena. Newton's mechanics is a deterministic system; but this does not mean that believing them commits us to determinism. We could say: of course nothing violates those axioms or the laws of the force of gravity. But animals, for example, run about the world in all sorts of paths and no path is dictated for them by those laws, as it is for planets. Thus in relation to the solar system (apart from questions like whether in the past some planet has blown up), the laws are like the rules of an infantile card game: once the cards are dealt we turn them up in turn, and make two piles each, one red, one black; the winner has the biggest pile of red ones. So once the cards are dealt the game is determined, and from any position in it you can derive all others back to the deal and forward to win or draw. But in relation to what happens on and inside a planet the laws are, rather, like the rules of chess; the play is seldom determined, though nobody breaks the rules.[2]

Why this difference? A natural answer is: the mechanics does not give the special laws of all the forces. Not, for example, for thermal, nuclear, electrical, chemical, muscular forces. And now the Newtonian model suggests the picture: given the laws of all the forces, then there is total coverage of what happens and then the whole game of motion is determined; for, by the first law, any acceleration implies a force of some kind, and must not forces have laws? My hypothetical physicist at least would think so; and would demand that they be deterministic. Nevertheless he still does not have to be a 'determinist'; for many forces, unlike gravity, can be switched on and off, are generated, and also shields can be put up against them. It is one thing to hold that in a clear-cut situation—an astronomical or a well-contrived experimental one designed to discover laws—'the result' should be determined: and quite another to say that in the hurly-burly of many crossing contingencies whatever happens next must be determined; or to say that the generation of forces (by human experimental procedures, among other things) is always determined in advance of the generating procedure; or to say that there is always a law of composition, of such a kind that the combined effect of a set of forces is determined in every situation.

Someone who is inclined to say those things, or implicitly to assume them, has almost certainly been affected by the impressive relation between Newton's mechanics and the solar system.

> We remember how it was in mechanics. By knowing the position and velocity of a particle at one single instant, by knowing the acting forces, the whole future path of the particle could be foreseen. In Maxwell's theory, if we know the field at one instant only, we can deduce from the equations of the theory how the whole field will change in space and time. Maxwell's equations enable us to follow the history of the field, just as the mechanical equations enabled us to follow the history of material particles ... With the help of Newton's laws we can deduce the motion of the earth from the force acting between the sun and the earth.[3]

"By knowing the acting forces"—that must of course include the future acting forces, not merely the present ones. And similarly for the equations which enable us to follow the history of the field; a change may be produced by an external influence. In reading both Newton and later writers one is often led to ponder that word "external". Of course, to be given 'the acting forces' is to be given the external forces too and any new forces that may later be introduced into the situation. Thus those first sentences are true, if true, without the special favour of fate, being general truths of mechanics and physics, but the last one is true by favour, by the brute fact that only the force acting between earth and sun matters for the desired deductions.

The concept of necessity, as it is connected with causation, can be explained as follows: a cause C is a necessitating cause of an effect E when (I mean: on the occasions when) if C occurs it is certain to cause E unless something prevents it. C and E are to be understood as general expressions, not singular terms. If 'certainty' should seem too epistemological a notion: a necessitating cause C of a given kind of effect E is such that it *is* not possible (on the occasion) that C should occur and should not cause an E, given that there is nothing that prevents an E from occurring. A non-necessitating cause is then one that can fail of its effect without the intervention of anything to frustrate it. We may discover *types* of necessitating and non-necessitating cause; e.g. rabies is a necessitating cause of death, because it is not possible for one who has rabies to survive without treatment. We don't have to tie it to the occasion. An example of a non-necessitating cause is mentioned by Feynman: a bomb is connected with a Geiger counter, so that it will go off if the Geiger counter registers a certain reading; whether it will or not is not determined, for it is so placed near some radioactive material that it may or may not register that reading.

There would be no doubt of the cause of the reading or of the explosion if the bomb did go off. Max Born is one of the people who has been willing to dissociate causality from determinism: he explicates cause and effect in terms of dependence of the effect on the cause. It is not quite clear what 'dependence' is supposed to be, but at least it seems to imply that you would not get the effect without the cause. The trouble about this is that you might from some other cause. That this effect was produced by this cause does not at all show that it could not, or would not, have been produced by something else in the absence of this cause.

Indeterminism is not a possibility unconsidered by philosophers. C. D. Broad, in his inaugural lecture, given in 1934, described it as a possibility; but added that whatever happened without being determined was accidental. He did not explain what he meant by being accidental; he must have meant more than not being necessary. He may have meant being uncaused; but, if I am right, not being determined does not imply not being caused. Indeed, I should explain indeterminism as the thesis that not all physical effects are necessitated by their causes. But if we think of Feynman's bomb, we get some idea of what is meant by "accidental". It was random: it 'merely happened' that the radio-active material emitted particles in such a way as to activate the Geiger counter enough to set off the bomb. Certainly the motion of the Geiger counter's needle is caused; and the actual emission is caused too; it occurs because there is this mass of radioactive material here. (I have already indicated that, contrary to the opinion of Hume, there are many different sorts of causality.) But all the same the *causation* itself is, one could say, *mere hap*. It is difficult to explain this idea any further.

Broad used the idea to argue that indeterminism, if applied to human action, meant that human actions are 'accidental'. Now he had a picture of choices as being determining causes, analogous to determining physical causes, and of choices in their turn being either determined or accidental. To regard a choice as such—i.e. any case of choice—as a predetermining causal event, now appears as a naive mistake in the philosophy of mind, though that is a story I cannot tell here.

It was natural that when physics went indeterministic, some thinkers should have seized on this indeterminism as being just what was wanted for defending the freedom of the will. They received severe criticism on two counts: one, that this 'mere hap' is the very last thing to be invoked as the physical correlate of 'man's ethical behaviour'; the other, that quantum laws predict statistics of events when situations are repeated; interference with these, by the *will's* determining individual events which the laws of nature leave undetermined, would be as much a violation of natural law as would have been interference which falsified a deterministic mechanical law.

Ever since Kant it has been a familiar claim among philosophers, that one can believe in both physical determinism and 'ethical' freedom. The reconciliations have always seemed to me to be either so much gobbledegook, or to make the alleged freedom of action quite unreal. My actions are mostly physical movements; if these physical movements are physically predetermined by processes which I do not control, then my freedom is perfectly illusory. The truth of physical indeterminism is thus indispensable if we are to make anything of the claim to freedom. But certainly it is insufficient. The physically undetermined is not thereby 'free'. For freedom at least involves the power of acting according to an idea, and no such thing is ascribed to whatever is the subject (what would be the relevant subject?) of unpredetermination in indeterministic physics. Nevertheless, there is nothing unacceptable about the idea that that 'physical haphazard' should be the only physical correlate of human freedom of action; and perhaps also of the voluntariness and intentionalness in the conduct of other animals which we do not call 'free'. The freedom, intentionalness and voluntariness are not to be analysed as the same thing as, or as produced by, the physical haphazard. Different sorts of pattern altogether are being spoken of when we mention them, from those involved in describing elementary processes of physical causality.

The other objection is, I think, more to the point. Certainly if we have a statistical law, but undetermined individual events, and then enough of these are supposed to be pushed by will in one direction to falsify the statistical law, we have again a supposition that puts will into conflict with natural laws. But it is not at all clear that the same train of minute physical events should have to be the regular correlate of the same action; in fact, that suggestion looks immensely implausible. It is, however, required by the objection.

Let me construct an analogy to illustrate this point. Suppose that we have a large glass box full of millions of extremely minute coloured particles, and the box is constantly shaken. Study of the box and particles leads to statistical laws, including laws for the random generation of small unit patches of uniform colour. Now the box is remarkable for also presenting the following phenomenon: the word "Coca-Cola" formed like a mosaic, can always be read when one looks at one of the sides. It is not always the same shape in the formation of its letters, not always the same size or in the same position, it varies in its colours; but there it always is. It is not at all clear that those statistical laws concerning the random motion of the particles and their formation of small unit patches of colour would have to be supposed violated by the operation of a cause for this phenomenon which did not derive it from the statistical laws.

It has taken the inventions of indeterministic physics to shake the rather common dogmatic conviction that determinism is a presupposition or perhaps a conclusion, of scientific knowledge. Not that that conviction has been very much shaken even so. Of course, the belief that the laws of nature are deterministic has been shaken. But I believe it has often been supposed that this makes little difference to the assumption of macroscopic determinism: as if undeterminedness were always encapsulated in systems whose internal workings could be described only by statistical laws, but where the total upshot, and in particular the outward effect, was as near as makes no difference always the same. What difference does it make, after all, that the scintillations, whereby my watch dial is luminous, follow only a statistical law—so long as the gross manifest effect is sufficiently guaranteed by the statistical law? Feynman's example of the bomb and Geiger counter smashes this conception; but as far as I can judge it takes time for the lesson to be learned. I find deterministic assumptions more common now among people at large, and among philosophers, than when I was an undergraduate.

The lesson is welcome, but indeterministic physics (if it succeeds in giving the lesson) is only culturally, not logically, required to make the deterministic picture doubtful. For it was always a mere extravagant fancy, encouraged in the 'age of science' by the happy relation of Newtonian mechanics to the solar system. It ought not to have mattered whether the laws of nature were or were not deterministic. For them to be deterministic is for them, together with the description of the situation, to entail unique results in situations defined by certain relevant objects and measures, and where no part is played by inconstant factors external to such definition. If that is right, the laws' being deterministic does not tell us whether 'determinism' is true. It is the total coverage of every motion that happens, that is a fanciful claim. But I do not mean that any motions lie outside the scope of physical laws, or that one cannot say, in any given context, that certain motions would be violations of physical law. Remember the contrast between chess and the infantile card game.

Meanwhile in non-experimental philosophy it is clear enough what are the dogmatic slumbers of the day. It is over and over again assumed that any singular causal proposition implies a universal statement running "Always when this, then that"; often assumed that true singular causal statements are derived from such 'inductively believed' universalities. Examples indeed are recalcitrant, but that does not seem to disturb. Even a philosopher acute enough to be conscious of this, such as Davidson, will say, without offering any reason at all for saying it, that a singular causal statement implies *that there is* such a true universal proposition[4]—though perhaps we can never have knowledge of it. Such a thesis needs some reason for believing it! 'Regularities in nature': that is not a reason. The most neglected of the key topics in this subject are: interference and prevention.

Notes

1. My colleague Ian Hacking has pointed out C. S. Peirce to me as an exception to this generalization.

2. I should have made acknowledgements to Gilbert Ryle (*Concept of Mind*, p. 77) for this comparison. But his use of the openness of chess is somewhat ambiguous and is not the same as mine. For the contrast with a closed card game I was indebted to A. J. P. Kenny.

3. Albert Einstein and Leopold Infeld, *The Evolution of Physics* (New York, 1938; paperback edn 1967), p. 146.

4. 'Causal Relations', *Journal of Philosophy*, 64 (November 1967).

Part II

The Analysis of Freedom: Compatibilist and Libertarian Accounts

---

5

Freedom of the Will and the Concept of a Person

HARRY FRANKFURT

What philosophers have lately come to accept as analysis of the concept of a person is not actually analysis of *that* concept at all. Strawson, whose usage represents the current standard, identifies the concept of a person as "the concept of a type of entity such that *both* predicates ascribing states of consciousness *and* predicates ascribing corporeal characteristics ... are equally applicable to a single individual of that single type."[1] But there are many entities besides persons that have both mental and physical properties. As it happens—though it seems extraordinary that this should be so—there is no common English word for the type of entity Strawson has in mind, a type that includes not only human beings but animals of various lesser species as well. Still, this hardly justifies the misappropriation of a valuable philosophical term.

Whether the members of some animal species are persons is surely not to be settled merely by determining whether it is correct to apply to them, in addition to predicates ascribing corporeal characteristics, predicates that ascribe states of consciousness. It does violence to our language to endorse the application of the term 'person' to those numerous creatures which do have both psychological and material properties but which are manifestly

From the *Journal of Philosophy* LXVIII, 1 (January 1971): 5–20. Reprinted by permission of the author and the *Journal of Philosophy*.

not persons in any normal sense of the word. This misuse of language is doubtless innocent of any theoretical error. But although the offense is "merely verbal," it does significant harm. For it gratuitously diminishes our philosophical vocabulary, and it increases the likelihood that we will overlook the important area of inquiry with which the term 'person' is most naturally associated. It might have been expected that no problem would be of more central and persistent concern to philosophers than that of understanding what we ourselves essentially are. Yet this problem is so generally neglected that it has been possible to make off with its very name almost without being noticed and, evidently, without evoking any widespread feeling of loss.

There is a sense in which the word 'person' is merely the singular form of 'people' and in which both terms connote no more than membership in a certain biological species. In those senses of the word which are of greater philosophical interest, however, the criteria for being a person do not serve primarily to distinguish the members of our own species from the members of other species. Rather, they are designed to capture those attributes which are the subject of our most humane concern with ourselves and the source of what we regard as most important and most problematical in our lives. Now these attributes would be of equal significance to us even if they were not in fact peculiar and common to the members of our own species. What interests us most in the human condition would not interest us less if it were also a feature of the condition of other creatures as well.

Our concept of ourselves as persons is not to be understood, therefore, as a concept of attributes that are necessarily species-specific. It is conceptually possible that members of novel or even of familiar nonhuman species should be persons; and it is also conceptually possible that some members of the human species are not persons. We do in fact assume, on the other hand, that no member of another species is a person. Accordingly, there is a presumption that what is essential to persons is a set of characteristics that we generally suppose—whether rightly or wrongly—to be uniquely human.

It is my view that one essential difference between persons and other creatures is to be found in the structure of a person's will. Human beings are not alone in having desires and motives, or in making choices. They share these things with the members of certain other species, some of whom even appear to engage in deliberation and to make decisions based upon prior thought. It seems to be peculiarly characteristic of humans, however, that they are able to form what I shall call "second-order desires" or "desires of the second order."

Besides wanting and choosing and being moved to *do* this or that, men may also want to have (or not to have) certain desires and motives. They are capable of wanting to be different, in their preferences and purposes, from what they are. Many animals appear to have the capacity for what I shall call "first-order desires" or "desires of the first order," which are simply desires to do or not do one thing or another. No animal other than man, however, appears to have the capacity for reflective self-evaluation that is manifested in the formation of second-order desires.[2]

I

The concept designated by the verb 'to want' is extraordinarily elusive. A statement of the form "*A* wants to *X*"—taken by itself, apart from a context that serves to amplify or to specify its meaning—conveys remarkably little information. Such a statement may be consistent, for example, with each of the following statements: (a) the prospect of doing *X* elicits no sensation or introspectible emotional response in *A*; (b) *A* is unaware that he wants to *X*; (c) *A* believes that he does not want to *X*; (d) *A* wants to refrain from *X*-ing; (e) *A* wants to *Y* and believes that it is impossible for him both to *Y* and to *X*; (f) *A* does not "really" want to *X*; (g) *A* would rather die than *X*; and so on. It is therefore hardly sufficient to formulate the distinction between first-order and second-order desires, as I have done, by suggesting merely that someone has a first-order desire when he wants to do or not to do such-and-such, and that he has a second-order desire when he wants to have or not to have a certain desire of the first order.

As I shall understand them, statements of the form "*A* wants to *X*" cover a rather broad range of possibilities.[3] They may be true even when statements like (a) through (g) are true: when *A* is unaware of any feelings concerning *X*-*ing*, when he is unaware that he wants to *X*, when he deceives himself about what he wants and believes falsely that he does not want to *X*, when he also has other desires that conflict with his desire to *X*, or when he is ambivalent. The desires in question may be conscious or unconscious, they need not be univocal, and *A* may be mistaken about them. There is a further source of uncertainty with regard to statements that identify someone's desires, however, and here it is important for my purposes to be less permissive.

Consider first those statements of the form "*A* wants to *X*" which identify first-order desires—that is, statements in which the term 'to *X*' refers to an action. A statement of this kind does not, by itself, indicate the relative strength of *A*'s desire to *X*. It does not make it clear whether this desire is at all likely to play a decisive role in what *A* actually does or tries to do. For it may correctly be said that *A* wants to *X* even when his desire to *X* is only one among his desires and when it is far from being paramount among them. Thus, it may be true that *A* wants to *X* when he strongly prefers to do something else instead; and it may be true that he wants to *X* despite the fact that, when he acts, it is not the desire to *X* that motivates him to do what he does. On the other hand, someone who states that *A* wants to *X* may mean to convey that it is this desire that is motivating or moving *A* to do what he is actually doing or that A will in fact be moved by this desire (unless he changes his mind) when he acts.

It is only when it is used in the second of these ways that, given the special usage of 'will' that I propose to adopt, the statement identifies A's will. To identify an agent's will is either to identify the desire (or desires) by which he is motivated in some action he performs or to identify the desire (or desires) by which he will or would be motivated when or if he acts. An agent's will, then, is identical with one or more of his first-order desires. But the notion of the will, as I am employing it, is not coextensive with the notion of first-order desires. It is not the notion of something that merely inclines an agent in some degree to act in a certain way. Rather, it is the notion of an *effective* desire—one that moves (or will or would move) a person all the way to action. Thus the notion of the will is not coextensive with the notion of what an agent intends to do. For even though someone may have a settled intention to do X, he may nonetheless do something else instead of doing X because, despite his intention, his desire to do X proves to be weaker or less effective than some conflicting desire.

Now consider those statements of the form "A wants to X" which identify second-order desires—that is, statements in which the term 'to X' refers to a desire of the first order. There are also two kinds of situation in which it may be true that A wants to want to X. In the first place, it might be true of A that he wants to have a desire to X despite the fact that he has a univocal desire, altogether free of conflict and ambivalence, to refrain from X-ing. Someone might want to have a certain desire, in other words, but univocally want that desire to be unsatisfied.

Suppose that a physician engaged in psychotherapy with narcotics addicts believes that his ability to help his patients would be enhanced if he understood better what it is like for them to desire the drug to which they are addicted. Suppose that he is led in this way to want to have a desire for the drug. If it is a genuine desire that he wants, then what he wants is not merely to feel the sensations that addicts characteristically feel when they are gripped by their desires for the drug. What the physician wants, insofar as he wants to have a desire, is to be inclined or moved to some extent to take the drug.

It is entirely possible, however, that, although he wants to be moved by a desire to take the drug, he does not want this desire to be effective. He may not want it to move him all the way to action. He need not be interested in finding out what it is like to take the drug. And insofar as he now wants only to *want* to take it, and not to *take* it, there is nothing in what he now wants that would be satisfied by the drug itself. He may now have, in fact, an altogether univocal desire *not* to take the drug; and he may prudently arrange to make it impossible for him to satisfy the desire he would have if his desire to want the drug should in time be satisfied.

It would thus be incorrect to infer, from the fact that the physician now wants to desire to take the drug, that he already does desire to take it. His second-order desire to be moved to take the drug does not entail that he has a first-order desire to take it. If the drug were now to be administered to him, this might satisfy no desire that is implicit in his desire to want to take it. While he wants to want to take the drug, he may have *no* desire to take it; it may be that *all* he wants is to taste the desire for it. That is, his desire to have a certain desire that he does not have may not be a desire that his will should be at all different than it is.

Someone who wants only in this truncated way to want to X stands at the margin of preciosity, and the fact that he wants to want to X is not pertinent to the identification of his will. There is, however, a second kind of situation that may be described by 'A wants to want to X'; and when the statement is used to describe a situation of this second kind, then it does pertain to what A wants his will to be. In such cases the statement means that A wants the desire to X to be the desire that moves him effectively to act. It is not merely that he wants the desire to X to be among the desires by which, to one degree or another, he is moved or inclined to act. He wants this desire to be effective—that is, to provide the motive in what he actually does. Now when the statement that A wants to want to X is used in this way, it does entail that A already has a desire to X. It could not be true both that A wants the desire to X to move him into action and that he does not want to X. It is only if he does want to X that he can coherently want the desire to X not merely to be one of his desires but, more decisively, to be his will.[4]

Suppose a man wants to be motivated in what he does by the desire to concentrate on his work. It is necessarily true, if this supposition is correct, that he already wants to concentrate on his work. This desire is now among his desires. But the question of whether or not his second-order desire is fulfilled does not turn merely on whether the desire he wants is one of his desires. It turns on whether this desire is, as he wants it to be, his effective desire or will. If, when the chips are down, it is his desire to concentrate on his work that moves him to do what he does, then what he wants at that time is indeed (in the relevant sense) what he wants to want. If it is some other desire that actually moves him when he acts, on the other hand, then what he wants at that time is not (in the relevant sense) what he wants to want. This will be so despite the fact that the desire to concentrate on his work continues to be among his desires.

II

Someone has a desire of the second order either when he wants simply to have a certain desire or when he wants a certain desire to be his will. In situations of the latter kind, I shall call his second-order desires "second-order volitions" or "volitions of the second order." Now it is having second-order volitions, and not having second-order desires generally, that I regard as essential to being a person. It is logically possible, however unlikely, that there should be an agent with second-order desires but with no volitions of the second order. Such a creature, in my view, would not be a person. I shall use the term 'wanton' to refer to agents who have first-order desires but who are not persons because, whether or not they have desires of the second order, they have no second-order volitions.[5]

The essential characteristic of a wanton is that he does not care about his will. His desires move him to do certain things, without its being true of him either that he wants to be moved by those desires or that he prefers to be moved by other desires. The class of wantons includes all nonhuman animals that have desires and all very young children. Perhaps it also includes some adult human beings as well. In any case, adult humans may be more or less wanton; they may act wantonly, in response to first-order desires concerning which they have no volitions of the second order, more or less frequently.

The fact that a wanton has no second-order volitions does not mean that each of his first-order desires is translated heedlessly and at once into action. He may have no opportunity to act in accordance with some of his desires. Moreover, the translation of his desires into action may be delayed or precluded either by conflicting desires of the first order or by the intervention of deliberation. For a wanton may possess and employ rational faculties of a high order. Nothing in the concept of a wanton implies that he cannot reason or that he cannot deliberate concerning how to do what he wants to do. What distinguishes the rational wanton from other rational agents is that he is not concerned with the desirability of his desires themselves. He ignores the question of what his will is to be. Not only does he pursue whatever course of action he is most strongly inclined to pursue, but he does not care which of his inclinations is the strongest.

Thus a rational creature, who reflects upon the suitability to his desires of one course of action or another, may nonetheless be a wanton. In maintaining that the essence of being a person lies not in reason but in will, I am far from suggesting that a creature without reason may be a person. For it is only in virtue of his rational capacities that a person is capable of becoming critically aware of his own will and of forming volitions of the second order. The structure of a person's will presupposes, accordingly, that he is a rational being.

The distinction between a person and a wanton may be illustrated by the difference between two narcotics addicts. Let us suppose that the physiological condition accounting for the addiction is the same in both men, and that both succumb inevitably to their periodic desires for the drug to which they are addicted. One of the addicts hates his addiction and always struggles desperately, although to no avail, against its thrust. He tries everything that he thinks might enable him to overcome his desires for the drug. But these desires are too powerful for him to withstand, and invariably, in the end, they conquer him. He is an unwilling addict, helplessly violated by his own desires.

The unwilling addict has conflicting first-order desires: he wants to take the drug, and he also wants to refrain from taking it. In addition to these first-order desires, however, he has a volition of the second order. He is not a neutral with regard to the conflict between his desire to take the drug and his desire to refrain from taking it. It is the latter desire, and not the former, that he wants to constitute his will; it is the latter desire, rather than the former, that he wants to be effective and to provide the purpose that he will seek to realize in what he actually does.

The other addict is a wanton. His actions reflect the economy of his first-order desires, without his being concerned whether the desires that move him to act are desires by which he wants to be moved to act. If he encounters problems in obtaining the drug or in administering it to himself, his responses to his urges to take it may involve deliberation. But it never occurs to him to consider whether he wants the relations among his desires to result in his having the will he has. The wanton addict may be an animal, and thus incapable of being concerned about his will. In any event he is, in respect of his wanton lack of concern, no different from an animal.

The second of these addicts may suffer a first-order conflict similar to the first-order conflict suffered by the first. Whether he is human or not, the wanton may (perhaps due to conditioning) both want to take the drug and want to refrain from taking it. Unlike the unwilling addict, however, he does not prefer that one of his conflicting desires should be paramount over the other; he does not prefer that one first-order desire rather than the other should constitute his will. It would be misleading to say that he is neutral as to the conflict between his desires, since this would suggest that he regards them as equally acceptable. Since he has no identity apart from his first-order desires, it is true neither that he prefers one to the other nor that he prefers not to take sides.

It makes a difference to the unwilling addict, who is a person, which of his conflicting first-order desires wins out. Both desires are his, to be sure; and whether he finally takes the drug or finally succeeds in refraining from taking it, he acts to satisfy what is in a literal sense his own desire. In either case he does something he himself wants to do, and he does it not because of some external influence whose aim happens to coincide with his own but because of his desire to do it. The unwilling addict identifies himself, however, through the formation of a second-order volition, with one rather than with the other of his conflicting first-order desires. He makes one of them more truly his own and, in so doing, he withdraws himself from the other. It is in virtue of this identification and withdrawal, accomplished through the formation of a second-order volition, that the unwilling addict may meaningfully make the analytically puzzling statements that the force moving him to take the drug is a force other than his own, and that it is not of his own free will but rather against his will that this force moves him to take it.

The wanton addict cannot or does not care which of his conflicting first-order desires wins out. His lack of concern is not due to his inability to find a convincing basis for preference. It is due either to his lack of the capacity for reflection or to his mindless indifference to the enterprise of evaluating his own desires and motives.[6] There is only one issue in the struggle to which his first-order conflict may lead: whether the one or the other of his conflicting desires is the stronger. Since he is moved by both desires, he will not be altogether satisfied by what he does no matter which of them is effective. But it makes no difference *to him* whether his craving or his aversion gets the upper hand. He has no stake in the conflict between them and so, unlike the unwilling addict, he can neither win nor lose the struggle in which he is engaged. When a *person* acts, the desire by which he is moved is either the will he wants or a will he wants to be without. When a *wanton* acts, it is neither.

III

There is a very close relationship between the capacity for forming second-order volitions and another capacity that is essential to persons—one that has often been considered a distinguishing mark of the human condition. It is only because a person has volitions of the second order that he is capable both of enjoying and of lacking freedom of the will. The concept of a person is not only, then, the concept of a type of entity that has both first-order desires and volitions of the second order. It can also be construed as the concept of a type of entity for whom the freedom of its will may be a problem. This concept excludes all wantons, both infrahuman and human, since they fail to satisfy an essential condition for the enjoyment of freedom of the will. And it excludes those suprahuman beings, if any, whose wills are necessarily free.

Just what kind of freedom is the freedom of the will? This question calls for an identification of the special area of human experience to which the concept of freedom of the will, as distinct from the concepts of other sorts of freedom, is particularly germane. In dealing with it, my aim will be primarily to locate the problem with which a person is most immediately concerned when he is concerned with the freedom of his will.

According to one familiar philosophical tradition, being free is fundamentally a matter of doing what one wants to do. Now the notion of an agent who does what he wants to do is by no means an altogether clear one: both the doing and the wanting, and the appropriate relation between them as well, require elucidation. But although its focus needs to be sharpened and its formulation refined, I believe that this notion does capture at least part of what is implicit in the idea of an agent who *acts* freely. It misses entirely, however, the peculiar content of the quite different idea of an agent whose *will* is free.

We do not suppose that animals enjoy freedom of the will, although we recognize that an animal may be free to run in whatever direction it wants. Thus, having the freedom to do what one wants to do is not a sufficient condition of having a free will. It is not a necessary condition either. For to deprive someone of his freedom of action is not necessarily to undermine the freedom of his will. When an agent is aware that there are certain things he is not free to do, this doubtless affects his desires and limits the range of choices he can make. But suppose that someone, without being aware of it, has in fact lost or been deprived of his freedom of action. Even though he is no longer free to do what he wants to do, his will may remain as free as it was before. Despite the fact that he is not free to translate his desires into actions or to act according to the determinations of his will, he may still form those desires and make those determinations as freely as if his freedom of action had not been impaired.

When we ask whether a person's will is free we are not asking whether he is in a position to translate his first-order desires into actions. That is the question of whether he is free to do as he pleases. The question of the freedom of his will does not concern the relation between what he does and what he wants to do. Rather, it concerns his desires themselves. But what question about them is it?

It seems to me both natural and useful to construe the question of whether a person's will is free in close analogy to the question of whether an agent enjoys freedom of action. Now freedom of action is (roughly, at least) the freedom to do what one wants to do. Analogously, then, the statement that a person enjoys freedom of the will means (also roughly) that he is free to want what he wants to want. More precisely, it means that he is free to will what he wants to will, or to have the will he wants. Just as the question about the freedom of an agent's action has to do with whether it is the action he wants to perform, so the question about the freedom of his will has to do with whether it is the will he wants to have.

It is in securing the conformity of his will to his second-order volitions, then, that a person exercises freedom of the will. And it is in the discrepancy between his will and his second-order volitions, or in his awareness that their coincidence is not his own doing but only a happy chance, that a person who does not have this freedom feels its lack. The unwilling addict's will is not free. This is shown by the fact that it is not the will he wants. It is also true, though in a different way, that the will of the wanton addict is not free. The wanton addict neither has the will he wants nor has a will that differs from the will he wants. Since he has no volitions of the second order, the freedom of his will cannot be a problem for him. He lacks it, so to speak, by default.

People are generally far more complicated than my sketchy account of the structure of a person's will may suggest. There is as much opportunity for ambivalence, conflict, and self-deception with regard to desires of the second order, for example, as there is with regard to first-order desires. If there is an unresolved conflict among someone's second-order desires, then he is in danger of having no second-order volition; for unless this conflict is resolved, he has no preference concerning which of his first-order desires is to be his will. This condition, if it is so severe that it prevents him from identifying himself in a sufficiently decisive way with *any* of his conflicting first-order desires, destroys him as a person. For it either tends to paralyze his will and to keep him from acting at all, or it tends to remove him from his will so that his will operates without his participation. In both cases he becomes, like the unwilling addict though in a different way, a helpless bystander to the forces that move him.

Another complexity is that a person may have, especially if his second-order desires are in conflict, desires and volitions of a higher order than the second. There is no theoretical limit to the length of the series of desires of higher and higher orders; nothing except common sense and, perhaps, a saving fatigue prevents an individual from obsessively refusing to identify himself with any of his desires until he forms a desire of the next higher order. The tendency to generate such a series of acts of forming desires, which would be a case of humanization run wild, also leads toward the destruction of a person.

It is possible, however, to terminate such a series of acts without cutting it off arbitrarily. When a person identifies himself *decisively* with one of his first-order desires, this commitment "resounds" throughout the potentially endless array of higher orders. Consider a person who, without reservation or conflict, wants to be motivated by the desire to concentrate on his work. The fact that his second-order volition to be moved by this desire is a decisive one means that there is no room for questions concerning the pertinence of desires or volitions of higher orders. Suppose the person is asked whether he wants to want to want to concentrate on his work. He can properly insist that this question concerning a third-order desire does not arise. It would be a mistake to claim that, because he has not considered whether he wants the second-order volition he has formed, he is indifferent to the question of whether it is with this volition or with some other that he wants his will to accord. The decisiveness of the commitment he has made means that he has decided that no further question about his second-order volition, at any higher order, remains to be asked. It is relatively unimportant whether we explain this by saying that this commitment implicitly generates an endless series of confirming desires of higher orders, or by saying that the commitment is tantamount to a dissolution of the pointedness of all questions concerning higher orders of desire.

Examples such as the one concerning the unwilling addict may suggest that volitions of the second order, or of higher orders, must be formed deliberately and that a person characteristically struggles to ensure that they are satisfied. But the conformity of a person's will to his higher-order volitions may be far more thoughtless and spontaneous than this. Some people are naturally moved by kindness when they want to be kind, and by nastiness when they want to be nasty, without any explicit forethought and without any need for energetic self-control. Others are moved by nastiness when they want to be kind and by kindness when they intend to be nasty, equally without forethought and without active resistance to these violations of their higher-order desires. The enjoyment of freedom comes easily to some. Others must struggle to achieve it.

IV

My theory concerning the freedom of the will accounts easily for our disinclination to allow that this freedom is enjoyed by the members of any species inferior to our own. It also satisfies another condition that must be met by any such theory, by making it apparent why the freedom of the will should be regarded as desirable. The enjoyment of a free will means the satisfaction of certain desires—desires of the second or of higher orders—whereas its absence means their frustration. The satisfactions at stake are those which accrue to a person of whom it may be said that his will is his own. The corresponding frustrations are those suffered by a person of whom it may be said that he is estranged from himself, or that he finds himself a helpless or a passive bystander to the forces that move him.

A person who is free to do what he wants to do may yet not be in a position to have the will he wants. Suppose, however, that he enjoys both freedom of action and freedom of the will. Then he is not only free to do what he wants to do; he is also free to want what he wants to want. It seems to me that he has, in that case, all the freedom it is possible to desire or to conceive. There are other good things in life, and he may not possess some of them. But there is nothing in the way of freedom that he lacks.

It is far from clear that certain other theories of the freedom of the will meet these elementary but essential conditions: that it be understandable why we desire this freedom and why we refuse to ascribe it to animals. Consider, for example, Roderick Chisholm's quaint version of the doctrine that human freedom entails an absence of causal determination.[7] Whenever a person performs a free action, according to Chisholm, it's a miracle. The motion of a person's hand, when the person moves it, is the outcome of a series of physical causes; but some event in this series, "and presumably one of those that took place within the brain, was caused by the agent and not by any other events" (18). A free agent has, therefore, "a prerogative which some would attribute only to God: each of us, when we act, is a prime mover unmoved" (23).

This account fails to provide any basis for doubting that animals of sub-human species enjoy the freedom it defines. Chisholm says nothing that makes it seem less likely that a rabbit performs a miracle when it moves its leg than that a man does so when he moves his hand. But why, in any case, should anyone *care* whether he can interrupt the natural order of causes in the way Chisholm describes? Chisholm offers no reason for believing that there is a discernible difference between the experience of a man who miraculously initiates a series of causes when he moves his hand and a man who moves his hand without any such breach of the normal causal sequence. There appears to be no concrete basis for preferring to be involved in the one state of affairs rather than in the other.[8]

It is generally supposed that, in addition to satisfying the two conditions I have mentioned, a satisfactory theory of the freedom of the will necessarily provides an analysis of one of the conditions of moral responsibility. The most common recent approach to the problem of understanding the freedom of the will has been, indeed, to inquire what is entailed by the assumption that someone is morally responsible for what he has done. In my view, however, the relation between moral responsibility and the freedom of the will has been very widely misunderstood. It is not true that a person is morally responsible for what he has done only if his will was free when he did it. He may be morally responsible for having done it even though his will was not free at all.

A person's will is free only if he is free to have the will he wants. This means that, with regard to any of his first-order desires, he is free either to make that desire his will or to make some other first-order desire his will instead. Whatever his will, then, the will of the person whose will is free could have been otherwise; he could have done otherwise than to constitute his will as he did. It is a vexed question just how 'he could have done otherwise' is to be understood in contexts such as this one. But although this question is important to the theory of freedom, it has no bearing on the theory of moral responsibility. For the assumption that a person is morally responsible for what he has done does not entail that the person was in a position to have whatever will he wanted.

This assumption *does* entail that the person did what he did freely, or that he did it of his own free will. It is a mistake, however, to believe that someone acts freely only when he is free to do whatever he wants or that he acts of his own free will only if his will is free. Suppose that a person has done what he wanted to do, that he did it because he wanted to do it, and that the will by which he was moved when he did it was his will because it was the will he wanted. Then he did it freely and of his own free will. Even supposing that he could have done otherwise, he would not have done otherwise; and even supposing that he could have had a different will, he would not have wanted his will to differ from what it was. Moreover, since the will that moved him when he acted was his will because he wanted it to be, he cannot claim that his will was forced upon him or that he was a passive bystander to its constitution. Under these conditions, it is quite irrelevant to the evaluation of his moral responsibility to inquire whether the alternatives that he opted against were actually available to him.[9]

In illustration, consider a third kind of addict. Suppose that his addiction has the same physiological basis and the same irresistible thrust as the addictions of the unwilling and wanton addicts, but that he is altogether delighted with his condition. He is a willing addict, who would not have things any other way. If the grip of his addiction should somehow weaken, he would do whatever he could to reinstate it; if his desire for the drug should begin to fade, he would take steps to renew its intensity.

The willing addict's will is not free, for his desire to take the drug will be effective regardless of whether or not he wants this desire to constitute his will. But when he takes the drug, he takes it freely and of his own free will. I am inclined to understand his situation as involving the overdetermination of his first-order desire to take the drug. This desire is his effective desire because he is physiologically addicted. But it is his effective desire also because he wants it to be. His will is outside his control, but, by his second-order desire that his desire for the drug should be effective, he has made this will his own. Given that it is therefore not only because of his addiction that his desire for the drug is effective, he may be morally responsible for taking the drug.

My conception of the freedom of the will appears to be neutral with regard to the problem of determinism. It seems conceivable that it should be causally determined that a person is free to want what he wants to want. If this is conceivable, then it might be causally determined that a person enjoys a free will. There is no more than an innocuous appearance of paradox in the proposition that it is determined, ineluctably and by forces beyond their control, that certain people have free wills and that others do not. There is no incoherence in the proposition that some agency other than a person's own is responsible (even *morally* responsible) for the fact that he enjoys or fails to enjoy freedom of the will. It is possible that a person should be morally responsible for what he does of his own free will and that some other person should also be morally responsible for his having done it.[10]

On the other hand, it seems conceivable that it should come about by chance that a person is free to have the will he wants. If this is conceivable, then it might be a matter of chance that certain people enjoy freedom of the will and that certain others do not. Perhaps it is also conceivable, as a number of philosophers believe, for states of affairs to come about in a way other than by chance or as the outcome of a sequence of natural causes. If it is indeed conceivable for the relevant states of affairs to come about in some third way, then it is also possible that a person should in that third way come to enjoy the freedom of the will.

Notes

1. P. F. Strawson, *Individuals* (London: Methuen, 1959), pp. 101–102. Ayer's usage of 'person' is similar: "it is characteristic of persons in this sense that besides having various physical properties ... they are also credited with various forms of consciousness" [A. J. Ayer, *The Concept of a Person* (New York: St. Martin's, 1963), p. 82]. What concerns Strawson and Ayer is the problem of understanding the relation between mind and body, rather than the quite different problem of understanding what it is to be a creature that not only has a mind and a body but is also a person.

2. For the sake of simplicity, I shall deal only with what someone wants or desires, neglecting related phenomena such as choices and decisions. I propose to use the verbs 'to want' and 'to desire' interchangeably, although they are by no means perfect synonyms. My motive in forsaking the established nuances of these words arises from the fact that the verb 'to want', which suits my purposes better so far as its meaning is concerned, does not lend itself so readily to the formation of nouns as does the verb 'to desire'. It is perhaps acceptable, albeit graceless, to speak in the plural of someone's "wants." But to speak in the singular of someone's "want" would be an abomination.

3. What I say in this paragraph applies not only to cases in which 'to *X*' refers to a possible action or inaction. It also applies to cases in which 'to *X*' refers to a first-order desire and in which the statement that '*A* wants to *X*' is therefore a shortened version of a statement—"*A* wants to want to *X*"—that identifies a desire of the second order.

4. It is not so clear that the entailment relation described here holds in certain kinds of cases, which I think may fairly be regarded as nonstandard, where the essential difference between the standard and the nonstandard cases lies in the kind of description by which the first-order desire in question is identified. Thus, suppose that *A* admires *B* so fulsomely that, even though he does not know what *B* wants to do, he wants to be effectively moved by whatever desire effectively moves *B*; without knowing what *B*'s will is, in other words, *A* wants his own will to be the same. It certainly does not follow that *A* already has, among his desires, a desire like the

one that constitutes *B*'s will. I shall not pursue here the questions of whether there are genuine counterexamples to the claim made in the text or of how, if there are, that claim should be altered.

5. Creatures with second-order desires but no second-order volitions differ significantly from brute animals, and, for some purposes, it would be desirable to regard them as persons. My usage, which withholds the designation 'person' from them, is thus somewhat arbitrary. I adopt it largely because it facilitates the formulation of some of the points I wish to make. Hereafter, whenever I consider statements of the form "*A* wants to want to *X*," I shall have in mind statements identifying second-order volitions and not statements identifying second-order desires that are not second-order volitions.

6. In speaking of the evaluation of his own desires and motives as being characteristic of a person, I do not mean to suggest that a person's second-order volitions necessarily manifest a *moral* stance on his part toward his first-order desires. It may not be from the point of view of morality that the person evaluates his first-order desires. Moreover, a person may be capricious and irresponsible in forming his second-order volitions and give no serious consideration to what is at stake. Second-order volitions express evaluations only in the sense that they are preferences. There is no essential restriction on the kind of basis, if any, upon which they are formed.

7. "Freedom and Action," in K. Lehrer, ed., *Freedom and Determinism* (New York: Random House, 1966), pp. 11–44.

8. I am not suggesting that the alleged difference between these two states of affairs is unverifiable. On the contrary, physiologists might well be able to show that Chisholm's conditions for a free action are not satisfied, by establishing that there is no relevant brain event for which a sufficient physical cause cannot be found.

9. For another discussion of the considerations that cast doubt on the principle that a person is morally responsible for what he has done only if he could have done otherwise, see my "Alternate Possibilities and Moral Responsibility," *Journal of Philosophy*, LXVI, 23 (Dec. 4, 1969): 829–839.

10. There is a difference between being *fully* responsible and being *solely* responsible. Suppose that the willing addict has been made an addict by the deliberate and calculated work of another. Then it may be that both the addict and this other person are fully responsible for the addict's taking the drug, while neither of them is solely responsible for it. That there is a distinction between full moral responsibility and sole moral responsibility is apparent in the following example. A certain light can be turned on or off by flicking either of two switches and each of these switches is simultaneously flicked to the "on" position by a different person, neither of whom is aware of the other. Neither person is solely responsible for the light's going on, nor do they share the responsibility in the sense that each is partially responsible; rather, each of them is fully responsible.

6

Free Agency

GARY WATSON

In this essay I discuss a distinction that is crucial to a correct account of free action and to an adequate conception of human motivation and responsibility.

I

According to one familiar conception of freedom, a person is free to the extent that he is able to do or get what he wants. To circumscribe a person's freedom is to contract the range of things he is able to do. I think that, suitably qualified, this account is correct, and that the chief and most interesting uses of the word 'free' can be explicated in its terms. But this general line has been resisted on a number of different grounds. One of the most important objections—and the one upon which I shall concentrate in this paper—is that this familiar view is too impoverished to handle talk of free actions and free will.

Frequently enough, we say, or are inclined to say, that a person is not in control of his own actions, that he is not a 'free agent' with respect to them, even though his behaviour is intentional. Possible examples of this sort of action include those which are explained by addictions, manias, and phobias of various sorts. But the concept of free action would seem to be

From the *Journal of Philosophy* LXXII, 8 (April 1975): 205–220. Reprinted by permission of the author and the *Journal of Philosophy*.

pleonastic on the analysis of freedom in terms of the ability to get what one wants. For if a person does something intentionally, then surely he was able at that time to do it. Hence, on this analysis, he was free to do it. The familiar account would not seem to allow for any further questions, as far as freedom is concerned, about the action. Accordingly, this account would seem to embody a conflation of free action and intentional action.

Philosophers who have defended some form of compatibilism have usually given this analysis of freedom, with the aim of showing that freedom and responsibility are not really incompatible with determinism. Some critics have rejected compatibilism precisely because of its association with this familiar account of freedom. For instance, Isaiah Berlin asks: if determinism is true,

> ... what reasons can you, in principle, adduce for attributing responsibility or applying moral rules to [people] which you would not think it reasonable to apply in the case of compulsive choosers—kleptomaniacs, dipsomaniacs, and the like?[1]

The idea is that the sense in which actions would be free in a deterministic world allows the actions of 'compulsive choosers' to be free. To avoid this consequence, it is often suggested, we must adopt some sort of 'contra-causal' view of freedom.

Now, though compatibilists from Hobbes to J. J. C. Smart have given the relevant moral and psychological concepts an exceedingly crude treatment, this crudity is not inherent in compatibilism, nor does it result from the adoption of the conception of freedom in terms of the ability to get what one wants. For the difference between free and unfree actions—as we normally discern it—has nothing at all to do with the truth or falsity of determinism.

In the subsequent pages, I want to develop a distinction between wanting and valuing which will enable the familiar view of freedom to make sense of the notion of an unfree action. The contention will be that, in the case of actions that are unfree, the agent is unable to get what he most wants, *or values*, and this inability is due to his own 'motivational system'. In this case the obstruction to the action that he most wants to do is his own will. It is in this respect that the action is unfree: the agent is obstructed in and by the very performance of the action.

I do not conceive my remarks to be a defence of compatibilism. This point of view may be unacceptable for various reasons, some of which call into question the coherence of the concept of responsibility. But these reasons do not include the fact that compatibilism relies upon the conception of freedom in terms of the ability to get what one wants, nor must it conflate free action and intentional action. If compatibilism is to be shown to be wrong, its critics must go deeper.

II

What must be true of people if there is to be a significant notion of free action? Our talk of free action arises from the apparent fact that what a person most wants may not be what he is finally moved to get. It follows from this apparent fact that the extent to which one wants something is not determined solely by the *strength of* one's desires (or 'motives') as measured by their effectiveness in action. One (perhaps trivial) measure of the strength of the desire or want is that the agent acts upon that desire or want (trivial, since it will be nonexplanatory to say that an agent acted upon that desire because it was the strongest). But, if what one most wants may not be what one most strongly wants, by this measure, then in what sense can it be true that one wants it?[2]

To answer this question, one might begin by contrasting, at least in a crude way, a Humean with a Platonic conception of practical reasoning. The ancients distinguished between the rational and the irrational parts of the soul, between Reason and Appetite. Hume employed a superficially similar distinction. It is important to understand, however, that (for Plato at least) the rational part of the soul is not to be identified with what Hume called 'Reason' and contradistinguished from the 'Passions'. On Hume's account, Reason is not a source of motivation, but a faculty of determining what is true and what is false, a faculty concerned solely with 'matters of fact' and 'relations among ideas'. It is completely dumb on the question of what to do. Perhaps Hume could allow Reason this much practical voice: given an initial set of wants and beliefs about what is or is likely to be the case, particular desires are generated in the process. In other words, a Humean might allow Reason a crucial role in deliberation. But its essential role would not be to supply motivation—Reason is not that kind of thing—but rather to calculate, within a context of desires and ends, how to fulfil those desires and serve those ends. For Plato, however, the rational part of the soul is not some kind of inference mechanism. It is itself a source motivation. In general form, the desires of Reason are desires for 'the Good'.

Perhaps the contrast can be illustrated by some elementary notions from decision theory. On the Bayesian model of deliberation, a preference scale is imposed upon various states of affairs contingent upon courses of action open to the agent. Each state of affairs can be assigned a numerical value (initial value) according to its place on the scale; given this assignment, and the probabilities that those states of affairs will obtain if the actions are performed, a final numerical value (expected desirability) can be assigned to the actions themselves. The rational agent performs the action with the highest expected desirability.

In these terms, on the Humean picture, Reason is the faculty that computes probabilities and expected desirabilities. Reason is in this sense neutral with respect to actions, for it can operate equally on any given assignment of initial values and probabilities—it has nothing whatsoever to say about the assignment of initial values. On the Platonic picture, however, the rational part of the soul itself determines what has *value* and how much, and thus is responsible for the original ranking of alternative states of affairs.

It may appear that the difference between these conceptions is merely a difference as to what is to be called 'Reason' or 'rational', and hence is not a substantive difference. In speaking of Reason, Hume has in mind a sharp contrast between what is wanted and what is thought to be the case. What contrast is implicit in the Platonic view that the ranking of alternative states of affairs is the task of the rational part of the soul?

The contrast here is not trivial; the difference in classificatory schemes reflects different views of human psychology. For one thing, in saying this (or what is tantamount to this) Plato was calling attention to the fact that it is one thing to think a state of affairs good, worth while, or worthy of promotion, and another simply to desire or want that state of affairs to obtain. Since the notion of value is tied to (cannot be understood independently of) those of the good and worthy, it is one thing to value (think good) a state of affairs and another to desire that it obtain. However, to think a thing good is at the same time to desire it (or its promotion). Reason is thus an original spring of action. It is because valuing is essentially related to thinking or *judging* good that it is appropriate to speak of the wants that are (or perhaps arise from) evaluations as belonging to, or originating in, the rational (that is, *judging)* part of the soul; values provide *reasons* for action. The contrast is with desires, whose objects may not be thought good and which are thus, in a natural sense, blind or irrational. Desires are mute on the question of what is good.[3]

Now it seems to me that—given the view of freedom as the ability to get what one wants—there can be a problem of free action only if the Platonic conception of the soul is (roughly) correct. The doctrine I shall defend is Platonic in the sense that it involves a distinction between valuing and desiring which depends upon there being independent sources of motivation. No doubt Plato meant considerably more than this by his parts-of-the-soul doctrine; but he meant at least this. The Platonic conception provides an answer to the question I posed earlier: in what sense can what one most wants differ from that which is the object of the strongest desire? The answer is that the phrase 'what one most wants' may mean either 'the object of the strongest desire' or 'what one most *values*'. This phrase can be interpreted in terms of strength or in terms of ranking order or preference. The problem of free action arises because what one desires may not be what one values, and what one most values may not be what one is finally moved to get.[4]

The tacit identification of desiring or wanting with valuing is so common[5] that it is necessary to cite some examples of this distinction in order to illustrate how evaluation and desire may diverge. There seem to be two ways in which, in principle, a discrepancy may arise. First, it is possible that what one desires is not *to any degree* valued, held to be worth while, or thought good; one assigns *no* value whatever to the object of one's desire. Second, although one may indeed value what is desired, the strength of one's desire may not properly reflect the degree to which one values its object; that is, although the object of a desire is valuable, it may not be deemed the most valuable in the situation and yet one's desire for it may be stronger than the want for what is most valued.

The cases in which one in no way values what one desires are perhaps rare, but surely they exist. Consider the case of a woman who has a sudden urge to drown her bawling child in the bath; or the case of a squash player who, while suffering an ignominious defeat, desires to smash his opponent in the face with the racquet. It is just false that the mother values her child's being drowned or that the player values the injury and suffering of his opponent. But they desire these things none the less. They desire them in spite of themselves. It is not that they assign to these actions an initial value which is then outweighed by other considerations. These activities are not even represented by a positive entry, however small, on the initial 'desirability matrix'.

It may seem from these examples that this first and radical sort of divergence between desiring and valuing occurs only in the case of momentary and inexplicable urges or impulses. Yet I see no conclusive reason why a person could not be similarly estranged from a rather persistent and pervasive desire, and one that is explicable enough. Imagine a man who thinks his sexual inclinations are the work of the devil, that the very fact that he has sexual inclinations bespeaks his corrupt nature. This example is to be contrasted with that of the celibate who decides that the most fulfilling life for him will be one of abstinence. In this latter case, *one* of the things that receive consideration in the process of reaching his all-things-considered judgement is the value of sexual activity. There is something, from his point of view, to be said for sex, but there is more to be said in favour of celibacy. In contrast, the man who is estranged from his sexual inclinations does not acknowledge even a prima-facie reason for sexual activity; that he is sexually inclined toward certain activities is not even *a* consideration. Another way of illustrating the difference is to say that, for the one man, foregoing sexual relationships constitutes a *loss*, even if negligible compared with the gains of celibacy; whereas from the standpoint of the other person, no loss is sustained at all.

Now, it must be admitted, any desire may provide the basis for a reason in so far as non-satisfaction of the desire causes suffering and hinders the pursuit of ends of the agent. But it is important to notice that the reason generated in this way by a desire is a reason for *getting rid* of the desire, and one may get rid of a desire either by satisfying it or by eliminating it in some other manner (by tranquillizers, or cold showers). Hence this kind of reason differs importantly from the reasons based upon the evaluation of the activities or states of affairs in question. For, in the former case, attaining the object of desire is simply a means of eliminating discomfort or agitation, whereas in the latter case that attainment is the end itself. Normally, in the pursuit of the objects of our wants we are not attempting chiefly to relieve ourselves. We aim to satisfy, not just eliminate, desire.

Nevertheless, aside from transitory impulses, it may be that cases wherein nothing at all can be said in favour of the object of one's desire are rare. For it would seem that even the person who conceives his sexual desires to be essentially evil would have to admit that indulgence would be pleasurable, and surely that is something. (Perhaps not even this should be admitted. For indulgence may not yield pleasure at all in a context of anxiety. Furthermore it is not obvious that pleasure is intrinsically good, independently of the worth of the pleasurable object.) In any case, the second sort of divergence between evaluation and desire remains: it is possible that, in a particular context, what one wants most strongly is not what one most values.

The distinction between valuing and desiring is not, it is crucial to see, a distinction among desires or wants according to their content. That is to say, there is nothing in the specification of the objects of an agent's desires that singles out some wants as based upon that agent's values. The distinction in question has rather to do with the *source* of the want or with its role in the total 'system' of the agent's desires and ends. It has to do with why the agent wants what he does.

Obviously, to identify a desire or want simply in terms of its content is not to identify its source(s). It does not follow from my wanting to eat that I am hungry. I may want to eat because I want to be well-nourished; or because I am hungry; or because eating is a pleasant activity. This single desire may have three independent sources. (These sources may not be altogether independent. It may be that eating is pleasurable only because I have appetites for food.) Some specifications of wants or desires—for instance, as cravings—pick out (at least roughly) the source of the motivation.

It is an essential feature of the appetites and the passions that they engender (or consist in) desires whose existence and persistence are independent of the person's judgement of the good. The appetite of hunger involves a desire to eat which has a source in physical needs and physiological states of the hungry organism. And emotions such as anger and fear partly consist in spontaneous inclinations to do various things—to attack or to flee the object of one's emotion, for example. It is intrinsic to the appetites and passions that appetitive and passionate beings can be motivated in spite of themselves. It is because desires such as these arise independently of the person's judgement and values that the ancients located the emotions and passions in the irrational part of the soul;[6] and it is because of this sort of independence that a conflict between valuing and desiring is possible.[7]

These points may suggest an inordinately dualistic view according to which persons are split into inevitably alien, if not always antagonistic, halves. But this view does not follow from what has been said. As central as it is to human life, it is not often noted that some activities are valued only to the extent that they are objects of the appetites. This means that such activities would never be regarded as valuable constituents of one's life were it not for one's susceptibility to 'blind' motivation—motivation independent of one's values. Sexual activity and eating are again examples. We may value the activity of eating to the degree that it provides nourishment. But we may also value it because it is an enjoyable activity, even though its having this status depends upon our appetites for food, our hunger. In the case of sex, in fact, if we were not erotic creatures, certain activities would not only lose their value to us, they might not even be physiologically possible.

These examples indicate, not that there is no distinction between desiring and valuing, but that the value placed upon certain activities depends upon their being the fulfilment of desires that arise and persist independently of what we value. So it is not that, when we value the activity of eating, we think there are reasons to eat no matter what other desires we have; rather, we value eating when food appeals to us; and, likewise, we value sexual relationships when we are aroused. Here an essential part of the *content* of our evaluation is that the activity in question be motivated by certain appetites. These activities may have value for us only in so far as they are appetitively motivated, even though to have these appetites is not *ipso facto* to value their objects.

Part of what it means to value some activities in this way is this: we judge that to cease to have such appetites is to lose something of worth. The judgement here is not merely that, if someone has these appetites, it is worth while *(ceteris paribus)* for him to indulge them. The judgement is rather that it is of value to have and (having them) to indulge these appetites. The former judgement does not account for the eunuch's loss or sorrow, whereas the latter does. And the latter judgement lies at the bottom of the discomfort one may feel when one envisages a situation in which, say, hunger is consistently eliminated and nourishment provided by insipid capsules.

It would be impossible for a nonerotic being or a person who lacked the appetite for food and drink fully to understand the value most of us attach to sex and to dining. Sexual activity must strike the nonerotic being as perfectly grotesque. Or consider an appetite that is in fact 'unnatural' (i.e. acquired): the craving for tobacco. To a person who has never known the enticement of Lady Nicotine, what could be more incomprehensible than the filthy practice of consummating a fine meal by drawing into one's lungs the noxious fumes of a burning weed?

Thus, the relationship between evaluation and motivation is intricate. With respect to many of our activities, evaluation depends upon the possibility of our being moved to act independently of our judgement. So the distinction I have been pressing—that between desiring and valuing—does not commit one to an inevitable split between Reason and Appetite, Appetitively motivated activities may well constitute for a person the most worthwhile aspects of his life.[8] But the distinction does commit us to the possibility of such a split. If there are sources of motivation independent of the agent's values, then it is possible that sometimes he is motivated to do things he does not deem worth doing. This possibility is the basis for the principal problem of free action: a person may be obstructed by his own will.

A related possibility that presents considerable problems for the understanding of free agency is this: some desires, when they arise, may 'color' or influence what appear to be the agent's evaluations, but only temporarily. That is, when and only when he has the desire, is he inclined to think or say that what is desired or wanted is worthwhile or good. This possibility is to be distinguished from another, according to which one thinks it worthwhile to eat when one is hungry or to engage in sexual activity when one is so inclined. For one may think this even on the occasions when the appetites are silent. The possibility I have in mind is rather that what one is disposed to say or judge is temporarily affected by the presence of the desire in such a way that, both before and after the onslaught of the desire, one judges that the desire's object is worth pursuing (in the circumstances) whether or not one has the desire. In this case one is likely, in a cool moment, to think it a matter for regret that one had been so influenced and to think that one should guard against desires that have this property. In other cases it may not be the desire itself that affects one's judgement, but the set of conditions in which those desires arise—e.g. the conditions induced by drugs or alcohol. (It is noteworthy that we say: 'under the influence of alcohol'.) Perhaps judgements made in such circumstances are often in some sense self-deceptive. In any event, this phenomenon raises problems about the identification of a person's values.

Despite our examples, it would be mistaken to conclude that the only desires that exhibit an independence of evaluation are appetitive or passionate desires. In Freudian terms, one may be as dissociated from the demands of the superego as from those of the id. One may be disinclined to move away from one's family, the thought of doing so being accompanied by compunction; and yet this disinclination may rest solely upon acculturation rather than upon a current judgement of what one is to do, reflecting perhaps an assessment of one's 'duties' and interests. Or, taking another example, one may have been habituated to think that divorce is to be avoided in all cases, so that the aversion to divorce persists even though one sees no justification for maintaining one's marriage. In both of these cases, the attitude has its basis solely in acculturation and exists independently of the agent's judgement. For this reason, acculturated desires are irrational (better: nonrational) in the same sense as appetitive and passionate desires. In fact, despite the inhibitions acquired in the course of a puritan upbringing, a person may deem the pursuit of sexual pleasure to be worthwhile, his judgement siding with the id rather than the superego. Acculturated attitudes may seem more akin to evaluation than to appetite in that they are often expressed in evaluative language ('divorce is wicked') and result in feelings of guilt when one's actions are not in conformity with them. But, since conflict is possible here, to want something as a result of acculturation is not thereby to value it, in the sense of 'to value' that we want to capture.

It is not easy to give a nontrivial account of the sense of 'to value' in question. In part, to value something is, in the appropriate circumstances, to want it, and to attribute a want for something to someone is to say that he is disposed to try to get it. So it will not be easy to draw this distinction in behavioural terms. Apparently the difference will have to do with the agent's attitude towards the various things he is disposed to try to get. We might say that an agent's values consist in those principles and ends which he—in a cool and non-self-deceptive moment—articulates as definitive of the good, fulfilling, and defensible life. That most people have articulate 'conceptions of the good', coherent life-plans, *systems* of ends, and so on, is of course something of a fiction. Yet we all have more or less long-term aims and normative principles that we are willing to defend. It is such things as these that are to be identified with our values.

The valuation system of an agent is that set of considerations which, when combined with his factual beliefs (and probability estimates), yields judgements of the form: the thing for me to do in these circumstances, all things considered, is *a*. To ascribe free agency to a being presupposes it to be a being that makes judgements of this sort. To be this sort of being, one must assign values to alternative states of affairs, that is, rank them in terms of worth.

The motivational system of an agent is that set of considerations which move him to action. We identify his motivational system by identifying what motivates him. The possibility of unfree action consists in the fact that an agent's valuational system and motivational system may not completely coincide. Those systems harmonize to the extent that what determines the agent's all-things-considered judgements also determines his actions.

Now, to be sure, since to value is also to want, one's valuational and motivational systems must to a large extent overlap. If, in appropriate circumstances, one were never inclined to action by some alleged evaluation, the claim that that was indeed one's evaluation would be disconfirmed. Thus one's valuational system must have some (considerable) grip upon one's motivational system. The problem is that there are motivational factors other than valuational ones. The free agent has the capacity to translate his values into action; his actions flow from his evaluational system.

One's evaluational system may be said to constitute one's standpoint, the point of view from which one judges the world. The important feature of one's evaluational system is that one cannot coherently dissociate oneself from it *in its entirety*. For to dissociate oneself from the ends and principles that constitute one's evaluational system is to disclaim or repudiate them, and any ends and principles so disclaimed (self-deception aside) cease to be constitutive of one's valuational system. One can dissociate oneself from one set of ends and principles only from the standpoint of another such set that one does not disclaim. In short, one cannot dissociate oneself from all normative judgements without forfeiting all standpoints and therewith one's identity as an agent.

Of course, it does not follow from the fact that one must assume some standpoint that one must have only one, nor that one's standpoint is completely determinate. There may be ultimate conflicts, irresolvable tensions, and things about which one simply does not know what to do or say. Some of these possibilities point to problems about the unity of the person. Here the extreme case is pathological. I am inclined to think that when the split is severe enough, to have more than one standpoint is to have none.

This distinction between wanting and valuing requires far fuller explication than it has received so far. Perhaps the foregoing remarks have at least shown *that* the distinction exists and is important, and have hinted at its nature. This distinction is important to the adherent of the familiar view— that talk about free action and free agency can be understood in terms of the idea of being able to get what one wants—because it gives sense to the claim that in unfree actions the agents do not get what they really or most want. This distinction gives sense to the contrast between free action and intentional action. Admittedly, further argument is required to show that such unfree agents are *unable* to get what they want; but the initial step toward this end has been taken.

At this point, it will be profitable to consider briefly a doctrine that is in many respects like that which I have been developing. The contrast will, I think, clarify the claims that have been advanced in the preceding pages.

III

In an important and provocative article,[9] Harry Frankfurt has offered a description of what he takes to be the essential feature of 'the concept of a person', a feature which, he alleges, is also basic to an understanding of 'freedom of the will'. This feature is the possession of higher-order volitions as well as first-order desires. Frankfurt construes the notion of a person's will as "the notion of an *effective* desire—one that moves (or will or would move) a person all the way to action" [80, above]. Someone has a second-order volition, then, when he wants "a certain desire to be his will." (Frankfurt also considers the case of a second-order desire that is not a second-order volition, where one's desire is simply to have a certain desire and not to act upon it. For example, a man may be curious to know what it is like to be addicted to drugs; he thus desires to desire heroin, but he may not desire his desire for heroin to be effective, to be his will. In fact, Frankfurt's actual example is somewhat more special, for here the man's desire is not simply to have a desire for heroin: he wants to have a desire for heroin which has a certain source, i.e., is addictive. He wants to know what it is like to *crave* heroin.) Someone is a *wanton* if he has no second-order volitions. Finally, "it is only because a person has volitions of the second order that he is capable both of enjoying and of lacking freedom of the will" [84, above].

Frankfurt's thesis resembles the Platonic view we have been unfolding in so far as it focuses upon "the structure of a person's will" [78, above]. I want to make a simple point about Frankfurt's paper: namely that the 'structural' feature to which Frankfurt appeals is not the fundamental feature for either free agency or personhood; it is simply insufficient to the task he wants it to perform.

One job that Frankfurt wishes to do with the distinction between lower and higher orders of desire is to give an account of the sense in which some wants may be said to be more truly the agent's own than others (though in an obvious sense all are wants of the agent), the sense in which the agent 'identifies' with one desire rather than another and the sense in which an agent may be unfree with respect to his own 'will'. This enterprise is similar to our own. But we can see that the notion of 'higher-order volition' is not really the fundamental notion for these purposes, by raising the question: Can't one be a wanton, so to speak, with respect to one's second-order desires and volitions?

In a case of conflict, Frankfurt would have us believe that what it is to identify with some desire rather than another is to have a volition concerning the former which is of higher order than any concerning the latter. That the first desire is given a special status over the second is due to its having an n-order volition concerning it, whereas the second desire has at most an *(n* − 1)-order volition concerning it. But why does one necessarily care about one's higher-order volitions? Since second-order volitions are themselves simply desires, to add them to the context of conflict is just to increase the number of contenders; it is not to give a special place to any of those in contention. The agent may not care which of the second-order desires win out. The same possibility arises at each higher order.

Quite aware of this difficulty, Frankfurt writes:

> There is no theoretical limit to the length of the series of desires of higher and higher orders; nothing except common sense and, perhaps, a saving fatigue prevents an individual from obsessively refusing to identify himself with any of his desires until he forms a desire of the next higher order. [86, above.]

But he insists that:

> It is possible ... to terminate such a series of acts [i.e. the formation of ever higher-order volitions] without cutting it off arbitrarily. When a person identifies himself decisively with one of his first-order desires, this commitment 'resounds' throughout the potentially endless array of higher orders.... The fact that his second-order volition to be moved by this desire is a decisive one means that there is no room for questions concerning the pertinence of volitions of higher orders.... The decisiveness of the commitment he has made means that he has decided that no further question about his second-order volition, at any higher order, remains to be asked. [86–87, above.]

But either this reply is lame or it reveals that the notion of a higher-order volition is not the fundamental one. We wanted to know what prevents wantonness with regard to one's higher-order volitions. What gives these volitions any special relation to 'oneself'? It is unhelpful to answer that one makes a 'decisive commitment', where this just means that an interminable ascent to higher orders is not going to be permitted. This *is* arbitrary.

What this difficulty shows is that the notion of orders of desires or volitions does not do the work that Frankfurt wants it to do. It does not tell us why or how a particular want can have, among all of a person's 'desires', the special property of being peculiarly his 'own'. There may be something to the notions of acts of identification and of decisive commitment, but these are in any case different notions from that of a second- (or n-) order desire. And if these are the crucial notions, it is unclear why these acts of identification cannot be themselves of the first order—that is, identification with or commitment to courses of action (rather than with or to desires)—in which case, no ascent is necessary, and the notion of higher-order volitions becomes superfluous or at least secondary.

In fact, I think that such acts of 'identification and commitment' (if one finds this way of speaking helpful) are generally to courses of action, that is, are first-order. Frankfurt's picture of practical judgement seems to be that of an agent with a given set of (first-order) desires concerning which he then forms second-order volitions. But this picture seems to be distorted. As I see it, agents frequently formulate values concerning alternatives they had not hitherto desired. Initially, they do not (or need not usually) ask themselves which of their desires they want to be effective in action; they ask themselves which course of action is most worth pursuing. The initial practical question is about courses of action and not about themselves.

Indeed, practical judgements are connected with 'second-order volitions'. For the same considerations that constitute one's on-balance reasons for doing some action, *a*, are reasons for wanting the 'desire' to do *a* to be effective in action, and for wanting contrary desires to be ineffective. But in general, evaluations are prior and of the first order. The first-order desires that result from practical judgements generate second-order volitions because they have this special status; they do not have the special status that Frankfurt wants them to have because there is a higher-order desire concerning them.

Therefore, Frankfurt's position resembles the platonic conception in its focus upon the structure of the 'soul'.[10] But the two views draw their divisions differently; whereas Frankfurt divides the soul into higher and lower orders of desire, the distinction for Plato—and for my thesis—is among independent sources of motivation.[11]

IV

In conclusion, it can now be seen that one worry that blocks the acceptance of the traditional view of freedom—and in turn, of compatibilism—is unfounded. To return to Berlin's question above, it is false that determinism entails that all our actions and choices have the same status as those of 'compulsive choosers' such as 'kleptomaniacs, dipsomaniacs, and the like'. What is distinctive about such compulsive behaviour, I would argue, is that the desires and emotions in question are more or less radically independent of the evaluational systems of these agents. The compulsive character of a kleptomaniac's thievery has nothing at all to do with determinism. (His desires to steal may arise quite randomly.) Rather, it is because his desires express themselves independently of his evaluational judgements that we tend to think of his actions as unfree.

The truth, of course, is that God (traditionally conceived) is the only free agent without qualification. In the case of God, who is omnipotent and omniscient, there can be no disparity between valuational and motivational systems. The dependence of motivation upon evaluation is total, for there is but a single source of motivation: his presumably benign judgement.[12] In the case of the Brutes, as well, motivation has a single source: appetite and (perhaps) passion. The Brutes (or so we normally think) have no evaluational systems. But human beings are only more or less free agents, typically less. They are free agents only in some respects. With regard to the appetites and passions, it is plain that in some situations the motivational systems of human beings exhibit an independence from their values which is inconsistent with free agency; that is to say, people are sometimes moved by their appetites and passions in conflict with their practical judgements.[13]

As Nietzsche said (probably with a rather different point in mind): "Man's belly is the reason why man does not easily take himself for a god."[14]

Notes

I have profited from discussions with numerous friends, students, colleagues, and other audiences, on the material of this essay; I would like to thank them collectively. However, special thanks are due to Joel Feinberg, Harry Frankfurt, and Thomas Nagel.

1. *Four Essays on Liberty* (Oxford University Press, 1969), xx–xxi.

2. I am going to use 'want' and 'desire' in the very inclusive sense now familiar in philosophy, whereby virtually any motivational factor that may figure in the explanation of intentional action is a want; 'desire' will be used mainly in connection with the appetites and passions.

3. To quote just one of many suggestive passages: "We must ... observe that within each one of us there are two sorts of ruling or guiding principle that we follow. One is an innate desire for pleasure, the other an acquired judgement that aims at what is best. Sometimes these internal guides are in accord, sometimes at variance; now one gains the mastery, now the other. And when judgement guides us rationally toward what is best, and has the mastery, that mastery is called temperance, but when desire drags us irrationally toward pleasure, and has come to rule within us, the name given to that rule is wantonness" *(Phaedrus,* 237e–238e; Hackforth trans.).

For a fascinating discussion of Plato's parts-of-the-soul doctrine, see Terry Penner's "Thought and Desire in Plato", in Gregory Vlastos, ed., *Plato: A Collection of Critical Essays*, vol. ii (New York: Anchor, 1971). As I see it (and here I have been influenced by Penner's article), the distinction I have attributed to Plato was meant by him to be a solution to the Socratic problem of *akrasia*.

I would argue that this distinction, though necessary, is insufficient for the task, because it does not mark the difference between ('mere') incontinence or weakness of will and psychological compulsion. This difference requires a careful examination of the various things that might be meant in speaking of the strength of a desire.

4. Here I shall not press the rational/nonrational contrast any further than this, though Plato would have wished to press it further. However, one important and anti-Humean implication of the minimal distinction is this: it is not the case that, if a person desires to do X, he therefore has (or even regards himself as having) a reason to do X.

5. For example, I take my remarks to be incompatible with the characterization of value R. B. Perry gives in *General Theory of Value* (Harvard University Press, 1950). In ch. 5, Perry writes: "This, then, we take to be the original source and constant feature of all value. That which is an object of interest is *eo ipso* invested with value." And 'interest' is characterized in the following way: "... liking and disliking, desire and aversion, will and refusal, or seeking and avoiding. It is to this all-pervasive characteristic of the motor-affective life, this *state, act, attitude* or *disposition of favour* or disfavor, to which we propose to give the name of 'interest'."

6. Notice that most emotions differ from passions like lust in that they involve beliefs and some sort of valuation (cf. resentment). This may be the basis for Plato's positing a third part of the soul which is in a way partly rational—namely, *Thumos*.

7. To be sure, one may attempt to cultivate or eliminate certain appetites and passions, so that the desires that result may be in this way dependent upon one's evaluations. Even so, the resulting desires will be such that they can persist independently of one's values. It is rather like jumping from an airplane.

8. It is reported that H. G. Wells regarded the most important themes of his life to have been (1) the attainment of a World Society, and (2) sex.

9. "Freedom of the Will and the Concept of a Person," *Journal of Philosophy,* 1971, 5–20.

10. Frankfurt's idea of a wanton, suitably construed, can be put to further illuminating uses in moral psychology. It proves valuable, I think, in discussing the problematic phenomenon of psychopathy or sociopathy.

11. Some very recent articles employ distinctions, for similar purposes, very like Frankfurt's and my own. See, for example, Richard C. Jeffrey, "Preferences among Preferences," *Journal of Philosophy*, 1974, 377–91. In "Freedom and Desire," *Philosophical Review*, 1974, 32–54, Wright Neely appeals to higher-order desires, apparently unaware of Frankfurt's development of this concept.

12. God could not act *akratically.* In this respect, Socrates thought people were distinguishable from such a being only by ignorance and limited power.

13. This possibility is a definitive feature of appetitive and passionate wants.

14. *Beyond Good and Evil,* s. 141.

7

Identification, Decision, and Treating as a Reason

MICHAEL E. BRATMAN

I. Frankfurt's Challenge

In his 1991 presidential address to the American Philosophical Association, Harry Frankfurt describes the "notion of identification ... [as] fundamental to any philosophy of mind and of action."[1] This is a striking claim. Standard philosophies of action tend to be rather minimalist. Some are extremely minimalist and include only belief, desire and action. Others introduce distinctive forms of valuation. Yet others insist further on the need to include, at a basic level, intentions and plans, and the decisions which are their normal source.[2] Frankfurt's effort to focus our attention on "identification" poses a two-fold challenge: we need to know what identification is, and we need to know if recognizing this phenomenon requires yet a further, fundamental addition to our model of our agency.

Frankfurt emphasizes that an agent may sometimes see her motivation as "external" even though it is in one straightforward sense hers. This may be the attitude a drug addict takes toward her overwhelming desire for the drug, or a person takes toward his "jealously spiteful desire to injure" an acquaintance, or someone takes towards a "spasm of emotion" that "just

From *Philosophical Topics*, vol. 24, no. 2 (1996), pp. 1–18. Reprinted by permission of the author and *Philosophical Topics*.

came over" him.[3] Seeing one's motivation as external may frequently involve characteristic feelings of estrangement, though Frankfurt does not seem to see these as essential.[4] In contrast, one may sometimes on reflection "identify" with one's motivation; one sees it as grounding action that is, in a sense that needs to be clarified, fully one's own. This is what the person in the second example might do when he eschews the desire to injure and instead identifies with, and acts on, a desire to benefit. Such identification seems to involve at least some sort of (perhaps inchoate) reflective consideration of one's motivation, and some sort of (again, perhaps inchoate) endorsement in light of that reflection. In identifying with one's desire, Frankfurt says, "a person is active with respect to" that desire and he "takes responsibility" for ensuing action.[5]

How can we best make systematic sense of such talk of identification? Frankfurt has tried to do this on several different occasions, as have some of his commentators and critics. I want to reflect on this debate and sketch a proposal that is to some extent in the spirit of Frankfurt's view in the 1987 paper, "Identification and Wholeheartedness,"[6] a view that Frankfurt rejects in his presidential address.

A preliminary caveat. One might try to see identification as a key to a compatibilist view of moral responsibility; but I will not focus here on these broader issues. My primary concern here will simply be to provide a coherent characterization of the phenomena that are the target of such talk of identification. It is possible that this is a mistake. Perhaps there is no single phenomenon of identification but instead a variety of complexly inter-related phenomena whose main commonality lies in their connection to judgments of responsibility and the like. But I want to see if we can, instead, describe—without independent appeal to judgments of responsibility—a fairly unified phenomenon plausibly seen as the target of such talk of identification. My conjecture is that we can do this, and that what is central are phenomena of deciding to treat, and of treating, certain of one's desires as reason-giving in one's practical reasoning and planning.

II. Hierarchies of Desire and Valuational Systems

Let us begin at the beginning. In his 1971 paper, "Freedom of the Will and the Concept of a Person," Frankfurt used the idea of desires of higher orders to sketch an account of the "structure of a person's will".[7] Frankfurt focused on cases in which an agent had conflicting "first-order" desires concerning what to do—whether or not to take a certain drug, for example. If the agent were appropriately reflective (and not a "wanton") she might consider which of these desires she wants to control her conduct. She might thereby arrive at a second-order desire—in Frankfurt's terminology, a second-order "volition"—that a certain first-order desire control her conduct and in that sense be her "will".

The agent might also experience conflict at the second-order level and need to reflect at a yet higher level. However, at some level—perhaps simply at the second-order level, perhaps at a higher level—the agent might arrive at a relevant and uncontested highest-order volition. Frankfurt suggests that in at least some such cases the "person identifies himself *decisively* with one of his first-order desires."[8] If, despite such an identification with a given first-order desire, the agent is moved to action by a conflicting first-order desire, that effective first-order desire may count as a "force other than his own"[9]—and this is how Frankfurt describes the case of the "unwilling addict".

Now, in this original paper there is a tension between two competing views. One view is that identification with a first-order desire can be reduced to the state of affairs in which one's relevant highest-order volition favors one's being moved by that desire. The second, weaker view is that identification with a first-order desire involves such a highest-order volition in its favor, but is not simply reducible to such a highest-order volition.

The first, reductive view seems wrong, however. As Gary Watson has put it: "[H]igher-order volitions are just, after all, desires, and nothing about their level gives them any special authority with respect to externality."[10] Perhaps I have a desire to make an aggressive public statement, as well as a desire not to. Perhaps I also have a second-order desire that my first-order desire not to make the statement be my will; but perhaps my reflection has not gone beyond that. It still may be an open question for me whether to see my second-order volition as an overly deferential and fearful "hang up". The mere fact that it is second-order does not suffice to ensure that through it I identify with the desire not to make the aggressive public statement.

This suggests that we try taking the second tack: identification involves an associated highest-order volition, but it also involves something else. But now we are without a suitably complete account of the nature of identification.

Watson made these points in his 1975 paper, "Free Agency".[11] His view there was that we could not analyze identification in terms of orders of desire, but that we could get at the relevant phenomena instead by appeal to a distinction between the agent's motivational and valuational systems. An addict might be moved to act on a desire for a drug even though her valuational system favored rejecting that course of action; in such a case she acts on motivation with which she does not identify. Similar remarks could be made concerning the person who is overwhelmed by a sudden passion. The conjecture, then, was that the motivational/valuational distinction could do the work that the distinction between orders of desires failed to do: tell us what we are talking about when we say that a person is moved by a desire with which she does (does not) identify. Roughly, one identifies with one's desire to A, and so (if that desire moves one to A) with one's A-ing, when A is favored by one's valuational system.[12]

Watson, however, gives up on this view in his 1987 paper, "Free Action and Free Will".[13] The problem he sees is that it seems possible to embrace—to identify with—a course of action that one does not think to be best, or to matter most, or to be what one cares about most deeply. As Watson says "it may not be thought best, but is fun, or thrilling; one loves doing it . . . ."[14] I am fully aware, let us suppose, that drinking beer with my friends tonight will undermine my efforts in an important interview tomorrow; but I nevertheless plump for the fun of social drinking. I am not compelled. The act is fully my own. But this is not an act favored by my evaluational system. Watson continues:

> Call such cases, if you like, perverse cases.... There is no estrangement here. One's will is fully behind what one does. Of course, a person's evaluational system might be defined just in terms of what that person does, without regret, when it comes right down to it, but that would be to give up on the explanation of identification by evaluation.[15]

I think that Watson is right here. Identification is not reducible, in a straightforward way, either to hierarchies of desires, or to features of the agent's evaluations of actions. So what, then, is identification?

III. Decisions About Desires

We have noted that some models of intentional agency include in a basic way decisions and the intentions in which they normally issue. Perhaps we can understand identification in terms of these further conceptual resources. Indeed, that is what Frankfurt suggests in a 1987 paper "Identification and Wholeheartedness".[16]

As early as his 1977 paper, "Identification and Externality", Frankfurt gave up the effort to reduce identification to hierarchies of desire.[17] He there describes a case in which "the relation of a person to his passions is established" "by making a particular kind of decision." He goes on to remark that "decisions, unlike desires or attitudes, do not seem to be susceptible both to internality and to externality."[18] In the 1987 paper, Frankfurt develops this suggestion by sketching an account of identification in terms of decision:

> it is characteristically by a decision ... that a sequence of desires or preferences of increasingly higher orders is terminated. When a decision is made without reservation, the commitment it entails is a decisive one.... The decision deter-

mines what the person really wants by making the desire upon which he decided fully his own.[19]

One "really wants" to A—one identifies with one's desire to A—when one's relevant highest-order desire favors A and one has decided in favor of that desire and its associated lower-order desires.

What is decision? Frankfurt does not provide a systematic answer, but he does offer a story about its normal roles in our agency. We are faced with two kinds of conflicts of desires.[20] Some conflicts call simply for ordering desires in terms of importance: an example might be a conflict between a desire to make more money and a desire for more leisure time. Other conflicts call instead for rejecting a desire as "an outlaw"[21]—as in the example of a "jealously spiteful desire to injure." In each case we can make a decision, but in the former case decision's role is one of "integration", in the latter case "segregation". In either case, a function of decision is to promote both a unified system of motivation and a coordinated pattern of actions over time: "a function of decision is to integrate the person both dynamically and statically".[22]

Decisions, as understood by Frankfurt, always concern, at least in part, desires of the agent. I do not simply decide not to take the drug. I decide in favor of my desire not to take it, and thereby identify with that desire and so with that action. If I simply opt for a course of action Frankfurt wants to say that I make a choice, but do not, strictly speaking, make a decision.[23]

I think that we do sometimes talk about a decision simply to act in a certain way, but the important point is not about terminology. The important point is the substantive claim that identification involves decisions that concern in part our desires. While we cannot understand identification solely in terms of hierarchies of desire, we also cannot do without a kind of decision that "essentially involves reflexivity".[24]

Suppose I see the conflict between my desire for money and my desire for leisure time as calling for ordering and integration. And suppose that this time I decide in favor of leisure time. I do not thereby treat the desire for money as "external": that is the point of the distinction between this kind of conflict and the kind that calls for "segregation". But my decision is to pursue leisure time, not to pursue money. So how can the model account for the idea that I still may "identify" with both of these conflicting desires?

The answer, I take it, is that my decision is complex: it is a decision both to order these desires in this way on this occasion, and to pursue leisure time on this occasion. Though it is a decision that favors one of the conflicting options, it nevertheless treats both desires as desires that are my own. I may identify with a desire even if, on the present occasion, this desire is not favored by my relevant, highest-order volition: in the case at hand, after all, my highest-order volition is that my desire to pursue leisure time be my will.

In trying to provide a conceptual framework adequate to the phenomenon of identification we have moved from hierarchies of desire and valuational systems to decisions about our desires. And we have been led to a more complex relation between identification and highest-order volition. I think these are moves in the right direction; though a full story would need to say more about what decisions are.[25] But now we need to consider a challenge to the idea that identification is a kind of decision about our desires.

IV. Unwitting Decisions and Reflective Satisfaction

J. David Velleman has argued that an appeal to decision will not work, for there can be "unwitting" decisions with which the agent does not identify.[26] Velleman describes a case in which comments of a friend provoke me to raise my voice in anger. On later reflection I realize that earlier "grievances had crystallized in my mind ... into a resolution to sever our friendship." But this earlier decision was unwitting, and I did not, at the time of action, identify with it. At that time "it was my resentment speaking, not I."[27]

The unwitting decision to which Velleman alludes is first-order: it is a decision to sever the friendship. Frankfurt might insist it is merely a choice and so does not challenge his point about decisions. But Velleman's case could be developed so as to involve an unwitting decision in favor of executing the desire to break off the friendship. The challenge remains to Frankfurt's suggestion that "decisions ... do not seem to be susceptible both to internality and to externality."

Indeed, in his presidential address Frankfurt gives up this effort to see identification as a kind of decision. His reason there seems similar in spirit to the reason suggested by Velleman's example. Concerning any mental act or occurrence, even a decision, one can raise the question of whether or not the agent identifies with it. So identification cannot consist simply in some actual mental act or occurrence.[28] So Frankfurt seeks a different approach.

"Identification" Frankfurt now says "is constituted neatly by an endorsing higher-order desire with which the person is satisfied."[29] To be satisfied with a higher-order desire one need not take some further attitude towards it. If some further attitude were needed there would be a threat of a regress; for we could ask about that further attitude whether or not the agent identified with it. It is enough for satisfaction if one is content, in an appropriate way, with that desire:

> Being genuinely satisfied is not a matter, then, of choosing to leave things as they are or of making some judgment or decision concerning the desirability of

change. It is a matter of simply *having no interest* in making changes. What it requires is that psychic elements of certain kinds *do not occur*.... [this] absence must nonetheless be reflective. In other words, the fact that the person is not moved to change things must derive from his understanding and evaluation of how things are with him. Thus, the essential non-occurrence is neither deliberatively contrived nor wantonly unselfconscious.[30]

Reflective satisfaction, while reflective, is nevertheless a "non-occurrence". Such a reflective non-occurrence is to do the work that decision was to do on the (now rejected) 1987 view.

Suppose I am reflecting on a higher-order desire and wondering whether to challenge it. So far I have reached no decision to challenge it; but that is because my reflections are so far incomplete and inconclusive. My reflections have as yet reached no conclusion. I am not (yet) moved to "change things" and this derives from my "understanding and evaluation [so far] of how things are" with me. Yet I do not (yet) identify with that desire: its standing remains a genuinely open question for me. Granted, I also have not (yet) come to see this desire as an "outlaw"; but the mere absence of such a rejection of my desire is not yet enough for identification. Identification seems to require that I somehow settle the question of the status of my desire. To settle that question my reflections need to reach closure—they need to reach a conclusion. But that seems to mean that my reflections need to reach some sort of decision about whether or not to challenge that higher-order desire or to "leave things as they are": the mere absence of motivation to "change things" seems not to suffice.

Is that right? Is a decision really needed for identification? Suppose I discover that I am not moved to change things and then simply stop there and "leave things as they are." Why would that not suffice for identification? The answer is that one may leave things as they are because of some sort of enervation or exhaustion or depression or the like. If in such a case one has not actually decided to leave things as they are one has not, I think, identified with how things are with one.

This is not completely to reject Frankfurt's strategy in this address. While decision may be needed for identification, it may not be all that is needed. Perhaps what is needed is, in part, a decision with which one is "satisfied". I will argue below for such a view.

V. Decisions to Treat as Reason-Giving

If identification involves decision, what kind of decision is it?

We cannot simply say that identification with a desire to *A* is a decision to act on that desire. There are two main reasons why. Return first to the drug addict. Suppose that faced with a powerful desire for the drug he grudgingly decides to go ahead and take it. He might even go ahead and reason grudgingly about preliminary steps and/or relevant means to the end of his getting the drug. Yet he might still see his desire for the drug as an "outlaw", as external; he might still not identify with that desire. So a decision to act on one's desire to A does not ensure identification with that desire.

Second, recall Frankfurt's distinction between two kinds of conflict of desire: conflicts that call for ordering the desires, and conflicts that call instead for rejecting a desire outright. Suppose I see a conflict as calling for ordering and integration and proceed to make a decision. To return to an earlier example: I decide this time to pursue more leisure time rather than more money. I can still treat my desire for money as my own: the mere fact that on this occasion I have decided in favor of leisure time does not ensure that I do not identify with the desire on the losing side. So identification with a desire to A does not require a decision to act on that desire.

Perhaps we have mis-identified what it is that one decides when one identifies with one's desire to A. To identify with the losing desire for more money one need not decide to pursue more money. But identification may still involve a kind of decision about that desire.

What kind of decision? T.M. Scanlon emphasizes that in practical reasoning we sometimes "select among considerations to be taken into account in deciding what to do." Scanlon gives an example of a person who needs to decide whether, in playing tennis, she will "play to win".[31] This is, he suggests, a decision about whether to count the promotion of victory as a reason in reasoning about whether, say, to charge the net.

Suppose a tennis player normally desires to win but decides not to treat the promotion of victory as a reason for action when she is playing against her young son.[32] This is not yet to treat her desire for victory as, in Frankfurt's terms, an "outlaw". After all, our tennis player only decides not to treat her desire for victory as reason-giving in certain special circumstances. But suppose, in contrast, she comes to despair about her extreme competitiveness and decides she will no longer treat her desire for victory as reason-giving in any circumstance: she will no longer treat it as setting an end for her practical reasoning and action. At this point she seems to be treating that desire as "external".[33] This is the kind of decision an agent might reach concerning (to recall some of Frankfurt's examples) a "jealously spiteful desire to injure" someone, or a "spasm of emotion".[34]

If this is what it is to treat a desire as external, what is it to identify with a desire? We might try saying that I identify with my desire to A just in case I so desire and do not treat it as external—I do not, that is, decide not to treat it as a reason in any circumstance. But, as I remarked in discussing Frankfurt's presidential address, such a mere non-occurrence of a decision is compatible with an agent's seeing the issue of the desire's status as genuinely open, and so with an agent's not (yet) identifying with the desire.

This suggests that to identify with a desire to A one needs actually to decide to treat that desire as reason-giving in one's practical reasoning and planning concerning some relevant circumstances. In requiring such a decision, and not merely the non-occurrence of a decision not to treat the desire as a reason in any circumstance, we allow for cases that lie between identifying with a desire and treating it as external, namely: cases in which one reaches neither such decision. Identification so-conceived requires an actual (though, perhaps, inchoate) endorsement, not merely the absence of explicit rejection.

This leaves open the possibility that I identify with a desire even though, in a circumstance in which I treat it as reason-giving, I do not decide to act on it; for I might decide to treat a desire as reason-giving and still also decide not to act on this reason this time. This may happen concerning my desire for money in the face of conflict with my desire for more leisure time.

But what does it mean to treat a desire as reason-giving? Is it, in short, to identify with that desire? Are we moving in a circle?

What is needed for our purposes here is a modest understanding of what it is to treat a desire as reason-giving, one that allows us to avoid unacceptable circularity in our story about identification. One way to try to do this is to appeal to the idea that I treat my desire as reason-giving in the relevant sense when I treat it as end-setting—where to treat it as end-setting is, in part, to treat it as potentially justifying, at least to some extent, my performance of relevant means and/or relevant preliminary steps. This is, at best, only part of the story. A desire in favor of a side-constraint on action, for example, might be reason-giving without being end-setting.[35] But let us limit our attention here to the basic case of an end-setting desire. If this proves useful in understanding identification we can return later to address further complexities.

The suggestion so far, then, is that to identify with a desire to A one needs to decide to treat that desire as reason-giving in at least some of one's relevant practical reasoning and planning. One treats one's desire as reason-giving when one treats it as setting an end that can to some extent justify means and/or preliminary steps. This is not to say that one treats one's desire as reason-giving only if one decides so to treat it. In many cases we simply and unreflectively treat our desires in this way without some further decision so to treat them. The suggestion so far is only that the special phenomenon of identifying with one's desire involves a decision to treat that desire as a reason.

VI. Being Satisfied with a
Decision to Treat as Reason-Giving

Return to our grudging addict. Suppose that he gives in and decides to take the drug, in response to his powerful desire for the drug. Having reached this decision he proceeds to reason concerning means and preliminary steps to the end of taking the drug. Does that mean that he is treating his desire for the drug as reason-giving? If so, might he not have decided to treat it in this way?

There seem to be two different cases. Sometimes the addict's reasoning treats his desire for the drug as a kind of threat of future pain and the like. Sarah Buss describes such a case:

> Since the addict is confident that his desire for drugs will soon so overpower him as to prevent him from acting intentionally, and since the struggle to remain drug-free is extremely painful, he decides to cease resisting his desire, and to take the steps necessary for satisfying it.[36]

In such a case he is trying to respond to his desire for drugs in the way one might try to respond to one's feeling that one will sneeze violently unless one takes certain steps. To respond in this way is not to treat that desire as reason-giving in the relevant sense. So the approach we are taking promises to explain the sense in which such an addict does not identify with his desire for the drug. The problem is that there also seem to be cases in which the addict grudgingly treats his desire as end-setting, and reasons about means and preliminary steps towards that end. In such reasoning he is treating his desire for the drug as reason-giving in our modest sense. Yet it seems that he may still not identify with this desire.

A reply might be to challenge the idea that there can be cases of the second sort of addictive action, cases in which one really does treat the addiction-based desire for the drug as reason-giving and yet does not identify with it.[37] In a related spirit, one might try saying instead that such an addict, though perhaps he does treat his desire for the drug as reason-giving, does not *decide* so to treat it. I am, however, skeptical that these strategies will work for all cases. This is no argument, though; and I am unsure how to settle this issue convincingly. What I propose, instead, is to sketch an alternative strategy in defense of the idea that identification involves a decision to treat as reason-giving. I think we can learn from this strategy even if it turns out that it is not the only one available.

The key, I think, is to notice that a decision to treat as reason-giving might itself be incompatible with *other* standing decisions or policies of the agent's concerning what to treat as reason-giving. The grudging addict might have a general policy against treating his desire for the drug as reason-giving and yet, in the face of the present urgency of the desire, decide to treat it as reason-giving this time. It seems to me that such an addict does not identify with his desire for the drug, even though he decides to treat it as reason-giving this time.

We can develop the point by exploiting Frankfurt's terminology of being "satisfied"—only now we focus on satisfaction with a special kind of decision.[38] To identify with a desire, we can say, one needs both to decide to treat that desire as reason-giving in some of one's relevant practical reasoning, and to be satisfied with that decision. And what is it to be satisfied with such a decision? We should not require the complete absence of conflict concerning that decision. But we may require that one not have reached and retained a conflicting decision, intention, or policy concerning the treatment of one's desire as reason-giving. If one has a general policy of not treating a certain desire as reason-giving, and yet, in a particular situation and in the face of the urgency of the desire, decides to treat it as reason-giving this time, one's will would be divided.[39] To identify with a certain desire one needs to decide to treat it as reason-giving in some relevant practical reasoning and to be satisfied with that decision. One is satisfied with such a decision when one's will is, in relevant ways, not divided: the decision to treat as reason-giving does not conflict with other standing decisions and policies about which desires to treat as reason-giving.[40]

VII. A Success Condition

We need one final addition to the basic account of what it is to identify with a desire. In "The Importance of What We Care About" Frankfurt emphasizes that one can decide to care about something and yet "when the chips are down" fail to care about it.[41] Perhaps, similarly, I might decide to treat my desire, say, to seek a reconciliation with an old acquaintance as reason-giving and yet, when the chips are down, find myself unable to treat it this way. I might find that, despite my decision, and despite the fact that I am satisfied with that decision, I do not care enough about reconciliation.

In such a case it seems that I have not fully succeeded in identifying with my desire for reconciliation. For one to identify with a desire one would normally not only reach an appropriate decision to treat that desire as reason-giving, but would also treat it that way. We need, however, to be careful to allow for cases in which one identifies with a desire but, as it happens, does not find oneself in those circumstances with respect to which one has decided to treat it as reason-giving. Though one does not, in fact, find oneself in such circumstances one is fully prepared to treat the desire as reason-giving in such circumstances.

I think we can do justice both to these complexities and to Frankfurt's insight about the limits of decision in the following way: To identify with one's desire is (a) to reach a decision to treat that desire as reason-giving and to be satisfied with that decision, and (b_1) to treat that desire as reason-giving or, at least, (b_2) to be fully prepared to treat it as reason-giving were a relevant occasion to arise.

We can now return to Velleman's concern about "unwitting" decisions. The decision in Velleman's example is a decision to (execute the desire to) sever the friendship. It is not a decision to treat the desire to sever as reason-giving. It seems to me that when we turn to a decision to treat that desire as reason-giving, when we add that this is a decision with which the agent is satisfied, and when we also add that the agent does treat that desire as reason-giving, it will no longer be plausible for the agent to insist that "it was my resentment speaking, not I."[42]

VIII. Extending the Model

Recall that I might unreflectively treat a desire of mine as reason-giving without actually deciding to treat it that way. This suggests an objection:[43] Suppose I routinely and as a matter of course treat a given desire of mine as reason-giving. Suppose I have not actually decided to treat it this way, but have made no decision to the contrary. Do I not identify with that desire?

Frankfurt considers a related issue in his discussion of satisfaction:

> It is possible, of course, for someone to be satisfied with his first-order desires without in any way considering whether to endorse them. In that case, he is identified with those first-order desires. But insofar as his desires are utterly unreflective, he is to that extent not genuinely a person at all. He is merely a wanton.[44]

Though it is not completely clear from the passage, I take it that the view here is that such an agent, while "identified with" the first-order desire, does not identify with that desire; for to identify with a desire one must reflectively consider that desire. My initial response to the present objection is along similar lines. If one is unreflective about whether to treat one's desire as a reason one does not yet face the kind of problem to which identification is a response. If, however, one is to some extent reflective about this desire then one needs to decide, however inchoately, in order to settle the issue. So there will be intentional actions whose motivating desires are ones which the agent treats as reason-giving and does not treat as external, but with which, strictly speaking, he does not identify.

That, as I said, is my initial response. But I want also to note a natural way in which, in response to the present objection and in light of Frankfurt's remarks, we might find it useful to extend the account. We might go on to say that a person is, in an extended sense, identified with a desire if (*i*) she treats it as reason-giving, (*ii*) she does not treat it as external, and (*iii*) she would decide to continue to treat it as reason-giving, be satisfied with that decision, and continue to treat it as reason-giving, if she were to reflect on the matter.[45] One may, in this extended sense, be identified with a desire even if one has not reflected on that desire in ways needed for one to identify with it.

IX. Three Concerns

Let us see how this approach would respond to a trio of concerns:

First, suppose an addict is so depressed and resigned to his addiction that he does not try to resist.[46] Instead, he decides to treat his desire for the drug as reason-giving, proceeds to do so and, because of his resignation to his addiction, has no policy to the contrary. But he still sees the desire as criticizible.

I think such an example shows that one can identify with a desire one thinks is criticizible if one really does arrive at, and is satisfied with, a decision to treat it as reason-giving, and does in fact treat it that way. Perhaps this is a result of resignation or depression, but that is a different matter.[47]

Second, suppose my decision to treat my desire for money as reason-giving is motivated by a bet I make with you.[48] I win the bet if I spend the next ten years treating this desire in this way, even though I think so acting is, to say the least, undignified.[49] I am satisfied with this decision, but only because I want to win the bet. Do I identify with my desire for money? I think that it is plausible to say "yes": I identify with it in order to win the bet. This is a nonstandard ground for identification and may be a bad way to live one's life, but that is a different matter.

Third, what about Watson's "perverse" cases? A person might identify with her desire in favor of something "thrilling" without thinking this best, or caring most about it. But if she really does identify with it she endorses it in some way; and the present proposal seems a plausible story about what that way is. Though she thinks so acting is not best, she still decides to treat her desire for the thrilling thing as reason-giving; and she goes on to treat it this way. If she is satisfied with her decision to treat that desire as reason-giving, she identifies with that desire.

X. Conclusion

I have tried to understand identification by appeal to phenomena of deciding to treat, and of treating, a desire of one's as reason-giving in one's practical reasoning, planning, and action. Is identification, so understood, "fundamental," as Frankfurt says, "to any philosophy of mind and of action"? Well, we have seen reason to include in our model of intentional agency such phenomena of deciding to treat, and of treating, certain of one's desires as reason-giving. Identification, at bottom, consists in such phenomena—or so I have proposed. Given that such phenomena are important in our practical lives we may agree with Frankfurt that identification is, in this sense, "fundamental".

Notes

I would like to thank Nomy Arpaly, Larry Beyer, Sarah Buss, Rachel Cohon, John Fischer, Alfred Mele, Elijah Millgram, Jennifer Rosner, Timothy Schroeder, David Velleman, and Gideon Yaffe for their helpful comments.

1. Harry Frankfurt, "The Faintest Passion," *Proceedings and Addresses of the APA* 66:3 (1992): 5–16; the quotation appears on 12. For earlier remarks in a similar spirit see his "Three Concepts of Free Action," in Harry Frankfurt, *The Importance of What We Care About* (Cambridge, England: Cambridge University Press, 1987), 47–57, esp. 54.

2. The desire-belief model remains the standard model of intentional agency in many areas of philosophy. See e.g., Fred Dretske, *Explaining Behavior: Reasons in a World of Causes* (Cambridge: Bradford/MIT Press, 1988). Gary Watson has emphasized the need to introduce forms of evaluation not reducible to desire. See his "Free Agency," *Journal of Philosophy* 72 (1975): 205–220. My own view is a version of the last view, one that emphasizes the distinctiveness and importance of intention. To decide is to form an intention in a standard way. See Michael E. Bratman, *Intention, Plans, and Practical Reason* (Cambridge: Harvard University Press, 1987). See also Gilbert Harman, *Change in View* (Cambridge: MIT Press, 1986) and Hector-Neri Castaneda, *Thinking and Doing* (Dordrecht: Reidel, 1975).

3. The first example is from Frankfurt, "Freedom of the Will and the Concept of a Person," *Journal of Philosophy* 68 (1971), reprinted in *The Importance of What We Care About*, 11–25. The last two examples are from Frankfurt, "Identification and Externality," in Amelie Rorty, ed., *The Identities of Persons* (University of California Press, 1977), reprinted in *The Importance of What We Care About*, 58–68. (The examples are on 67 and 63 respectively.) Page references will be to *The Importance of What We Care About*.

4. See Frankfurt, "Identification and Externality," 63. In "Alienation and Externality," *Canadian Journal of Philosophy* 29 (1999): 371–88. Timothy Schroeder and Nomy Arpaly emphasize the significance of such feelings for an account of externality.

5. Frankfurt, "Three Concepts of Free Action," 54.

6. "Identification and Wholeheartedness," originally published in Ferdinand David Schoeman, ed., *Responsibility, Character and the Emotions: New Essays in Moral Psychology* (New York: Cambridge University Press, 1987); reprinted in *The Importance of What We Care About*, 159–176. Page references will be to the latter volume.

7. Frankfurt, "Freedom of the Will and the Concept of a Person," 12.

8. Ibid., 21.

9. Ibid., 18.

10. Gary Watson, "Free Action and Free Will," *Mind* 96 (1987): 145–172; the quotation appears on 149.

11. Watson, "Free Agency".

12. In his later paper, "Free Action and Free Will," Watson tries to avoid an overly "rationalistic" flavor of this model by replacing talk of valuing with talk of caring about something. Susan Wolf has proposed a similar, friendly amendment, appealing to talk about "things which *matter* to a person in some positive way." See her *Freedom Within Reason* (New York: Oxford University Press, 1990), 31. (Wolf goes on to criticize the use of this approach in defense of a form of compatibilism.) And there are aspects of Frankfurt's discussion in his later "The Importance of What We Care About" (in *The Importance of What We Care About*, 80–94) that have a similar structure. But these friendly amendments do not by themselves protect the view from the concerns to be noted, concerns about what Watson calls "perverse" cases.

13. Watson, "Free Action and Free Will".

14. Ibid., 150.

15. Ibid.

16. Frankfurt, "Identification and Wholeheartedness".

17. Frankfurt, "Identification and Externality," 66.

18. Ibid., 68 and 68n.

19. Frankfurt, "Identification and Wholeheartedness," 170.

20. See ibid.; see also Frankfurt, "Identification and Externality," 66–67.

21. Frankfurt, "Identification and Wholeheartedness," 170.

22. Ibid., 175. I have argued in a similar spirit for the importance of similar roles for intentions and plans—the normal upshots and, so to speak, traces of decisions. By articulating the roles of intentions in coordinating plans we go a long way toward saying what intention—and so, decision—is. (See my *Intention, Plans, and Practical Reason*.) We also arrive at a model of a policy as an intention that is suitably general. (See my "Intention and Personal Policies," *Philosophical Perspectives* 3 (1989): 443–469.) I discuss related matters in my "Responsibility and Planning," *The Journal of Ethics* 1 (1997): 27–43, esp. 29–30.

23. See Frankfurt, "Identification and Wholeheartedness," 172.

24. Ibid., 176. Contrast with Watson's emphasis on first-order evaluations of actions in his "Free Agency," 219.

25. As I indicate in note 23, I think that the planning theory of intention can help us do this by seeing intentions as normal products of decisions, and then providing a plausible account of the nature of intention.

26. See J. David Velleman, "What Happens When Someone Acts?" *Mind* 101 (1992): 461–481.

27. Ibid., 464–465.

28. This is suggested by Frankfurt's comments in "The Faintest Passion," 13. It was anticipated, but not applied to decisions, in "Identification and Externality," 65–66.

29. Frankfurt, "The Faintest Passion," 14.

30. Ibid., 13–14.

31. See T. M. Scanlon, *What We Owe to Each Other* (Cambridge, Mass.: Harvard University Press, 1998), the quotes are on 46 and 51, respectively. Rachel Cohon has introduced a somewhat similar idea in her "Internalism about Reasons for Action," *Pacific Philosophical Quarterly* 74 (1993): 265–288. Cohon supposes that rational agents have "standards of practical rationality" which specify "what is a reason and what isn't" (274–75). Cohon explicitly notes that that "an agent's standards might not count some of his desires as providing any reasons at all" (275). Cohon sees such standards as, in effect, views about what are, as a matter of fact, reasons for action; whereas decisions and policies to treat as reason-giving, of the sort I will be appealing to below, need not commit one to the idea that one can get such a thing right or wrong. (Though one may, of course, have that idea.) Allan Gibbard also discusses "norms that say to treat R as weighing in favor of doing X," in his *Wise Choices, Apt Feelings* (Cambridge, Mass.: Harvard University Press, 1990), at 163. Neither Cohon nor Gibbard nor Scanlon, to my knowledge, consider the relation between their ideas about decisions or standards or norms about reasons for action and questions about the nature of identification in the sense that Frankfurt and his critics are after. What I am trying to do here is to draw on ideas to some extent in the spirit of such work in a way that sheds light on identification.

32. Such a decision would function as what Joseph Raz calls an "exclusionary reason." See his *Practical Reason and Norms* (London: Hutchinson, 1975; reprint, Princeton, N.J.: Princeton University Press, 1990), 35–48.

33. This may be one way of interpreting Frankfurt's remark that the agent, in a case of conflict that calls for "segregation," "places the rejected desire outside the scope of his preferences, so that it is not a candidate for satisfaction at all." (Frankfurt, "Identification and Externality," 67; see also "Identification and Wholeheartedness," 170.) Frankfurt, though, does not here explicitly invoke ideas of seeing or treating one's desire as a *reason*; so he may not welcome such an interpretation.

34. This kind of decision may involve characteristic feelings of estrangement of a sort emphasized by Schroeder and Arpaly, op. cit. I do not see that such feelings are necessary, though. In any case, my concern here is rather with the role of such a decision in one's reasoning and action.

35. See Robert Nozick, *Anarchy, State, and Utopia* (New York: Basic Books, 1974), 29–33.

36. Sarah Buss, "Autonomy Reconsidered" in Peter A. French, Theodore E. Uehling, Jr., and Howard K. Wettstein, eds., *Midwest Studies in Philosophy XIX: Philosophical Naturalism* (Notre Dame, Ind.: University of Notre Dame Press, 1994), 95–121; the quotation appears on 101. (Nomy Arpaly and Timothy Schroeder present a somewhat similar picture of the unwilling addict in their "Praise, Blame and the Whole Self," *Philosophical Studies* 93 (1999): 161–188.)

37. Sarah Buss (op. cit.) suggests such a view, as did David Velleman in correspondence. Elijah Millgram's complex discussion of what he calls the "clear-headed addict" may also point toward such a challenge, though he does seem to allow that such an addict might treat his "urge", if not strictly speaking his "desire", as end-setting. See his *Practical Induction* (Cambridge, Mass.: Harvard University Press, 1997), 29–31.

38. There are similarities between what I say here and Frankfurt's remarks about the wholeheartedness of a decision in "Identification and Wholeheartedness." Frankfurt there alludes to a case in which a

> decision, no matter how apparently conscientious and sincere, is not wholehearted: Whether the person is aware of it or not, he has other intentions, intentions incompatible with the one the decision established.... (174).

Elsewhere, though, Frankfurt seems to indicate that wholeheartedness can be undermined not only by conflicting intentions, but also by conflicting desires (ibid., 175) or by a conflict with what the person cares about ("The Importance of What We Care About," 84). My approach, like that suggested in the above quote from Frankfurt, but unlike some of Frankfurt's remarks elsewhere, sees a conflict of intentions, decisions, or policies as basic.

39. Frankfurt says that "choosing not to do X ... is incompatible with choosing to do X." ("Concerning the Freedom and Limits of the Will," *Philosophical Topics* 17 [1989]: 119–130; the quotation appears on 127.) In the case I am describing, however, one decision concerns a general policy (not to treat the desire as a reason) and one concerns a particular instance (of treating it as a reason). Such a general policy is a "self-governing intention" of the sort I discuss in my *Intention, Plans, and Practical Reason*, esp. 159.

40. As suggested in notes 33 and 38, the idea that identification with a desire involves a decision to treat that desire as a reason, along with being satisfied with the decision, may be one interpretation of Frankfurt's view in "Identification and Wholeheartedness". However, as is also suggested in these notes, it is not clear that this is an interpretation he would welcome.

In *The Sources of Normativity* (Cambridge University Press, 1996), Christine Korsgaard also connects, but in a different way, identification with treating as a reason. Like Frankfurt, Korsgaard emphasizes the reflective structure of our conscious agency. (Korsgaard refers to Frankfurt's 1971 paper—at 99 n. 8—but does not try to chart Frankfurt's later views.) Korsgaard believes that when a reflective agent acts on a desire that agent "must say to itself that the desire is a reason."(94) To see a desire as a reason is, for Korsgaard, to see it as fitting with a relevant normative conception one has of one's identity: the connection with one's conception of one's identity is what makes the desire a reason. On my view, in contrast, to identify with a desire is, in large part, to reach a certain kind of decision about treating that desire as a reason. Such a decision will itself normally be grounded in some way, and I would grant that in many cases it is grounded in some general conception of one's identity. But (as G.A. Cohen suggests in his "Reason, Humanity, and the Moral Law," in *The Sources of Normativity*, 167–188, at 185) it is not clear that the decision must be grounded in this way. In any case, it is the decision to treat as a reason, and the actual treating-as-a-reason, not the grounds for the decision, which, on my view, constitute identification with a desire.

41. Frankfurt, "The Importance of What We Care About," 84–85. See also his remarks in "Identification and Wholeheartedness," 174. Thoughtful comments from Sarah Buss helped me see the need to address issues raised by this aspect of Frankfurt's views.

42. This is a good point to reflect briefly on Velleman's positive proposal in his "What Happens When Someone Acts?" and its relation to the view I am sketching here. Velleman seeks a component of the agent's motivational machinery that plays what is seen by commonsense as the role of the agent. Velleman argues that what plays this role is "the desire to act in accordance with reasons."(478) More specifically, it is the desire "to see which [motives] provide stronger reasons for acting, and then to ensure that they prevail over those whose rational force is weaker."(ibid.) In a sense, the agent is to be identified with this particular desire as it functions in her psychology: "the agent *is* [this] motive, functionally speaking."(480) My approach, in contrast, understands identification in terms of deciding to treat, and of treating, a desire as a reason, rather than in terms of a desire to act in accordance with the strongest reasons. This allows my approach to provide what seems a more natural treatment of identification with desires on the losing side. My approach can also see both the motives with which there is identification, and the decisions and policies which help ensure such identification, as the agent's "own". That said, my view is in the spirit of Velleman's (as he helped me see in correspondence) in understanding identification in part by appeal to a way in which one may bring one's desire into one's practical reasoning.

Another useful comparison may be with Sarah Buss's treatment in "Autonomy Reconsidered"; for Buss also appeals to how one brings, or does not bring, one's desire into one's practical reasoning. Buss writes that a "person's desires ... can figure in her practical reasoning as some of the things she considers.... Sometimes, however, these very same states exert a *non*rational influence on a person's reasoning."(106) Buss argues that this distinction is crucial to the idea that some desires are external: "their status as external influences depends on how they relate to her practical reasoning. Rather than being *constituents of* this reasoning ... they influence reasoning from without."(107). (Buss goes on to say that not every such "nonrational influence is autonomy undermining." [108]) I am agreeing with Buss that it is important whether or not one treats one's desire as a reason—as Buss puts it, a thing "*considered*" in one's reasoning (107). But I am also emphasizing that we make decisions and have policies about such matters and that such decisions and policies are important to identification.

43. This objection is due to Nomy Arpaly and Timothy Schroeder.

44. Frankfurt, "The Faintest Passion," 14.

45. Though there will be cases in which there is no clear answer to the question of what an agent would decide if she were to reflect on such a matter. Jennifer Rosner explores related issues about what she calls "counterfactual stability under reflective evaluation" in her *Reflective Evaluation, Autonomy, and Self-Knowledge* (Ph.D. thesis, Stanford University, 1998).

46. This example is due to John Fischer.

47. Note that this example differs from one noted earlier in which one's depression prevents one from making any decision about whether to treat one's desire as reason-giving. Now, in "Identification and Externality," Frankfurt writes: "A person may acknowledge to himself that passions of which he dispproves are undeniably and unequivocally his ..." (65). I am suggesting that there are two different versions of the case to which Frankfurt here alludes: one in which the person is simply resigned to the passion of which he disapproves, another in which the person

goes on, perhaps out of resignation, to decide to treat that passion as reason-giving. On my view, this difference matters to identification.

48. This example is due to Alfred Mele.

49. If I win the bet, I get something other than money that I value highly. Perhaps I get to marry Turandot.

8

Human Freedom and the Self

RODERICK M. CHISHOLM

'A staff moves a stone, and is moved by a hand, which is moved by a man.'
Aristotle, *Physics*, 256a.

1. The metaphysical problem of human freedom might be summarized in the following way: Human beings are responsible agents; but this fact appears to conflict with a deterministic view of human action (the view that every event that is involved in an act is caused by some other event); and it also appears to conflict with an indeterministic view of human action (the view that the act, or some event that is essential to the act, is not caused at all.) To solve the problem, I believe, we must make somewhat far-reaching assumptions about the self or the agent—about the man who performs the act.

Perhaps it is needless to remark that, in all likelihood, it is impossible to say anything significant about this ancient problem that has not been said before.[1]

2. Let us consider some deed, or misdeed, that may be attributed to a responsible agent: one man, say, shot another. If the man *was* responsible for what he did, then, I would urge, what was to happen at the time of the shooting was something that was entirely up to the man himself. There was a moment at which it was true, both that he could have fired the shot

The Lindley Lecture, 1964, pp. 3–15. Copyright by the Department of Philosophy, University of Kansas. Reprinted by permission of the Department of Philosophy of the University of Kansas, Lawrence, Kansas, USA.

and also that he could have refrained from firing it. And if this is so, then, even though he did fire it, he could have done something else instead. (He didn't find himself firing the shot 'against his will', as we say.) I think we can say, more generally, then, that if a man is responsible for a certain event or a certain state of affairs (in our example, the shooting of another man), then that event or state of affairs was brought about by some act of his, and the act was something that was in his power either to perform or not to perform.

But now if the act which he *did* perform was an act that was also in his power *not* to perform, then it could not have been caused or determined by any event that was not itself within his power either to bring about or not to bring about. For example, if what we say he did was really something that was brought about by a second man, one who forced his hand upon the trigger, say, or who, by means of hypnosis, compelled him to perform the act, then since the act was caused by the *second* man it was nothing that was within the power of the *first* man to prevent. And precisely the same thing is true, I think, if instead of referring to a second man who compelled the first one, we speak instead of the *desires and beliefs* which the first man happens to have had. For if what we say he did was really something that was brought about by his own beliefs and desires, if these beliefs and desires in the particular situation in which he happened to have found himself caused him to do just what it was that we say he did do, then, since *they* caused it, *he* was unable to do anything other than just what it was that he did do. It makes no difference whether the cause of the deed was internal or external; if the cause was some state or event for which the man himself was not responsible, then he was not responsible for what we have been mistakenly calling his act. If a flood caused the poorly constructed dam to break, then, given the flood and the constitution of the dam, the break, we may say, *had* to occur and nothing could have happened in its place. And if the flood of desire caused the weak-willed man to give in, then he, too, had to do just what it was that he did do and he was no more responsible than was the dam for the results that followed. (It is true, of course, that if the man is responsible for the beliefs and desires that he happens to have, then he may also be responsible for the things they lead him to do. But the question now becomes: *is* he responsible for the beliefs and desires he happens to have? If he is, then there was a time when they were within his power either to acquire or not to acquire, and we are left, therefore, with our general point.)

One may object: But surely if there were such a thing as a man who is really *good,* then he would be responsible for things that he would do; yet, he would be unable to do anything other than just what it is that he does do, since, being good, he will always choose to do what is best. The answer, I think, is suggested by a comment that Thomas Reid makes upon an ancient author. The author had said of Cato, "He was good because he could not be otherwise", and Reid observes: "This saying, if understood literally and strictly, is not the praise of Cato, but of his constitution, which was no more the work of Cato than his existence".[2] If Cato was himself responsible for the good things that he did, then Cato, as Reid suggests, was such that, although he had the power to do what was not good, he exercised his power only for that which was good.

All of this, if it is true, may give a certain amount of comfort to those who are tender-minded. But we should remind them that it also conflicts with a familiar view about the nature of God—with the view that St. Thomas Aquinas expresses by saying that "every movement both of the will and of nature proceeds from God as the Prime Mover".[3] If the act of the sinner *did* proceed from God as the Prime Mover, then God was in the position of the second agent we just discussed—the man who forced the trigger finger, or the hypnotist—and the sinner, so-called, was not responsible for what he did. (This may be a bold assertion, in view of the history of western theology, but I must say that I have never encountered a single good reason for denying it.)

There is one standard objection to all of this and we should consider it briefly.

3. The objection takes the form of a stratagem—one designed to show that determinism (and divine providence) is consistent with human responsibility. The stratagem is one that was used by Jonathan Edwards and by many philosophers in the present century, most notably, G. E. Moore.[4]

One proceeds as follows: The expression

(a)   He could have done otherwise,

it is argued, means no more nor less than

(b)   If he had chosen to do otherwise, then he would have done otherwise.

(In place of 'chosen', one might say 'tried', 'set out', 'decided', 'undertaken', 'willed'.) The truth of statement (b), it is then pointed out, is consistent with determinism (and with divine providence); for even if all of the man's actions were causally determined, the man could still be such that, *if* he had chosen otherwise, then he would have done otherwise. What the murderers saw, let us suppose, along with his beliefs and desires, *caused* him to fire the shot; yet he was such that *if*, just then, he had chosen or decided *not* to fire the shot, then he would not have fired it. All of this is certainly possible. Similarly, we could say, of the dam, that the flood caused it to break and also that the dam was such that, *if* there had been no flood or any similar pressure, then the dam would have remained intact. And therefore, the argument proceeds, if (b) is consistent with determinism, and if (a) and (b) say the same thing, then (a) is also consistent with determinism; hence we can say that the agent *could* have done otherwise even though he was caused to do what he did do; and therefore determinism and moral responsibility are compatible.

Is the argument sound? The conclusion follows from the premises, but the catch, I think, lies in the first premiss—the one saying that statement (a) tells us no more nor less than what statement (b) tells us. For (b), it would seem, could be true while (a) is false. That is to say, our man might be such that, if he had chosen to do otherwise, then he would have done otherwise, and yet *also* such that he could not have done otherwise. Suppose, after all, that our murderer could not have *chosen,* or could not have *decided,* to do otherwise. Then the fact that he happens also to be a man such that, if he had chosen not to shoot he would not have shot, would make no difference. For if he could *not* have chosen *not* to shoot, then he could not have done anything other than just what it was that he did do. In a word: from our statement (b) above ('If he had chosen to do otherwise, then he would have done otherwise'), we cannot make an inference to (a) above ('He could have done otherwise') unless we can *also* assert:

(c)   He could have chosen to do otherwise.

And therefore, if we must reject this third statement (c), then, even though we may be justified in asserting (b), we are not justified in asserting (a). If the man could not have chosen to do otherwise, then he would not have done otherwise—*even if* he was such that, if he *had* chosen to do otherwise, then he would have done otherwise.

The stratagem in question, then, seems to me not to work, and I would say, therefore, that the ascription of responsibility conflicts with a deterministic view of action.

4. Perhaps there is less need to argue that the ascription of responsibility also conflicts with an indeterministic view of action—with the view that the act, or some event that is essential to the act, is not caused at all. If the act—the firing of the shot—was not caused at all, if it was fortuitous or capricious, happening so to speak out of the blue, then, presumably, no one—and nothing—was responsible for the act. Our conception of action, therefore, should be neither deterministic nor indeterministic. Is there any other possibility?

5. We must not say that every event involved in the act is caused by some other event; and we must not say that the act is something that is not caused at all. The possibility that remains, therefore, is this: We should say that at least one of the events that are involved in the act is caused, not by any other events, but by something else instead. And this something else can only be the agent—the man. If there is an event that is caused, not by other events, but by the man, then there are some events involved in the act that are not caused by other events. But if the event in question is caused by the man then it *is* caused and we are not committed to saying that there is something involved in the act that is not caused at all.

But this, of course, is a large consequence, implying something of considerable importance about the nature of the agent or the man.

6. If we consider only inanimate natural objects, we may say that causation, if it occurs, is a relation between *events* or *states of affairs*. The dam's breaking was an event that was caused by a set of other events—the dam being weak, the flood being strong, and so on. But if a man is responsible for a particular deed, then, if what I have said is true, there is some event, or set of events, that is caused, *not* by other events or states of affairs, but by the agent, whatever he may be.

I shall borrow a pair of medieval terms, using them, perhaps, in a way that is slightly different from that for which they were originally intended. I shall say that when one event or state of affairs (or set of events or states of affairs) causes some other event or state of affairs, then we have an instance *of transeunt* causation. And I shall say that when an *agent,* as distinguished from an event, causes an event or state of affairs, then we have an instance of *immanent* causation.

The nature of what is intended by the expression 'immanent causation' may be illustrated by this sentence from Aristotle's *Physics:* "Thus, a staff moves a stone, and is moved by a hand, which is moved by a man." (VII, 5, 256a, 6–8) If the man was responsible, then we have in this illustration a number of instances of causation—most of them transeunt but at least one of them immanent. What the staff did to the stone was an instance of transeunt causation, and thus we may describe it as a relation between events: 'the motion of the staff caused the motion of the stone.' And similarly for what the hand did to the staff: 'the motion of the hand caused the motion of the staff'. And, as we know from physiology, there are still other events which caused the motion of the hand. Hence we need not introduce the agent at this particular point, as Aristotle does—we *need* not, though we *may.* We *may* say that the hand was moved by the man, but we may *also* say that the motion of the hand was caused by the motion of certain muscles; and we may say that the motion of the muscles was caused by certain events that took place within the brain. But some event, and presumably one of those that took place within the brain, was caused by the agent and not by any other events.

There are, of course, objections to this way of putting the matter; I shall consider the two that seem to me to be most important.

7. One may object, firstly: "If the *man* does anything, then, as Aristotle's remark suggests, what he does is to move the *hand*. But he certainly does not do anything to his brain—he may not even know that he *has* a brain. And if he doesn't do anything to the brain, and if the motion of the hand was caused by something that happened within the brain, then there is no point in appealing to "immanent causation" as being something incompatible with "transeunt causation"—for the whole thing, after all, is a matter of causal relations among events or states of affairs."

The answer to this objection, I think, is this: It is true that the agent does not do anything with his brain, or to his brain, in the sense in which he *does* something with his hand and does something to the staff. But from this it does not follow that the agent was not the immanent cause of something that happened within his brain.

We should note a useful distinction that has been proposed by Professor A. I. Melden—namely, the distinction between 'making something A happen' and 'doing A'.[5] If I reach for the staff and pick it up, then one of the things that I *do* is just that—reach for the staff and pick it up. And if it is something that I do, then there is a very clear sense in which it may be said to be something that I know that I do. If you ask me, 'Are you doing something, or trying to do something, with the staff?', I will have no difficulty in finding an answer. But in doing something with the staff, I also make various things happen which are not in this same sense things that I do: I will make various air-particles move; I will free a number of blades of grass from the pressure that had been upon them; and I may cause a shadow to move from one place to another. If these are merely things that I make happen, as distinguished from things that I do, then I may know nothing whatever about them; I may not have the slightest idea that, in moving the staff, I am bringing about any such thing as the motion of air-particles, shadows, and blades of grass.

We may say, in answer to the first objection, therefore, that it is true that our agent does nothing to his brain or with his brain; but from this it does not follow that the agent is not the immanent cause of some event within his brain; for the brain event may be something which, like the motion of the air-particles, he made happen in picking up the staff. The only difference between the two cases is this: in each case, he made something happen when he picked up the staff; but in the one case—the motion of the air-par-

ticles or of the shadows—it was the motion of the staff that caused the
event to happen; and in the other case—the event that took place in the
brain—it was this event that caused the motion of the staff.

The point is, in a word, that whenever a man does something A, then (by
'immanent causation') he makes a certain cerebral event happen, and this
cerebral event (by 'transeunt causation') makes A happen.

8. The second objection is more difficult and concerns the very concept of
'immanent causation', or causation by an agent, as this concept is to be interpreted here. The concept is subject to a difficulty which has long been associated with that of the prime mover unmoved. We have said that there
must be some event A, presumably some cerebral event, which is caused
not by any other event, but by the agent. Since A was not caused by any
other event, then the agent himself cannot be said to have undergone any
change or produced any other event (such as 'an act of will' or the like)
which brought A about. But if, when the agent made A happen, there was
no event involved other than A itself, no event which could be described as
making A happen, what did the agent's causation consist of? What, for example, is the difference between A's just happening, and the agents' *causing*
A to happen? We cannot attribute the difference to any event that took
place within the agent. And so far as the event A itself is concerned, there
would seem to be no discernible difference. Thus Aristotle said that the activity of the prime mover is nothing in addition to the motion that it produces, and Suarez said that 'the action is in reality nothing but the effect as
it flows from the agent'.[6] Must we conclude, then, that there is no more to
the man's action in causing event A than there is to the event A's happening
by itself? Here we would seem to have a distinction without a difference—
in which case we have failed to find a *via media* between a deterministic
and an indeterministic view of action.

The only answer, I think, can be this: that the difference between the
man's causing A, on the one hand, and the event A just happening, on the
other, lies in the fact that, in the first case but not the second, the event A
was caused and was caused by the man. There was a brain event A; the
agent did, in fact, cause the brain event; but there was nothing that he did
to cause it.

This answer may not entirely satisfy and it will be likely to provoke the
following question: 'But what are you really *adding* to the assertion that A
happened when you utter the words "The agent *caused* A to happen"?' As
soon as we have put the question this way, we see, I think, that whatever
difficulty we may have encountered is one that may be traced to the concept of causation generally—whether 'immanent'or 'transeunt'. The prob-

lem, in other words, is not a problem that is peculiar to our conception of human action. It is a problem that must be faced by anyone who makes use of the concept of causation at all; and therefore, I would say, it is a problem for everyone but the complete indeterminist.

For the problem, as we put it, referring just to 'immanent causation', or causation by an agent, was this: "What is the difference between saying, of an event A, that A just happened and saying that someone caused A to happen?" The analogous problem, which holds for 'transeunt causation', or causation by an event, is this: "What is the difference between saying, of two events A and B, that B happened and then A happened, and saying that B's happening was the *cause* of A's happening?" And the only answer that one can give is this—that in the one case the agent was the cause of A's happening and in the other case event B was the cause of A's happening. The nature of transeunt causation is no more clear than is that of immanent causation.

9. But we may plausibly say—and there is a respectable philosophical tradition to which we may appeal—that the notion of immanent causation, or causation by an agent, is in fact more clear than that of transeunt causation, or causation by an event, and that it is only by understanding our own causal efficacy, as agents, that we can grasp the concept of *cause* at all. Hume may be said to have shown that we do not derive the concept of *cause* from what we perceive of external things. How, then, do we derive it? The most plausible suggestion, it seems to me, is that of Reid, once again: namely that "the conception of an efficient cause may very probably be derived from the experience we have had...of our own power to produce certain effects."[7] If we did not understand the concept of immanent causation, we would not understand that of transeunt causation.

10. It may have been noted that I have avoided the term 'free will' in all of this. For even if there is such a faculty as 'the will', which somehow sets our acts agoing, the question of freedom, as John Locke said, is not the question *"whether the will be free"*; it is the question *"whether a man be free."*[8] For if there is a 'will', as a moving faculty, the question is whether the man is free to will to do these things that he does will to do—and also whether he is free *not* to will any of those things that he does will to do, and, again, whether he is free to will any of those things that he does not will to do. Jonathan Edwards tried to restrict himself to the question—"Is the man free to do what it is that he wills?"—but the answer to this question will not tell us whether the man is responsible for what it is that he *does* will to do. Using still another pair of medieval terms, we may say that the metaphysical problem of freedom does not concern the *actus imperatus*; it does not concern the question whether we are free to accomplish what-

ever it is that we will or set out to do; it concerns the *actus elicitus,* the question whether we are free to will or to set out to do those things that we do will or set out to do.

11. If we are responsible, and if what I have been trying to say is true, then we have a prerogative which some would attribute only to God: each of us, when we act, is a prime mover unmoved. In doing what we do, we cause certain events to happen, and nothing—or no one—causes us to cause those events to happen.

12. If we are thus prime movers unmoved and if our actions, or those for which we are responsible, are not causally determined, then they are not causally determined by our *desires.* And this means that the relation between what we want or what we desire, on the one hand, and what it is that we do, on the other, is not as simple as most philosophers would have it.

We may distinguish between what we might call the 'Hobbist approach' and what we might call the 'Kantian approach' to this question. The Hobbist approach is the one that is generally accepted at the present time, but the Kantian approach, I believe, is the one that is true. According to Hobbism, if we *know,* of some man, what his beliefs and desires happen to be and how strong they are, if we know what he feels certain of, what he desires more than anything else, and if we know the state of his body and what stimuli he is being subjected to, then we may *deduce,* logically, just what it is that he will do—or, more accurately, just what it is that he will try, set out, or undertake to do. Thus Professor Melden has said that "the connection between wanting and doing is logical".[9] But according to the Kantian approach to our problem, and this is the one that I would take, there is no such logical connection between wanting and doing, nor need there even be a causal connection. No set of statements about a man's desires, beliefs, and stimulus situation at any time implies any statement telling us what the man will try, set out, or undertake to do at that time. As Reid put it, though we may "reason from men's motives to their actions and, in many cases, with great probability", we can never do so "with absolute certainty".[10]

This means that, in one very strict sense of the terms, there can be no science of man. If we think of science as a matter of finding out what laws happen to hold, and if the statement of a law tells us what kinds of events are caused by what other kinds of events, then there will be human actions which we cannot explain by subsuming them under any laws. We cannot say, "It is causally necessary that, given such and such desires and beliefs, and being subject to such and such stimuli, the agent will do so and so." For at times the agent, if he chooses, may rise above his desires and do something else instead.

But all of this is consistent with saying that, perhaps more often than not, our desires do exist under conditions such that those conditions necessitate us to act. And we may also say, with Leibniz, that at other times our desires may "incline without necessitating."

13. Leibniz's phrase presents us with our final philosophical problem. What does it mean to say that a desire, or a motive, might "incline without necessitating"? There is a temptation, certainly, to say that 'to incline' means to cause and that 'not to necessitate' means not to cause, but obviously we cannot have it both ways.

Nor will Leibniz's own solution do. In his letter to Coste, he puts the problem as follows: "When a choice is proposed, for example to go out or not to go out, it is a question whether, with all the circumstances, internal and external, motives, perceptions, dispositions, impressions, passions, inclinations taken together, I am still in a contingent state, or whether I am necessitated to make the choice, for example, to go out; that is to say, whether this proposition true and determined in fact, *In all these circumstances taken together I shall choose to go out,* is contingent or necessary."[11] Leibniz's answer might be put as follows: in one sense of the terms 'necessary' and 'contingent', the proposition 'In all these circumstances taken together I shall choose to go out', may be said to be contingent and not necessary, and in another sense of these terms, it may be said to be necessary and not contingent. But the sense in which the proposition may be said to be contingent, according to Leibniz, is only this: there is no logical contradiction involved in denying the proposition. And the sense in which it may be said to be necessary is this: since 'nothing ever occurs without cause or determining reason', the proposition is causally necessary. "Whenever all the circumstances taken together are such that the balance of deliberation is heavier on one side than on the other, it is certain and infallible that that is the side that is going to win out." But if what we have been saying is true, the proposition 'In all these circumstances taken together I shall choose to go out', may be causally as well as logically contingent. Hence we must find another interpretation for Leibniz's statement that our motives and desires may incline us, or influence us, to choose without thereby necessitating us to choose.

Let us consider a public official who has some moral scruples but who also, as one says, could be had. Because of the scruples that he does have, he would never take any positive steps to receive a bribe—he would not actively solicit one. But his morality has its limits and he is also such that, if we were to confront him with a *fait accompli* or to let him see what's about to happen ($10,000 in cash is being deposited behind the garage), then he would succumb and be unable to resist. The general situation is a familiar one and this is one reason that people pray to be delivered from temptation. (It also justifies Kant's remark: "And how many there are who may have led a long blameless life, who are only *fortunate* in having escaped so many temptations."[12] Our relation to the misdeed that we contemplate may not be a matter simply of being able to bring it about or not to bring it about. As St. Anselm noted, there are at least four possibilities. We may illustrate them by reference to our public official and the event which is his receiving the bribe, in the following way: (i) he may be able to bring the event about himself *(facere esse),* in which case he would actively cause himself to receive the bribe; (ii) he may be able to refrain from bringing it about himself *(non facere esse),* in which case he would not himself do anything to insure that he receive the bribe; (iii) he may be able to do something to prevent the event from occurring *(facere non esse),* in which case he would make sure that the $10,000 was *not* left behind the garage; or (iv) he may be unable to do anything to prevent the event from occurring *(non facere non esse),* in which case, though he may not solicit the bribe, he would allow himself to keep it.[13] We have envisaged our official as a man who can resist the temptation to (i) but cannot resist the temptation to (iv): he can refrain from bringing the event about himself, but he cannot bring himself to do anything to prevent it.

Let us think of "inclination without necessitation," then, in such terms as these. First we may contrast the two propositions:

(1)   He can resist the temptation to do something in order to make A happen;

(2)   He can resist the temptation to allow A to happen (i.e. to do nothing to prevent A from happening).

We may suppose that the man has some desire to have A happen and thus has a motive for making A happen. His motive for making A happen, I suggest, is one that *necessitates* provided that, because of the motive, (1) is false; he cannot resist the temptation to do something in order to make A happen. His motive for making A happen is one that *inclines* provided that, because of the motive, (2) is false; like our public official, he cannot bring himself to do anything to prevent A from happening. And therefore we can say that this motive for making A happen is one that *inclines but does not necessitate* provided that, because of the motive, (1) is true and (2) is false; he can resist the temptation to make it happen but he cannot resist the temptation to allow it to happen.

Notes

1. The general position to be presented here is suggested in the following writings, among others: Aristotle, *Eudemian Ethics*, bk. ii ch. 6, *Nicomachean Ethics*, bk. iii, ch. 1–5; Thomas Reid, *Essays on the Active Powers of Man*, C. A. Campbell, "Is 'Free Will' a Pseudo-Problem?" *Mind*, 1951, 441–65; Roderick M. Chisholm, "Responsibility and Avoidability," and Richard Taylor, "Determination and the Theory of Agency," in *Determinism and Freedom in the Age of Modern Science*, ed. Sidney Hook (New York, 1958).

2. Thomas Reid, *Essays on the Active Powers of Man*, essay iv, ch. 4 (*Works*, 600).

3. *Summa Theologica*, First Part of the Second Part, qu. vi ("On the Voluntary and Involuntary").

4. Jonathan Edwards, *Freedom of the Will* (New Haven, 1957); G. E. Moore, *Ethics* (Home University Library, 1912), ch. 6.

5. A. I. Melden, *Free Action* (London, 1961), especially ch. 3. Mr. Melden's own views, however, are quite the contrary of those that are proposed here.

6. Aristotle, *Physics*, bk. iii, ch. 3; Suarez, *Disputations Metaphysicae*, Disputation 18, s. 10.

7. Reid, *Works*, 524.

8. *Essay concerning Human Understanding*, bk. ii, ch. 21.

9. Melden, 166.

10. Reid, *Works*, 608, 612.

11. "Lettre a Mr. Coste de la Nécessité et de la Contingence" (1707) in *Opera Philosophica*, ed. Erdmann, 447–9.

12. In the Preface to the *Metaphysical Elements of Ethics*, in Kant's *Critique of Practical Reason and Other Works on the Theory of Ethics*, ed. T. K. Abbott (London, 1959), 303.

13. Cf. D. P. Henry, "Saint Anselm's De 'Grammatico'," *Philosophical Quarterly*, X (1960), 115–26. St. Anselm noted that (i) and (iii), respectively, may be thought of as forming the upper left and the upper right corners of a square of opposition, and (ii) and (iv) the lower left and the lower right.

9

Indeterminist Free Action

LAURA WADDELL EKSTROM

Commitment to compatibilism concerning free will and determinism is for many sustained by the belief that no defensible incompatibilist account of the nature of freedom is available. Hence although incompatibilists have worked diligently to set out complex arguments demonstrating the thesis of incompatibilism,[1] compatibilists sometimes regard their arguments as impressive in their intricacy but dismissible in the end, since the arguments rely from the start on a deeply problematic notion of freedom. The dismissal of all incompatibilist free will accounts is too hasty, however.

I. Indeterminism and Randomness

The compatibilist's concern is admittedly a sympathetic one. Insofar as indeterminacy is associated with chaos and randomness, indeterminism seems not only not to be required for free action, but also to be positively antithetical to it. An act done of one's own free will is an act under one's own control *in excelsis*. Yet an act undetermined by a chain of previous events and hence subject to some indeterminacy seems an act produced from randomness and not under control.

Distinguishing a free act from a random event is hence the first fundamental problem facing the incompatibilist free will theorist. The second is

Portions of this essay are reprinted from Laura Waddell Ekstrom, *Free Will: A Philosophical Study* (Boulder: Westview Press, 2000), 81–129.

pinpointing a *helpful* location for indeterminism in the causal history of the free act. Positive arguments for incompatibilism rest on the requirement that an agent be able at the time of acting to do otherwise than she does, where this ability is understood in a categorical and not a conditional sense.[2] The arguments assume an understanding of freedom according to which it must be undetermined by natural laws and events of the past what the free agent will do next.

But holding fixed *everything* about the past up until the moment of action, including even the agent's preference or judgment about what to do next, and maintaining that crucial to the agent's freedom is her ability to do otherwise than what, at an immediately prior moment, she prefers or judges best to do, presents an extremely puzzling picture of free agency. Is this where the incompatibilist proposes to locate the requisite indeterminism: between the agent's preference for acting and her subsequent action? If not, then where else instead?

Some ways of responding to these problems generate accounts that are more susceptible to critics' charges of implausibility and "panicked" metaphysical speculation than are others. Accounts appealing to such factors as power centers that somehow transcend the empirical realm, noumenal selves, or the "Will" as uncaused homunculus within the agent are, in my view, examples.[3] More plausible options include both an account appealing to an *uncaused* volition or choice and, alternatively, an account resting on the idea of *causation* (of an act or a choice or an immediately executive intention) *by an agent as substance*. In sections II and III of this essay, I characterize these types of theory and briefly describe my reasons for declining to endorse either of them. In sections IV and V, I develop and defend an alternative account.

II. Free Acts as Uncaused Acts

Consider first the characterization of a free act that appeals to an *uncaused* event (either the act itself or some event immediately preceding the act, such as the formation of an intention or a volition or a choice). Carl Ginet is a prominent contemporary defender of an account of this sort. According to Ginet's account, at the core of every complex bodily free action is a simple mental act, a *volition*, that is itself uncaused.[4] The mental event of volition, as a simple act, has no internal causal structure. It counts as an action, according to Ginet, in virtue of its having a certain phenomenal quality, characterized by its *seeming* to the agent as if it were caused directly by him, although in fact it was not.[5]

A natural critical reaction to this type of account is that an uncaused volition is heteronomous. As R. E. Hobart remarks: "In proportion as an act of volition starts of itself without cause it is exactly, so far as the freedom of the individual is concerned, as if it had been thrown into his mind from without—'suggested to him by a freakish demon.'"[6]

Ginet might contend in response that a mental event compelled by a "freakish demon" is not uncaused and so cannot count as the volition crucial to the account of free action. But the problem is that a mental event's having an *actish phenomenal quality* is not sufficient to ground the source of the act in the self. An event with such a phenomenal quality *might* be produced by a demon. And in the case of a genuinely uncaused volition, if the agent as a substance does not causally produce the volition, and neither does any previous event causally produce it, then the simple mental event of volition is not causally produced by anything at all and hence only seems, but is not in fact, under the agent's control. As David Velleman observes, on Ginet's account the agential source of all actions is "tainted with illusion."[7]

What ought to be fully under the agent's control in cases of free action is what action he does. But an uncaused event is an event that derives from nothing, that has its source in nothing. This sort of event is mysterious; without any causal antecedents whatsoever, it is random. Free actions surely should not appear from nowhere. Hence a choice made for reasons, yet completely unconnected causally to either an agent or events of the past, is out of control. Likewise, a complex bodily action having at its center an uncaused mental act of volition is ultimately underivable from anything and hence is out of control.

III. Agent-Causation

A second incompatibilist strategy is to contend that some events are caused by an *agent*. The agent-causal relation consists in the obtaining of a causal connection between a person qua agent and a certain event which, depending on the particular agent-causal theory, is taken to be a decision, or the (free) act itself, or the formation of an intention-to-act-here-and-now. On an agent-causal account, a person acts freely just in case his act or the crucial precursor to his bodily movement (in the case of overt actions) is not causally determined by previous events but is rather causally determined directly by the agent as a persisting entity.

An agent-causation theory of freedom was famously defended by the eighteenth-century Scottish philosopher Thomas Reid and has been adopted and explicated in various ways as well by the contemporary philosophers C. A. Campbell, Roderick Chisholm, Richard Taylor, Timothy O'Connor, and Randolph Clarke, among others (although both Chisholm and Taylor later repudiated their agent-causal views).[8] The fundamental tenet of each of these accounts is the same—that some events are brought about by a *thing* or *substance,* where the causal relation between the substance and the event is a fundamentally irreducible notion. This causation by an agent Chisholm dubbed *immanent* (as opposed to *transeunt*—event or state of affairs—causation). In tracing event causation back to the agent, Chisholm maintains, we will reach an ultimate brain event that was made to happen by the agent, and not by other events. Of course the agent cannot change or do anything to cause the event in question, because then an event—namely, the event of the agent's willing to do it, or his change—would have been the cause of the act, and not the agent himself. This leads Chisholm to conclude that every agent must be a "prime mover unmoved."[9]

The reference to "prime movers unmoved," and to agent-causation more generally, has been subjected to a fair amount of philosophical heckling. The supposition of our having the ability to be unmoved movers has seemed to some to be merely an unlikely posit made in theoretical desperation, rather than a genuinely useful construct well supported by evidence. We do have experience of people doing things, *bringing about* events and states of affairs: I might cause a pen to move across my desk by flicking it; you might cause your eyes to widen. But in speaking of ourselves as being the cause of these events, just as when we say that the dog spilled the water, what we really mean is that certain events caused other events: the event of my flicking my finger caused the pen to move; the event of the dog's bumping the dish with sufficient force caused the water to spill. Speaking of an object or an agent as the cause of some event is just shorthand for the more specific event-causal explanation upon which the agent causal explanation supervenes.

Agent-causalists disagree. If we ever act freely, then it must be the case that we, as agents, sometimes stand in nonreducible relations with events. This is the only good way to account for incompatibilist intuitions about free agency: to posit the special agent-causal relation. Critics contend that the notion merely "labels" what libertarians need, without doing anything to "illuminate" the nature of free will.[10]

Agent-causal accounts do provide theoretical backing to the intuitively powerful idea that when we act freely, what we do is ultimately "up to us," that we ourselves, as agents, are the originators or source points of our acts. Free acts, intuitively, derive directly from the self; they are acts over which the self has full authority. Agent-causal theories take this idea seriously, capturing it in direct fashion, and this is their greatest strength. Moreover, agent-causal views have the virtue of providing a straightforward answer to the problem of agent control—decisions (or intention formations, or acts, depending on the version of the theory) are clearly and fully under the free agent's control, in virtue of the agent's standing in a direct, causally determining relationship with them. These virtues account for the attractiveness for many libertarians of the agent-causal approach.

But although an appeal to agent-causation may help to mitigate concerns about the *randomness* of an act undetermined by previous events, it nonetheless has seemed to many to generate more problems than it solves. Take a case of a putatively free act, in virtue of having at its core an agent-caused event: say, my making a promise to myself not to eat so much chocolate. I, the agent, existed prior to the occurrence of this act, and I continue to exist after I have made the promise to myself. But if I exist both prior to the act's occurring and after it is done, without the act's occurring at any of those other times, then what makes the difference at the time it does occur?

How can *I* as a persisting entity make something happen (or come to exist)? Normally when something happens, something else happened previous to it to cause it to occur. (For instance, before the dog's water spilled out of his dish, the dog bumped the dish, causing it to spill.) But I do not happen; I simply exist. And I exist both before and after the event in question. So what caused the promise to stop eating so much chocolate to occur when it did? The agent-causal account seems to lack the resources to explain why the agent-caused event occurs when it does, since nothing about the agent, no change he undergoes, can explain its happening then. Furthermore, how will the agent-causal account explain how two different forms of causation could systematically interact in a single human being?[11] Moreover, it is not clear that we have sufficient reason to believe that agents in fact have the requisite properties for subsisting the sort of causal power that agent-causalists envision: to directly cause, at will, actions or the coming to be of immediately executive intentions.[12]

Perhaps the appeal to a primitive notion of *agent-causation* is unnecessary. Chisholm once remarked against scoffers at the notion that philosophers do not have the right to make such jokes until they have a proposed analysis of such statements as "Jones killed his uncle" into purely event-causal statements, an analysis that captures the participation of the agent. Without such an analysis, he claims, "the joke is entirely on you."[13] David Velleman's reply to this remark is particularly apt: "The proper goal for the philosophy of action is to *earn* the right to make jokes about primitive agent-causation, by explaining how an agent's causal role supervenes on the causal network of events and states."[14] Although this comment is directed toward the philosophy of action in general, in my view it expresses precisely the right goal for libertarian free will theory.

In the remainder of this essay, I would therefore like to see how far we can get in constructing an indeterminist model of free will *without* making appeal to agent-causation as an irreducible notion. The goal is to produce a model that explains how our ordinary description of an agent's causing an event is in fact reducible to event-causal terms.[15]

IV. Action on Indeterministically Formed Preference

A third approach is one that builds on Anscombe's argument for a divorce between the notions of causation and necessitation.[16] Some causes might not necessitate their effects, but only make them probable, and thus it might be true that every event has an event as a cause while it is false that there is at every moment exactly one physically possible future. A *necessitating cause* C of an effect E is one such that it is not possible (on the occasion) that C occur and not cause E, given that there is nothing that prevents E from occurring. A *nonnecessitating cause* is one that can fail to produce its effect, even without the intervention of anything to frustrate it. Anscombe's example of a nonnecessitating cause is a collection of radioactive material that activates a Geiger counter that is connected to a bomb. Via the Geiger counter, the material causes the bomb to explode. It was not determined, but merely happened, that the radioactive material emitted particles in such a way as to activate the Geiger counter sufficiently to set off the bomb.

Many philosophers now admit cases of indeterministic causation. David Lewis, for instance, remarks:

> I certainly do not think that causation requires determinism.... Events that happen by chance may nevertheless be caused. Indeed, it seems likely that most actual causation is of just this sort. Whether that is so or not, plenty of people do think that our world is chancy; and chancy enough so that most things that happen had some chance, immediately beforehand, of not happening. These people are seldom observed to deny commonplace causal statements.... We had better provide for causation under indeterminism, causation of events for which prior conditions were not lawfully sufficient.[17]

Several accounts of indeterministic causation are available (e.g., those of Ellery Eells, I. J. Good, Christopher Hitchcock, David Lewis, Hans Reichenbach, Wesley Salmon, and Patrick Suppes).[18] These accounts share a certain motivating idea: that a cause increases the probability of the effect. Lewis's theory, in particular, differs from some other probabilistic accounts in two respects. First, it applies to causation by one particular event of another event, rather than conduciveness of one *kind* of event to another kind (so that its probabilities are single-case chances). And second, his analysis is in terms of counterfactual conditionals about probability rather than in terms of conditional probabilities (since Lewis is troubled by a certain difficulty raised for the attempt to use inequality of conditional probabilities to express that event C raises the probability of event E: namely, that the inequality may hold because C and E are both effects of a common cause. Some philosophers maintain that this problem can be handled by specifying suitable background conditions.)

Now suppose that mental states and events can be nonnecessitating or indeterministic causes of other mental states and events. And suppose that we begin delineating a positive indeterminist account of free action by refining the basic causal approach to analyzing action. According to the causal theory of action,[19] a certain complex of an agent's desires and beliefs causes an intention to act in a particular way, and the intention consequently causes corresponding bodily movements in execution of the intention. The motivating desires and beliefs are the agent's reasons for acting— they justify the act, in that the agent desires a certain end and believes that acting in a particular way will help him achieve that end. The reasons are also causes, and, provided that the causal processes between the desire-belief complex and the intention, and between the intention and the bodily movements, proceed in a nondeviant or "normal" sort of way, the agent's movements mark the achievement of an action.[20]

Consider an account of free action as *being able to act as one wants*. A number of philosophers have made familiar the point that although this is a natural root idea for characterizing free action, certain of one's wants or desires can, from an internal perspective, be repudiated or themselves unwanted by the agent, so that in acting on them one is enslaved, rather than free.[21] Rather than solving this problem by appealing to higher-order desires (or desires about desires and desires about desires about desires and so on), since this would necessitate a solution to a regress problem, consider the notion of an agent's *evaluated reasons*. We have reasons for doing and desiring and believing all sorts of things, but an agent's evaluated reasons are those that have survived a process of critical scrutiny with regard to what is true and what is good.[22] Call a desire—to act or to intend or to desire in some particular way—that has survived such a process of critical reflection with respect to the good a *preference*. Call the mental endorsement of a proposition formed by critical reflection with the aim of assenting to what is true an *acceptance*.[23]

Now consider the collection of preferences and acceptances of a person's psychology to be his *character*. And take the *self* to be a character, together with the capacity or faculty—call it the deliberative faculty—for forming and reforming that character.[24] That is, the agent's self or identity is constituted by this faculty for critical reflection with an eye toward truth and goodness, together with the preferences and acceptances formed as the outcome of that reflection.[25]

I will use the term 'decision' to refer to a process: the sequence of events that occurs when an agent's deliberative faculty considers various factors, leading up to the formation of a state of mind settling the agent's uncertainty. If the decision concerns what to desire (so that in deciding one asks oneself, what do I *desire* to do or to desire?), and if in the process of making the decision the agent centrally considers her acceptances concerning what is good, and as the outcome of that consideration reflectively endorses a certain desire or course of action, then the outcome of the decision—its settlement state—is a preference.[26] The event of preference formation thus settles the agent's indecision concerning what she wants to do.[27]

What happens in the case of a free action? When faced with alternatives, the agent considers various reasons, including standing desires, preferences, and acceptances, in favor of competing outcomes. This deliberation might proceed quickly or as a long, drawn-out process. Suppose that, as the outcome of this deliberation, the agent forms a preference concerning what to do and that this preference causes (in a normal sort of way) a corresponding intention to act, which in turn causes (in a normal sort of way) a corresponding piece of behavior. Then the agent's act is causally derived from an aspect of the self, as defined above partially in terms of preference. Needed in the model is some indeterminism in the production of the act.

The best *freedom-enhancing* place to locate the indeterminism, I believe, is just prior to the formation of the preference concerning what to do. So the idea is that as the free agent decides what to do, which preference she will form as the resolution of the decision process is causally undetermined by the past. In the case of a free agent, the entire state of the world at a moment prior to the settlement of her mind—including the agent's genetic constitution, memories, occurrent and nonoccurrent desires, preferences and beliefs—together with the natural laws, does *not* entail a unique decision outcome at the subsequent moment.

Of course, the preference ultimately formed does not simply appear from nowhere. If it did, it would be mysterious, and the action resulting from it would have dubious claim to being fully originated by the agent. Rather, in the case of free action, the formed preference has causal antecedents in the considerations that occur to the agent during the deliberative process. But the crucial point is that in the case of free action, the considerations *cause without determining* the deliberative outcome. That is to say, the considerations are probabilistic causes of the formation of a particular preference concerning what to do.

I have proposed that in the case of free action, certain considerations cause without determining the formation of a particular preference concerning what to do. The account needs an additional requirement, namely, that the agent is uncoerced by any external force or agent, such as an invisibly controlling neurosurgeon or evil demon, as she decides what to do. Adding this requirement to those above generates the following account: a free act is the effect of a pertinent intention (e.g., to perform the act here

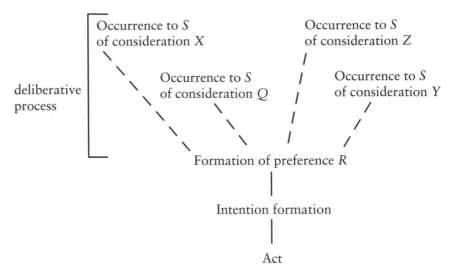

FIGURE 9.1 Proposed account of free action. Dashed lines represent causal connections that must be indeterministic in nature, and solid lines represent causal connections that need not be indeterministic.

and now) that was caused by a preference to act as specified in the content of the intention, a preference that itself was the uncoerced, causally indeterministic outcome of factors considered by the agent's deliberative faculty during the decision process. A free act, then, is *agent caused*—where this notion is given content by the proposed account of the self—and is not, prior to the agent's resolution of the decision process, causally determined by the past and the natural laws.

The proposed account of free action may be depicted in the manner shown in Figure 9.1.

A preference leading to a free act has what we might call *undefeated authorization*. Its claim to being authentic to the agent is not defeated by the claim that it is merely the causally deterministic outcome of the past and the laws—the sole physically possible outcome at the time. An act that one performs as the normal causal outcome of a preference with undefeated authorization then is self-determined in a way that is sufficient for that act's being free. Undefeated authorization is defined as follows:

> df, undefeated authorization: *S* is authorized in preferring *A* in a way that is undefeated if and only if *S*'s evaluative faculty was neither coerced nor causally determined by anything to form the preference for *A*, but rather the preference for *A* was indeterminately caused by *S*'s considerations.

Freedom of action may then be defined in terms of preferences with undefeated authorization. Many of us conceive of ourselves as an agent possessing a certain kind of power: the power to form and reform one's own character. This power, we suppose, is often an uncoerced and undetermined determinant of our actions. It is the correctness of this very conception, I suggest, that allows or would allow one to act freely. An agent enjoys freedom of action in performing an act at a particular time if and only if it is true that the agent's act results by a normal causal process from a preference (for the act) the authorization of which is undefeated.

To say that an act results from an *undetermined* preference is to say that the agent could have, before forming the preference, decided in a number of ways. Suppose, as an illustration, that Jane Eyre is deciding whether or not to leave Thornfield upon discovering that her beloved Mr. Rochester is already married to Berta Mason. The possible outcomes to her deliberation are the preference to remain with Mr. Rochester and live as his wife, the preference to remain yet to live as his platonic companion, and the preference to flee the situation altogether. Various considerations occur to her, including the thought that Mr. Rochester is intelligent and passionate, a desire for romantic love, a preference for lifelong companionship with someone who shares her interests, an acceptance that it is immoral to be romantically involved with a married man, a preference for acting in accordance with the divine will, an acceptance that it is the divine will for her to lead a morally upright life, a preference for having children of her own one day, a conviction that children are best off being born to married parents. Each of these deliberative inputs points rationally toward one or another of the differing conclusive preferences, and each raises the probability of one of the three potential deliberative outcomes.

Jane decides to flee Thornfield. If she acts freely in leaving, then her preference for leaving must have been neither coerced nor causally necessitated by the past: during the decision process, she was able to have formed any of the three potential outcome preferences.

Note that the compatibilist cannot require strictly sufficient conditions for an event in order for that event to be nonrandom. To do so is question-begging, for what the libertarian affirms is precisely that there is a third option between determined and random. The third option, according to this view, is that the decision is explicable by reference to the deliberative events that caused the decision to be what it was. Why did the free agent decide in that way? Because of reasons x, y, z, and so on. Why did those reasons lead him to decide as he did? The determinist would answer: because of a deterministic causal law linking such reasons to such a decision. But the proposed account answers: because the agent exercised her evaluative faculty in a particular way. Why? For reasons that favored but did not necessitate a particular outcome to her deliberation process. These causal statements report necessary but not strictly sufficient conditions for the decisively formed preference. In order to be explicable, the decisively formed preference need not be necessitated. But in order to be free, the decisively formed preference must not be necessitated. It may be tempting to suppose that a preference cannot be explained if it might have been otherwise, given all of the agent's considerations and holding fixed the natural laws. But this supposition is only what Christopher Hitchcock calls a "demon of determinism." Not all explanation is deterministic. [28]

Certainly a number of factors influence us as we deliberate—the media, friendly advice, the attitudes of one's colleagues, the desires of one's parents, subconscious needs, the political climate, concern for the environment, the interests of one's children or siblings, and regard for what is true and right. What we desire when focusing on freedom is that none of these factors necessitate particular outcomes of our decisions. We welcome the influence of such factors, if we are reasonable. But what we abhor, when concentrating on the value of freedom, is the causal determination of our deliberative process by any of them. It is disturbing to suppose that our deliberative process is driven down a single path by the past. Freedom is opposed to constraint, and *having* to form a preference to act in any particular way—no matter how appealing that way may be, or how objectively right it is, or how much one's parent approves of it—is constraining.

Notice that the preference-forming decisions central to the account need not immediately precede the act in time: one might form a preference for committing a certain act at a particular time in the future, leading to the formation of a future-directed intention which, together with the belief that the time has become appropriate, generates an immediately executive intention, which in turn—if all goes well and the agent does not change his mind—leads normally to the act. Alternatively, one might deliberately form a preference to act in a certain way in the future, not at a particular time, but whenever certain circumstances arise, such that one then has a *standing* preference from which free acts can arise without immediately following a deliberative process. For instance, the first time I chose a caregiver for my child, I may have engaged in an elaborate deliberation process, involving many considerations (concerning such matters as my values, my child's needs, and the qualifications of various candidates) before forming a preference concerning whom to hire. But subsequently when the need arises, I may simply phone the regular sitter and do so freely, without needing to elaborately reevaluate the matter, instead acting from a *standing* preference to use the person in question when he or she is available.

Thus, an agent may be unable *at t* (the time at which she performs some act A) to do otherwise than A and yet be free in doing A. She is free in performing A at t only if she is genuinely self-determined with respect to A— that is, she performs A for certain reasons *and* those reasons are genuinely her own, in that she was not coercively caused to have them and the reasons were not causally determined to be her preferences by previous deliberative events.

The proposed view has the benefit of not making it a matter of chance whether or not the free act follows an agent's decisively formed preference. The view of free action as *action on undefeated authorized preference* has other merits as well: (1) The account appropriately captures intuitions concerning what we *want* in valuing freedom. It proposes some causal openness in the construction of the self, so that who we are is not the necessary result of the past, given the natural laws. Yet what preferences we form is causally and rationally explicable. What is especially objectionable about determinism, it seems, is the thought that our characters were fully determined by genetic and environmental factors. (2) The account is a phenomenologically accurate one. It seems as if the ending point of deliberation is the outcome of our considerations, yet during deliberation there are genuinely available alternatives, multiple branching paths before us. (3) The view is consistent with a wholly naturalistic metaphysics. We need not believe in immaterial souls in order to believe in free will. We need not believe in an uncaused substance-event causal relation or that we are "unmoved movers." The view of free action as action on undefeated authorized preference leaves free acts within the realm of what is scientifically explicable, and there is no need in this account to deny the antecedently plausible principle that every event has a cause.

In short, given the power of the arguments for incompatibilism, *some* indeterminist model of free action must have a hold on us, and the proposed account, I believe, is the best of the available options.[29] When I act freely, the preference leading to the act is generated by the evaluative faculty that in part constitutes me, and the preference is not coerced by an external source. Hence when the appropriately formed preference leads to my act, what I do is "up to me," because I, quite literally, causally determine it.

V. Three Concerns

I will consider three objections to this account.

First is a potential regress problem. Consider the act of preference formation preceding a free act. Need it, itself, be a free act? If so, then it (call it preference$_1$) would have to be preceded by an intention and by a preference (call it preference$_2$). And if the preference-forming event preceding a free act need be a free act itself, then preference$_2$ preceding the free act of the formation of preference$_1$ would itself have to be a free act, requiring that it be preceded by an intention and by a prior free act of preference formation; and so on. And hence it seems that, in order to perform a free act, one would have to perform an infinite number of free acts; and this is, of course, highly implausible.

In response, I maintain that the preference-forming event preceding a free act need not be a free act itself. As long as the preference is the uncoerced, indeterministic outcome of the agent's deliberative process, the act resulting from the preference can be free.

Second, why should we think that the preference preceding a free act must have an indeterministic causal explanation? The objector claims that the indeterminism undercuts rather than adds to a person's freedom in and credit for performing the act.

In response, any incompatibilist model of freedom is going to have to locate the event-causal indeterminism somewhere in the history of the free act, and the specified place, between the considerations and the decisive formation of preference, seems the most reasonable place to locate it. One might, instead, locate the indeterminism *prior to* some of the considerations that occur to the agent during the deliberative process, so that what is undetermined is which particular considerations come into the agent's mind (and perhaps at what points during the process).[30] But if this were the only place specified for required indeterminism, then an act might be the purely causally deterministic outcome of the considerations that happen to occur to the agent and yet, on the proposal, count as free.

Such an account is too weak to ground agent freedom and responsibility because, given the occurrence of the particular considerations in any case, one particular act follows of physical necessity as the completely deterministic unfolding of previous events. Consider an agent whose act is, in such a sense, "libertarian free." A duplicate agent in exactly similar circumstances governed by the same natural laws and subject to the same occurrence of considerations at the same points in the deliberative process will form exactly the same judgment concerning the best thing to do and will act accordingly. But then, given the consideration pattern that occurs (but might not have), there is no wiggle room for the agent in forming an evaluative judgment—it simply drops, necessarily, from the consideration pattern. Hence such an account does not leave sufficient room for free agency.

Where causal indeterminism is best located, instead, is *after* the considerations (which in the usual case have been determined to occur by previous events, such as how much rest one has had, what one has recently eaten, with whom one has recently spoken, what one has read), yet *prior* to the decisive formation of preference, such that given the exact consideration pattern, the agent may decide to prefer *A* or may decide to prefer otherwise. The considerations themselves are indeterministic causes of the preference.

One might, out of dissatisfaction with the proposed model, opt to be a compatibilist. But then one must face the fact that the arguments for incompatibilism are powerful, and no response to them is particularly persuasive.[31] Furthermore, the intuitions underlying our deep-rooted notion of human dignity, our commonsensical conception of the future as we engage in practical deliberation, and commonly held judgments concerning deserved attributions of praise and blame are incompatibilist in nature. It is central to our self-image as practical deliberators that there are forks in the path in front of us representing causally open future alternatives. Thus some incompatibilist model of free action is needed. Where are the junctures that are important to us for acting freely? The proposed model, I have argued, appropriately locates them.

We could, in accounting for free action, appeal to agent-causation as a primitive notion, irreducible to causation among events. But the agent-causal theory seems, indeed, merely to label rather than to illuminate the problem of free agency. Alternatively, we could select an approach relying on the posit of an uncaused volition or choice. But to adopt such a view of free action requires that we believe in something—uncaused events—with which we have no familiarity in the physical world. Uncaused events of volition or choice can be explained by reference to the agent's purposes, but they cannot be causally explained; they derive from absolutely nothing. With regard to any uncaused volition or uncaused choice, we can answer the question "Why did it occur?" by citing the agent's goals, but it is impossible to answer the question "What *made* it occur?" This is not satisfying. According to the view I have defended, free actions result from preferences, and those preferences are formed noncoercively for reasons that are probabilistic causes of them.

Consider a third objection. A decision to form a particular preference should be reasonable for the agent rather than arbitrary, in order for the act resulting from that decision to be free. But if the agent's deliberative process produces the answer that, all things considered, A is the best-choice outcome, then it seems that choosing A would be inevitable. To require for freedom that her choice outcome remain undetermined by the reasons seems to require an odd ability: the ability to decide against the best reasons. That is, to require for freedom that an agent be able to choose otherwise in the categorical sense *after* the occurrence in her mind of various considerations—that she be able to choose A and that she be able to choose B, given the laws of nature and all of the facts about her and her past, including the deliberations of her evaluative faculty—seems to require for freedom the ability to act irrationally. But no one wants this ability. As Robert Kane expresses the problem, what is difficult to understand and in need of explanation is "how I could have reasonably chosen to do otherwise, how I could have reasonably chosen B, *given exactly the same prior deliberation* that led me to choose A, the same information deployed, the same consequences considered, the same assessments made, and so on."[32] To want the ability to act freely as I have characterized it, then, might seem to be, in the words of Susan Wolf, "not only to want the ability to make choices when there is no basis for choice, but to want the ability to make choices on no basis even when there is a basis. But the latter ability would seem to be an ability no one could ever have reason to want to exercise."[33]

However, it is not true of choice outcomes in the proposed account that they have no basis whatsoever. They are, rather, caused indeterministically by prior considerations. Suppose that my decision outcome is preference A. What does it mean to say that I could have reasonably formed preference B, given exactly the same prior deliberation that led me to choose A? We know what it means to say that I *could have* chosen otherwise than A: I had the skill required for forming some choice outcome other than A, and, given the past and the laws, it was undetermined what choice outcome would follow; the physical conditions and laws *left room* for the exercise of my skill. As to the question of how I could have *reasonably* chosen otherwise, suppose that I had decisively formed preference B (rather than preference A) and that preference B was uncoerced and was indeterminately caused by some of my prior considerations. Then preference B was *reasonable*. If formed, that is, the preference for B would have been caused and justified by reasons. In fact, so long as the choice outcome follows on reasons considered by the agent in the deliberative process, it is *reasonable* in the sense that it results for a reason, although it is not necessarily the most rational option, given the total set of the agent's reasons.

If the objector claims to prefer always being determined by the *best* considerations to being caused to decide as he does by just *any* considerations, then this merely shows something about the objector's values, namely, that he prizes being right over being free. Being pushed into deciding in a certain way by anything, whether one's grandmother, one's genetic blueprint, or overwhelmingly powerful considerations, is antithetical to free agency. Contrary to Wolf's claim about what we want, it seems to me that in deciding what to do and what sort of person to be, we do not want to be determined by anything. Rational and causal influence is one thing; determination of choice is another. Again, freedom is opposed to constraint, and *having* to choose in any particular way, no matter how rational or objectively right that way may be, is constraining.

According to the proposed account, then, before the agent's evaluative faculty is set to work, she can form preference A and can form preference B. Both preference A and preference B could be rational for the agent, if she has reasons supporting each preference. A preference probabilistically caused by considerations of the agent's is not a preference formed "on no basis." The objection might be construed as a request for an explanation of how either of two alternative, decisively formed preferences the agent could potentially form could be rational for that agent, if formed. The answer, then, is that whichever one *is* made, is rationally explicable by reference to the agent's evaluative process and its inputs. Suppose she decided to form preference *A*. Why did she do so? Because of prior considerations that reasonably supported that particular decision outcome. The decisions from which free acts result are those in which the agent decides on bases, but no basis is causally determinative of what she decides.

Notes

1. See, for instance, Peter van Inwagen, *An Essay on Free Will* (Oxford: Clarendon Press, 1983), chapter 3; John Martin Fischer, *The Metaphysics of Free Will* (Cambridge, MA: Blackwell, 1994), chapters 1–2; Laura Waddell Ekstrom, *Free Will: A Philosophical Study* (Boulder: Westview Press, 2000), chapter 2.

2. Thus it is not that the agent *could* or *would* do otherwise *if* certain circumstances had been different, but rather that the agent has at the moment more than one option for acting, given the past and the circumstances exactly as they are. The free agent is taken to be able to perform more than one action, given the reigning natural laws and conditions, and this ability means not only that the agent has the appropriate faculties for performing a multiple number of actions, but further that he or she can in the circumstances exercise them.

3. Robert Kane is a contemporary incompatibilist who also rejects such views as implausible. See his *Free Will and Values* (Albany: State University of New York Press, 1985) and *The Significance of Free Will* (New York: Oxford University Press, 1996).

4. Others taking *volition* to be central to the analysis of action include Hugh McCann, "Volition and Basic Action," *Philosophical Review* 83 (1974): 451–473, and Brian O'Shaughnessy, *The Will: A Dual Aspect Theory*, 2 vols. (Cambridge: Cambridge University Press, 1980).

5. Carl Ginet, *On Action* (Cambridge: Cambridge University Press, 1990), 13–32.

6. R. E. Hobart, "Free-Will as Involving Determination and Inconceivable Without It," *Mind*, 43 (1943): 1–27.

7. David Velleman, "What Happens When Someone Acts?" *Mind* 101 (1992): 461–481, reprinted in *Perspectives on Moral Responsibility*, ed. J. M. Fischer and M. Ravizza (Ithaca, NY: Cornell University Press, 1993), 194, note 3. For a discussion of this problem in Ginet's account, see Timothy O'Connor, "Why Agent Causation?" *Philosophical Topics* 24, no. 2 (1996): 146.

8. Thomas Reid, *Essays on the Active Powers of the Human Mind* (Cambridge: MIT Press, 1969); C. A. Campbell, *On Selfhood and Godhood* (London: George Allen and Unwin, 1957): 158–169; Roderick Chisholm, "Human Freedom and the Self," 1964, reprinted in *Free Will*, ed. Gary Watson (New York: Oxford University

Press, 1982), 24–35, and reprinted in this volume; Richard Taylor, *Metaphysics*, 4th edition (Englewood Cliffs, NJ: Prentice-Hall, 1992); Randolph Clarke, "Toward a Credible Agent-Causal Account of Free Will," *Noûs* 27 (1993): 191–203; O'Connor, "Why Agent Causation?"

9. Chisholm 1982, 32.

10. See Thomas Hobbes, *The English Works of Thomas Hobbes*, vol. 5, ed. W. Molesworth (London: Scientia Aalen, 1962), 35, 77, 113; Gary Watson, "Introduction," in *Free Will*, ed. Gary Watson (New York: Oxford University Press, 1982), 10; and John Bishop, *Natural Agency* (Cambridge: Cambridge University Press, 1989), 69.

11. As it stands, this question expresses only the suspicion of a problem; but the burden lies with the agent-causalist to show how his appeal to the special sort of causation fits together with the causation between neurological (and other physical) events.

12. Timothy O'Connor contends, in "Why Agent Causation?" (150–151), that we have evidence of our possessing the power to be agent-causes in the form of observations of it in our acting freely.

13. Roderick Chisholm, "Comments and Replies," *Philosophia* 7 (1978): 597–636 (quoted in Velleman, "What Happens When Someone Acts?").

14. Velleman, "What Happens When Someone Acts?" p. 197 in Fischer and Ravizza.

15. One might question the commitment to reductionism motivating this project. John Dupre argues, in *The Disorder of Things: Metaphysical Foundations of the Disunity of Science* (Cambridge, MA: Harvard University Press, 1993), that entities at many different levels of organization initiate causal chains. If Dupre is right, then to believe that human beings initiate causal chains is not so odd, since we are not the only genuine causal entities but have a great deal of company in the natural world. Even if the reductionism I presuppose in launching the project that follows is subject to controversy, however, it is not unreflectively presupposed. I find the project of working out a model of free action for one convinced of the success of incompatibilist arguments and at the same time skeptical of antireductionist arguments both intriguing and profitable.

16. Elizabeth Anscombe, "Causality and Determination," inaugural lecture, Cambridge University, 1971. [Essay 4 in this volume.]

17. David Lewis, postscript to "Causation," in his *Philosophical Papers*, vol. 2 (New York: Oxford University Press, 1982), 175.

18. Ellery Eells, *Probabilistic Causality* (Cambridge: Cambridge University Press, 1991); I. J. Good, "A Causal Calculus I–II," *British Journal for the Philosophy of Science* 11 (1961): 305–318; 12 (1962): 43–51; Christopher Hitchcock, "A Generalized Probabilistic Theory of Causal Relevance," *Synthese* 97 (1993): 335–364; David Lewis, "Causation," *Journal of Philosophy* 70 (1973): 556–567; Hans Reichenbach, *Philosophic Foundations of Quantum Mechanics* (Berkeley: University of California Press, 1946), and *The Philosophy of Space and Time* (New York: Dover Publications, 1957); Wesley Salmon, *Causality and Explanation* (New York: Oxford University Press, 1998); Patrick Suppes, *A Probabilistic Theory of Causality* (Amsterdam: North-Holland, 1970).

19. See Donald Davidson, *Essays on Actions and Events* (New York: Oxford University Press, 1980).

20. For discussion of the need for "normal" or nondeviant causal chains, see John Bishop, *Natural Agency* (Cambridge: Cambridge University Press, 1989), and Alfred Mele, *Springs of Action* (New York: Oxford University Press, 1992).

21. See, for instance, Harry Frankfurt, "Freedom of the Will and the Concept of a Person," *Journal of Philosophy* 68 (1971): 5–20. [Essay 5 in this volume.]

22. It may be that a counterfactual condition plausibly weakens this proposal: an evaluated reason could be described as either one that actually has survived critical scrutiny by the agent or one that *would* satisfy such evaluation *if* scrutinized. An amendment midway between this weak proposal and the strong one proposed in the body of this paper is one requiring the satisfaction of the counterfactual condition and requiring additionally of the *agent* that she be the sort of person who routinely engages in critical reflection so that her practical deliberative processes have been affected, such that she does not regularly allow desires to serve as reasons for action that would not survive explicit critical scrutiny. Arguably, a desire meeting the conditions of either of these weakened proposals could count as being formed as the "outcome" of critical reflection and so count as a *preference*.

I am inclined to uphold the strong version of the proposal on the grounds that it is through the process of critical engagement with the question of the *worth* of a desire that one makes that desire one's own, but with the explicit observation that this process need not be lengthy and involved or even proceed at the fully conscious level.

23. The notion of acceptance is Keith Lehrer's; see his *Theory of Knowledge* (Boulder: Westview Press, 1990).

24. I defend these conceptions of character and the self in "A Coherence Theory of Autonomy," *Philosophy and Phenomenological Research* 53 (September 1993): 599–616, and in *Free Will: A Philosophical Study* (Boulder: Westview Press, 2000). Surely the faculty for shaping the character—for evaluating desires, beliefs, and courses of action with respect to standards—ought to be taken as a constituent of the self. We clearly have some faculty for deciding what becomes a component of our character, what remains a component of our character, and what gets discarded as no longer an element of our character (although whether or not the operation of this faculty is causally necessitated by prior factors is less clear). And this conception of the *character* is plausible for several reasons. Unlike hierarchical conceptions of the self as structured solely by desire, the proposed conception of the self incorporates some beliefs. Our convictions concerning the truth are central to who we are. But, appropriately, not just any beliefs and desires count as parts of the character. Opinions that one holds unreflectively and passions that overtake one are too common, as well as too blindly had, to be part of the character. A character is the complex of attributes or features that mark and *distinguish* the individual. Elements of the character—preferences and acceptances—are the outputs of the individual's own evaluative activity.

25. I rely on a controversial conception of agential identity as a cluster of mental states and a capacity of a certain sort; I have not tried to give an account of the sort of relationships between the states that in part constitute the agent at different points in time serving to preserve personal identity through time.

26. The formation of the preference counts as an act in virtue of its causal history: in particular, in virtue of its being preceded by an intention to decide what to prefer (or the intention to form some preference or another). Likewise, in Mele's view, decisions to A are preceded not by intentions to decide to A but rather by intentions to decide what to do; see Alfred Mele, "Agency and Mental Action," in *Mind, Causation, and World*, ed. James E. Tomberlin, *Philosophical Perspectives*, vol. 11 (Boston: Blackwell, 1997).

27. This should not be taken to rule out an agent's realizing that she ought to rethink the matter and subsequently beginning another decision process.

28. Hitchcock writes: "It has become close to orthodoxy in the philosophy of science to believe that indeterministic explanation is possible. There are, no doubt, strong pre-theoretic intuitions linking explanation and determinism. Through a series of powerful arguments … , however, we have been trained to repress these intuitions. I wholeheartedly accept the conclusions of these arguments; nonetheless, it would be idle to deny that we still carry these intuitions; we are all occasionally haunted by the demons of determinism. It is even possible to entice these demons to rise by phrasing our questions in the right way: since the photon *could have* been absorbed, then surely we have not *fully explained* why the photon was transmitted? We must not give in to temptation." Christopher Hitchcock, "Contrastive Explanation and the Demons of Determinism," forthcoming, *British Journal for the Philosophy of Science*. He goes on to argue that not only is it possible to provide explanations of indeterministic outcomes, but also it is possible to provide *contrastive* explanations of those outcomes.

29. Consider an alternative but related account. Daniel Dennett, in "On Giving Libertarians What They Say They Want," in his *Brainstorms* (Montgomery, VT: Bradford Books, 1978), 286–299, sketches—without endorsing—what he contends is the best model of free agency available to a libertarian. Dennett describes a scenario in which an agent must make a decision about what to do, namely, to accept academic job offer A or to accept academic job offer B. According to the model, "it just might be the case that *exactly* which considerations occur to one in such circumstances is to some degree strictly undetermined" (294). In Dennett's example, considerations A through F occur to Jones, and on the basis of them, she decides to take a job at Swarthmore. But had consideration G also occurred to her, she would have taken a job at the University of Chicago instead. As it happened, G didn't occur to her, although it might have, given the past and the laws. The proposal is that the indeterminism required for a free act is quite far back in the causal history of the act: just prior to the events describable as certain considerations occurring to the agent as inputs to the process of deliberation over what to do.

Dennett's proposal—set out only on the way toward making the ultimate point that incompatibilist freedom is not really the sort of freedom we want—is closely related to the model of libertarian autonomy proposed—but, again, not endorsed—by Alfred Mele in his *Autonomous Agents: From Self-Control to Autonomy* (New York: Oxford University Press, 1995). Mele's proposal is this: what should be held by the libertarian to be causally undetermined is "which members of a shifting subset of Jones's relevant nonoccurrent beliefs will become occurrent and function in his deliberation" (214). So, some beliefs will come to mind and some won't, and of those that come to mind, a subset of them are undetermined by the past and the laws to occur—they just *happen* to occur when they do in the deliberation process, but they might not have. Mele takes judgments concerning what to do to be the outcome of practical deliberation. So, *what* an agent decisively judges best in the case of deliberation leading to free action remains causally open until deliberation ends, and *when* deliberation ends remains causally open, since it is causally open whether a certain belief will come to mind and prolong deliberation. As virtues of this account of modest libertarianism, Mele claims these: (1) compatibilists have no good reason to insist on determinism at this point in the deliberative process as a requirement for freedom; (2) this sort of internal indeterminism is, for all we know, a reality; and (3) such indeterminism does not diminish the agent's control over his deliberations. (See his *Autonomous Agents*, chapter 12.)

The views set out by Dennett and Mele offer another interesting libertarian alternative. But in my view they locate the indeterminism in the wrong place. Specifically, the views are too *weak* in virtue of its indeterminism location to secure agential freedom. In these views, the free agent is subject to luck in what thoughts come into his mind as he is deliberating about what to do. But once the thoughts occur and the last of them has occurred during deliberation, there is a deterministic causal connection between the particular pattern of beliefs that has happened to occur and the subsequent decision outcome. But this is problematic. I might be a free agent, according to Dennett's or Mele's account, while being a victim in what I judge best, and in what I consequently intend, and in what I consequently do, to what thoughts happened to occur to me at the time. Granted, there are "forks in the road" of some sort in this picture of free agency—alternative futures. But it is not up to me, the free agent, which one I take. Which one I take is decided by which considerations happen to come to mind, where this is indeterministically caused by some previous events. According to both Dennett's and Mele's views, once a certain pattern of considerations has happened to occur to the agent, a particular action follows of physical necessity and yet counts as free. Since neither of the views includes an account of the nature of the self, they leave unanswered the question of why an act that is the causally necessary outcome of whatever considerations have happened to occur is plausibly claimed to be originated by the agent.

30. See Mele 1995 and Dennett 1978.

31. I defend this claim in *Free Will*, chapter 2.

32. Kane, *Free Will and Values*, 57. Kane raises this objection and then goes on to answer it.

33. This sort of consideration is one of the reasons leading Wolf to conclude that the determination of one's choice by Reason does not compromise the freedom of that choice. Susan Wolf, *Freedom Within Reason* (New York: Oxford University Press, 1990), 55.

10

Responsibility, Luck and Chance: Reflections on Free Will and Indeterminism

ROBERT KANE

I. The Luck Principle

Wittgenstein once said that "to solve the problems of philosophers, you have to think even more crazily than they do."[1] This task (which became even more difficult after Wittgenstein than it was before him) is certainly required for the venerable problem of free will and determinism. Consider the following principle:

> (L) If an action is *undetermined* at a time t, then its happening rather than not happening at t would be a matter of *chance* or *luck*, and so it could not be a *free* and *responsible* action.

This principle (which we may call the "Luck Principle," or simply L) is false, as I shall explain shortly. Yet it seems true. L and a related principle to be considered later in this paper are fueled by many of those "intuition pumps," in Daniel Dennett's apt expression,[2] that support common intuitions about freedom and responsibility. L and related principles lie behind the widespread belief that indeterminism, so far from being required for

From *Journal of Philosophy* XCVI, 5 (May 1999), pp. 217–240. Reprinted by permission of the author and the *Journal of Philosophy*.

free will and responsibility, would actually undermine free will and responsibility. Dennett does not dwell on the intuition pumps of this sort, as I shall do in this paper. As a compatibilist, he is more interested in criticizing intuition pumps that lead people to think (mistakenly, on his view) that freedom and responsibility are not compatible with determinism; whereas intuition pumps that support L lead people to think freedom and responsibility are not compatible with *indeterminism*. Yet intuition pumps of the latter kind are every bit as pervasive and influential in free will debates as those Dennett dwells upon; and they are as much in need of deconstruction, since they play a significant role in leading people to believe that freedom and responsibility must be compatible with determinism.

For I think the modern route to compatibilism—which is the reigning view among contemporary philosophers—usually goes through principles like L at some point or other. In my experience, most ordinary persons start out as natural incompatibilists. They believe there is some kind of conflict between freedom and determinism; and the idea that freedom and responsibility might be compatible with determinism looks to them at first like a "quagmire of evasion" (William James) or "a wretched subterfuge" (Immanuel Kant). Ordinary persons have to be talked out of this natural incompatibilism by the clever arguments of philosophers—who, in the manner of their mentor, Socrates, are only too happy to oblige. To weaken natural incompatibilist instincts, philosophers first argue that what we mean by freedom in everyday life is the power or ability to do whatever we choose or desire to do—in short, an absence of coercion, compulsion, oppression and other impediments or constraints upon our behavior. They then point out that we can be free in these everyday senses to do what we choose or desire, even if our choices and desires are determined by causes that lie in our past.

But this line of argument does not usually dispose of incompatibilist intuitions by itself. Ordinary persons might grant that many everyday freedoms are compatible with determinism and still wonder if there is not also some deeper freedom—the freedom to have an *ultimate* say in what we choose or desire to do in the first place—that is incompatible with determinism. (I have argued elsewhere that this deeper freedom is what was traditionally meant by "free *will*."[3]) So the philosophers must add a second step to their case—an argument to the effect that any allegedly deeper freedom (of the will) that is not compatible with determinism is no intelligible freedom at all. And with this step, principles like L come into the picture. For, any freedom not compatible with determinism would require indeterminism; and what is undetermined, it seems, would happen by chance or luck and could not be a free and responsible action. This kind of argument is the one that usually puts the final nail in the coffin of incompatibilist instincts.

When philosophy professors go through this two-stage argument in the modern classroom, they are replicating the standard case against traditional (incompatibilist or libertarian) free will that is one of the defining characteristics of modernity. The goal is to consign incompatibilist freedom to the dustbin of history with other beliefs that a modern scientific age is encouraged to outgrow. Students and ordinary persons subjected to this argument may have an uneasy feeling they are being had by the clever arguments of philosophers. But, also seeing no obvious response, except an appeal to mystery, many of them become compatibilists.

II. Indeterminism, the Bogeyman

The second stage of this two stage argument in support of compatibilism will concern me in this paper, the one that goes through L and related principles in the attempt to show that indeterminism would not enhance, but in fact would undermine, freedom and responsibility. What is at stake here is not merely the clever arguments of philosophers. For it happens that the case for principles like L is a powerful one. It *is* difficult to see how indeterminism and chance can be reconciled with freedom and responsibility. Philosophers have tried to bring this out in a number of ways that will be addressed in this paper. We may think of these as the varied intuition pumps that support L and principles like it.

(i) We are often asked to consider, for example, that whatever is undetermined or happens by chance is not under the *control* of anything, and so is not under the control of the agent. But an action that is not under the control of the agent could not be a free and responsible action. (Here it is evident that the notion of control is involved in the case for L: indeterminism and chance imply lack of control to a degree that implies lack of freedom and responsibility.)

(ii) Another line of argument often heard is this: Suppose a choice occurred as the result of an undetermined event (say, a quantum jump) in one's brain. Would that be a free choice? Being undetermined, it would appear to be more of a fluke or accident than a free and responsible action. Some twentieth-century scientists and philosophers have suggested that free will might be rescued by supposing that undetermined quantum events in the brain could be amplified to have large-scale effects on choice or action.[4] Unfortunately, this modern version of the ancient Epicurean "swerve" of the atoms, seems to be subject to the same criticisms as its ancient counterpart. It seems that undetermined events in the brain or body, whether amplified or not, would occur spontaneously and would be more of a nuisance—or perhaps a curse, like epilepsy—than an enhancement of freedom and responsibility.

(iii) Nor would it help to suppose that the indeterminism or chance came *between* our choices (or intentions) and our actions. Imagine that

you are intending to make a delicate cut in a fine piece of cloth, but because of an undetermined twitching in your arm, you make the wrong cut.
Here, indeterminism is no enhancement of your freedom, but a *hindrance*
or *obstacle* to your carrying out your purposes as intended. Critics of libertarian freedom have often contended that this is what indeterminism
would always be—a hindrance or impediment to one's freedom. It would
get in the way, *diminishing* control, and hence responsibility, rather than
enhancing them.[5]

(iv) Even more absurd consequences follow if we suppose that indeterminism or chance is involved in the initiation of overt actions.
Schopenhauer imagined the case of a man who suddenly found his legs
start to move *by chance* carrying him across the room against his wishes.[6]
Such caricatures are popular among critics of indeterminist freedom for obvious reasons: undetermined or chance-initiated overt actions would represent the opposite of controlled and responsible actions.

(v) Going a little deeper, one may also note that if a choice or action is
undetermined, it might occur otherwise *given exactly the same past and
laws of nature* up to the moment when it does occurs. This means that if
Jane is deliberating about whether to vacation in Hawaii or Colorado, and
gradually comes to favor and choose Hawaii, she might have chosen otherwise (chosen Colorado), given *exactly the same deliberation* up to the moment of choice that in fact led her to favor and choose Hawaii (exactly the
same thoughts, reasonings, beliefs, desires, dispositions, and other characteristics—not a sliver of difference). It is difficult to make sense of this. The
choice of Colorado in such circumstances would seem irrational and inexplicable, capricious and arbitrary.[7] If it came about by virtue of undetermined events in Jane's brain, this would not be an occasion for rejoicing in
her freedom, but for consulting a neurologist about the waywardness of her
neural processes.

(vi) At this point, some defenders of incompatibilist freedom appeal to
Leibniz's celebrated dictum that prior reasons or motives need not determine choice or action, they may merely "incline without necessitating"—
i.e., they may incline the agent toward one option without determining the
choice of that option.[8] This may indeed happen. But it will not solve the
present problem. For it is precisely *because* Jane's prior reasons and motives
(beliefs, desires, etc.) incline her toward the choice of Hawaii that choosing
Colorado by chance at the end of exactly the same deliberation would be
irrational and inexplicable. Similarly, if her reasons had inclined her toward
Colorado, then choosing Hawaii by chance at the end of the same deliberation would have been irrational and inexplicable. And if prior reasons or
motives had not inclined her either way (the celebrated medieval "liberty of
indifference") and the choice was a matter of chance, then the choosing of
one rather than the other would have been all the more a matter of luck

and out her control. (One can see why libertarian freedom has often been ridiculed as a mere "liberty of indifference.")

(vii) Indeed, critics of indeterminist freedom have often argued that indeterminist free choices must always amount to *random* choices of this sort and hence the outcomes would be matters of mere luck or chance—like spinning a wheel to select among a set of alternatives. Perhaps there is a role for such random choices in our lives when we are genuinely indifferent to outcomes.[9] But to suppose that *all* of our free and responsible choices—including momentous ones, like whether to act heroically or treacherously—had to be by random selection in this way has been regarded by many philosophers as a *reductio ad absurdum* of the view that free will and responsibility require indeterminism.

(viii) Consider one final argument that cuts more deeply than the others and to which I will devote considerable attention. This paper was in fact prompted by new versions of this argument advanced in recent years against my incompatibilist account of free will by Galen Strawson, Alfred Mele, Bernard Berofsky, Bruce Waller, Richard Double, Mark Bernstein and Istiyaque Haji—though the argument is meant to apply generally to any view requiring that free actions be undetermined up to the moment when they occur.[10]

Suppose two agents had exactly the same pasts (as indeterminism requires) up to the point where they were faced with a choice between distorting the truth for selfish gain or telling the truth at great personal cost. One agent lies and the other tells the truth. As Waller puts it, if the pasts of these two agents "are really identical" in every way up to the moment of choice, "and the difference in their acts results from chance," would there "be any grounds for distinguishing between [them], for saying that one deserves censure for a selfish decision and the other deserves praise?"[11] Mele poses the problem in terms of a single agent in different possible worlds. Suppose in the actual world, John fails to resist the temptation to do what he thinks he ought to do, arrive at a meeting on time. If he could have done otherwise given the same past, then his counterpart, John* in a nearby possible world, which is the same as the actual world up to the moment of choice, resists the temptation and arrives on time. Mele then argues that "if there is nothing about the agents' powers, capacities, states of mind, moral character and the like that explains this difference in outcome, ... the difference is just a matter of luck." It would seem that John* got lucky in his attempt to overcome temptation, whereas John did not. Would it be just to reward the one and punish the other for what appears to be ultimately the luck of the draw?[12]

Considerations such as (i)–(viii) lie behind familiar and varied charges that undetermined choices or actions would be "arbitrary," "capricious," "random," "uncontrolled," "irrational," "inexplicable," or "matters of luck or chance," and hence not free and responsible actions. These are the charges that principles like L are meant to express. Responses to them in the history of philosophy have been many; but none to my mind has been entirely convincing. The charges have often led libertarians—those who believe in an incompatibilist free will—to posit "extra factors" in the form of unusual species of agency or causation (such as noumenal selves, immaterial egos, or non-occurrent agent causes) to account for what would otherwise be arbitrary, uncontrolled, inexplicable or mere luck or chance. I do not propose to appeal to any such extra factors in this paper in defense of libertarian freedom. Such appeals introduce additional problems of their own without, in my view, directly confronting the deep problems about indeterminism, chance and luck to which considerations (i)–(viii) are pointing. To directly confront these deep problems, I believe one has to rethink issues about indeterminism and responsibility from the ground up, without relying on appeals to additional causal factors—a task to which I now turn.

III. Indeterminism and Responsibility

First, one must question the intuitive connection in people's minds between "indeterminism's being involved in something's happening" and "its happening merely as a matter of chance or luck." "Chance" and "luck" are terms of ordinary language that carry the connotation of "its being out of my control" (as in (i) and (iv) and above). So using them already begs certain questions; whereas "indeterminism" is a technical term that merely precludes *deterministic* causation (though not causation altogether). Second, one must emphasize that indeterminism does not have to be involved in all free and responsible acts, even for incompatibilists or libertarians.[13] Frequently we act from a will already formed; and it may well be that our actions are determined in such cases by our then existing characters and motives. On such occasions, to do otherwise by chance *would* be a fluke or accident, irrational and inexplicable, as critics of indeterminist freedom contend (in (iii) and (iv) above).

Incompatibilists about free will should not deny this. What they should rather say is that when we act from a will already formed (as we frequently do), it is "our own free will" by virtue of the fact that we formed it (at least in part) by earlier choices or actions that were not determined and for which we could have done otherwise voluntarily, not merely as a fluke or accident. I call these earlier undetermined actions "self-forming actions" or SFAs.[14] Undetermined SFAs are a subset of all of the actions done of our own free wills (many of which may be determined by our earlier formed character and motives). But if there were no such undetermined self-forming actions in our lifetimes, there would have been nothing we could have ever voluntarily done to make ourselves different than we are—a condition that I think is inconsistent with our having the kind of responsibility for being what we are that genuine free will requires.

Now let us look more closely at these undetermined self-forming actions (SFAs). As I see it, they occur at times in life when we are torn between competing visions of what we should do or become. Perhaps we are torn between doing the moral thing or acting from self-interest, or between present desires and long term goals, or we are faced with difficult tasks for which we have aversions. In all such cases, we are faced with competing motivations and have to make an effort to overcome temptation to do something else we also strongly want. In the light of this picture, I suggest the following incompatibilist account of self-forming actions.[15] There is a tension and uncertainty in our minds at such times of inner conflict that is reflected in appropriate regions of our brains by movement away from thermodynamic equilibrium—in short, a kind of stirring up of chaos in the brain that makes it sensitive to micro-indeterminacies at the neuronal level. As a result, the uncertainty and inner tension we feel at such soul-searching moments of self-formation is reflected in the indeterminacy of our neural processes themselves. What is experienced phenomenologically as uncertainty corresponds physically to the opening of a window of opportunity that temporarily screens off complete determination by the past. (By contrast, when we act from predominant motives or settled dispositions, the uncertainty or indeterminism is muted. If it were involved then, it *would* be a mere nuisance or fluke, capricious or arbitrary, as critics contend (in (ii), (v) and (vi) above).)

When we do decide under such conditions of uncertainty, the outcome is not determined because of the preceding indeterminacy—and yet it can be willed (and hence rational and voluntary) either way owing to the fact that in such self-formation, the agents' prior wills are divided by conflicting motives. If we overcome temptation, it will be the result of our effort, and if we fail, it will be because we did not *allow* our effort to succeed. And this is owing to the fact that, while we wanted to overcome temptation, we also wanted to fail, for quite different and incommensurable reasons. When we decide in such circumstances, and the indeterminate efforts we are making become determinate choices, we *make* one set of competing reasons or motives prevail over the others then and there *by deciding*.

Return now to concerns about indeterminism and responsibility in the light of this picture. Consider a businesswoman who faces a conflict in her will of the kind typically involved in such SFAs. She is on the way to a meeting important to her career when she observes an assault in an alley. An inner struggle ensues between her moral conscience, to stop and call for help, and her career ambitions, which tell her she cannot miss this meeting—a struggle she eventually resolves by turning back to help the victim.

Now suppose this woman visits some future neuroscientists the next day and they tell her a story about what was going on in her brain at the time she chose, not unlike the story just told. Prior to choice, there was some indeterminacy in her neural processes stirred up by the conflict in her will. The indeterminism made it uncertain (and undetermined) whether she would go back to help or press onward.

Suppose further that two recurrent and connected neural networks are involved in the neuroscientists' story. Such networks circulate impulses and information in feedback loops and generally play a role in complex cognitive processing in the brain of the kind that one would expect to be involved in human deliberation. Moreover, recurrent networks are non-linear, thus allowing (as some recent research suggests) for the possibility of chaotic activity, which would contribute to the plasticity and flexibility human brains display in creative problem solving (of which practical deliberation is an example).[16] The input of one of these recurrent networks consists of the woman's moral motives and its output the choice to go back; the input of the other, her career ambitions and its output, the choice to go on to her meeting. The two networks are connected, so that the indeterminism which made it uncertain that she would do the moral thing was coming from her desire to do the opposite, and vice versa—the indeterminism thus arising, as we said, from a conflict in the will. When her effort to overcome self-interested desires succeeded, this corresponded to one of the neural pathways reaching an activation threshold, overcoming the indeterminism generated by the other.

To this picture, one might now pose the following objection: if it really was undetermined which choice the woman would make (in neural terms, which network would activate) right up to the moment when she chose, it seems that it would be a matter of luck or chance that one choice was made rather than the other, and so she could not be held responsible for the outcome. (Note that this is an expression of the Luck Principle, L.) The first step in response is to recall a point made earlier: we must be wary of moving too hastily from "indeterminism is involved in something's happening" to "its happening merely as a matter of chance or luck." "Luck" and "chance" have meanings in ordinary language that mere indeterminism may not have. The second step is to note that indeterminism of itself does not necessarily undermine control and responsibility.[17] Suppose you are trying to think through a difficult problem, say a mathematical problem, and there is some indeterminacy in your neural processes complicating the task—a kind of chaotic background. It would be like trying to concentrate and solve a problem with background noise or distraction. Whether you are going to succeed in solving the mathematical problem is uncertain and undetermined because of the distracting neural noise. Yet, if you concentrate and solve the problem nonetheless, I think we can say that you did it and are responsible for doing it even though it was undetermined whether you would succeed. The indeterministic noise would have been an obstacle to your solving the problem which you nevertheless overcame by your effort.

There are numerous other examples in the philosophical literature of this kind, where indeterminism functions as an obstacle to success without precluding responsibility. Consider an assassin who is trying to kill the prime minister, but might miss because of some undetermined events in his nervous system that might lead to a jerking or wavering of this arm. If he does hit his target, can he be held responsible? The answer (as J. L. Austin and Philippa Foot successfully argued decades ago) is yes, because he intentionally and voluntarily succeeded in doing what he was *trying* to do—kill the prime minister.[18] Yet, his killing the prime minister was undetermined. We might even say in a sense that he got lucky in killing the prime minister, when he could have failed. But it does not follow, if he succeeds, that killing the prime minister was not his action, not something he did; nor does it follow, as L would require, that he was not responsible for killing the prime minister. Indeed, if anything is clear, it is that he both killed the prime minister and was responsible for doing so.

Or consider a husband who, while arguing with his wife, swings his arm down in anger on her favorite glass table top, intending to break it. Again we suppose that some indeterminism in the husband's efferent neural pathways makes the momentum of his arm indeterminate, so it is undetermined if the table will break right up to the moment when it is struck. Whether the husband breaks the table or not is undetermined. Yet, it does not follow, if he succeeds, that breaking the table was not something he did; nor again does it follow, as L would require, that he was not responsible for breaking it.[19] The inference sanctioned by L from "it was undetermined" to "he was not responsible," is not valid. The above cases are counterexamples to it; and there are many more.

IV. Possible Worlds and L*

But one may grant this and still object that counterexamples to L of these kinds do not amount to genuine exercises of free will involving SFAs, such as the businesswoman's, where there is conflict in the wills of the agents and they are supposed to choose freely and responsibly *whichever* way they choose. If the assassin and husband succeed in doing what they are trying to do (kill the prime minister, break the table) they will do it *voluntarily* (in accordance with their wills) and *intentionally* (knowingly and purposely). But if they *fail* because of the indeterminism, they will not fail voluntarily and intentionally, but "by mistake" or "accident," or merely "by chance." Thus their "power" to do *otherwise* (if we should even call it a power) is not the usual power we associate with freedom of choice or action in self-formation, where the agents should be able to choose or act either way voluntarily or intentionally. The power to do otherwise of the assassin and the husband is more like Jane's "power" in (v) and (vi) of section 2, to choose to vacation in Colorado by a fluke or accident, after a long deliberation in which she had come to favor Hawaii.

As a consequence, while L may fail for cases like those of the assassin, husband, and mathematical problem-solver, another Luck Principle similar to L might still be applicable to genuine exercises of free will involving SFAs, like the businesswoman's: if it is undetermined at t whether an agent *voluntarily* and *intentionally* does A at t or *voluntarily* and *intentionally* does otherwise, then the agent's doing one of these rather than the other at t would be a matter of *luck* or *chance*, and so could not be a free and responsible action. This principle—let us call it L*—is fueled by the same intuitions that fuel L. Indeed it is a special case of L, but one that is more difficult to deal with because it is not subject to counterexamples like those of the husband and the assassin; and it seems to be applicable to SFAs, like the businesswoman's, where failure is not merely a matter of mistake or accident.

To explore further the difficulties posed by L*, let us look at the final and, I think, most powerful of the intuition pumps in support of L-type principles mentioned in section 2, namely, consideration (viii). This was the argument of Strawson, Mele, Berofsky, Waller, Double, Bernstein and Haji about two agents, or one agent in different possible worlds, with the same pasts.

Consider the version of this argument by Mele, which is a particularly revealing and challenging version. In the actual world, an agent John succumbs to the temptation to arrive late to a meeting, whereas his counterpart, John*, in a nearby possible world, whose physical and psychological history is the same as John's up to the moment of choice (as indeterminism requires), resists this temptation. Similarly, we can imagine a counterpart to the businesswoman, businesswoman*, in a nearby possible world who goes to her meeting rather than stopping to aid the assault victim, given the same past. But then, Mele argues, "if there is nothing about [these] agents' powers, capacities, states of mind, moral character and the like that explains this difference in outcome," since they are the same up to the moment of choice in the two possible worlds, "then the difference is just a matter of luck."[20] It would seem that John* got lucky in his attempt to overcome temptation, whereas John did not; and similarly, the businesswoman got lucky in her attempt to overcome temptation, while businesswoman* did not.

Let us first consider a general form of this argument that would support LP.

(1)   In the actual world, person P (e.g., John, the businesswoman) does A at t.

On the assumption that the act is undetermined at t, we may imagine that

(2)   In a nearby possible world which is the same as the actual world up to t, P* (P's counterpart with the same past) does otherwise (does B) at t.

(3)   But then (since their pasts are the same), there is nothing about the agents' powers, capacities, states of mind, characters, dispositions, motives, etc. prior to t that explains the difference in choices in the two possible worlds.

(4)   It is therefore a matter of luck or chance that P does A and P* does B at t.

(5)   P is therefore not responsible (praiseworthy or blameworthy, as the case may be) for A at t (and presumably P* is also not responsible for B).

Call this the "Luck Argument." The key assumption is the assumption of indeterminism, which leads to step (2). The remaining steps are meant to follow from (2), given (1).

Despite the fact that this argument looks like Mele's and has an initial plausibility, it is not his argument—and it is a good thing it is not. For the argument from (1)–(5) is invalid as it stands—for the same reasons that L was invalid. Consider the husband and husband* (his counterpart in a nearby world who fails to break the wife's table). If the outcome is undetermined, husband and husband* also have "the same powers, capacities, states of mind, characters, dispositions, motives etc." up to the moment of breaking or not breaking the table, as the argument requires; and it is a matter of luck or chance that the table breaks in one world and not the other. But for all that, it does not follow, as (5) requires, that the husband is not responsible for breaking the table. The husband would have quite a task persuading his wife that he was not responsible for breaking the table on the grounds that it was a matter of luck or chance that it broke. ("Luck or chance did it, not me" is an implausible excuse.)

But, of course, as we noted, husband* is not also responsible for *failing* to break the table, since he does not fail to break it voluntarily or intentionally. He is responsible only for the attempt, when he fails. Similarly, assassin* would be responsible for the attempted murder of the prime minister, when he missed. What has to be explicitly added to the argument (1)–(5) to avoid counterexamples like these is the L*-requirement that *both* P and P* *voluntarily* and *intentionally* do A and B respectively in their respective worlds. Specifically, we must add to premise (1) that P voluntarily and intentionally does A at t and to (2), that P* voluntarily and intentionally does B at t, and then make the corresponding additions to (4) and (5). This will yield what we might call the L*-version of the Luck Argument rather than the L-version. And the stronger L*-version is clearly the one Mele intends, since John's choice in his example is supposed to be an SFA, like the businesswoman's choice in my example, where the agents can go either way voluntarily and intentionally. Moreover, this version of the argument—like L* itself—is immune to counterexamples like those of the husband and the assassin.

V. Parallel Processing

Nonetheless, despite immunity from these counterexamples, I think the L*-version of the Luck Argument, and L* itself, also fail. But it is far less easy to show why. To do so, we have to take a closer look at SFAs and push the argument beyond where it has come thus far. Let it be granted that the businesswoman's case and other self-forming actions or SFAs like John's are not like the examples of the husband and the assassin. The wills of the husband and assassin are already "set" on doing what they intend, whereas the wills of agents in SFAs, like the businesswoman and John, are not already settled or "formed" until they choose (hence the designation "self-forming actions").[21]

Thus, to get from examples like those of the husband and assassin to genuine SFAs, I think we must do two things. First, we must put the indeterminacy involved in the efferent neural pathways of the husband and assassin into the central neural processes of the businesswoman and other agents, like John, who are making efforts of will to overcome moral, prudential and other temptations. This move has already been made in earlier sections. But to respond to L*-versions of the Luck Argument, like Mele's, I believe this move must also be combined with another—a kind of "doubling" of the example given earlier of solving the mathematical problem in the presence of background indeterministic noise.[22]

Imagine that the businesswoman is *trying* or making an effort to solve *two* cognitive problems at once, or to complete two competing (deliberative) tasks at once—to make a moral choice and to make a choice for her ambitions (corresponding to the two competing neural networks involved in the earlier description). With respect to each task, as with the mathematical problem, she is being thwarted in her attempt to do what she is trying to do by indeterminism. But in her case, the indeterminism does not have a mere external source; it is coming from her own will, from her desire to do the opposite. Recall that the two crossing neural networks involved are connected, so that the indeterminism which is making it uncertain that she will do the moral thing is coming from her desire to do the opposite, and vice versa. She may therefore fail to do what she is trying to do, just like the assassin, the husband and the person trying to solve the mathematical problem. But I argue that, if she nevertheless *succeeds*, then she can be held responsible because, like them, she will have succeeded in doing *what she was trying to do*. And the interesting thing is that this will be true of her, *whichever choice is made*, because she was trying to make both choices and one is going to succeed.

Does it make sense to talk about agents trying to do two competing things at once in this way? Well, we know the brain is a parallel processor and that capacity, I believe, is essential for the exercise of free will. In cases of self-formation, agents are simultaneously trying to resolve plural and competing cognitive tasks. They are, as we say, of two minds. But they are not therefore two separate persons. They are not disassociated from either task.[23] The businesswoman who wants to go back and help the assault victim is the same ambitious woman who wants to go on to her meeting and close the sale. She is a complex creature, like most of us who are often torn inside; but hers is the kind of complexity needed for free will. And when she succeeds in doing one of the things she is trying to do, she will endorse that as *her* resolution of the conflict in her will, voluntarily and intentionally, as L* requires. She will not disassociate from either outcome, as did Jane (in (v) of section 2), who wondered what "happened to" her when she chose Colorado, or like the husband and assassin who did not also want to fail.[24]

But one may still object that the businesswoman makes one choice rather than the other *by chance*, since it was undetermined right up to the last moment which choice she would make. If this is so, we may have the picture of her first making an effort to overcome temptation (to go on to her meeting) and do the moral thing, and then at the last minute "chance takes over" and decides the issue for her. But this is the wrong picture. On the view just described, you cannot separate the indeterminism from the effort to overcome temptation in such a way that *first* the effort occurs *followed by* chance or luck (or vice versa). One must think of the effort and the indeterminism as fused; the effort *is* indeterminate and the indeterminism is a property of the effort, not something separate that occurs after or before the effort. The fact that the woman's effort of will has this property of being indeterminate does not make it any less her *effort*. The complex recurrent neural network that realizes the effort in the brain is circulating impulses in feedback loops and there is some indeterminacy in these circulating impulses. But the whole process is her effort of will and it persists right up to the moment when the choice is made. There is no point at which the effort stops and chance "takes over." She chooses *as a result of* the effort, even though she might have failed because of the indeterminism.

And just as expressions like "she chose *by* chance" can mislead us in these contexts, so can expressions like "she got lucky." Ask yourself this question: why does the inference "he got lucky, *so he was not responsible?*" *fail* when it does fail, as in the cases of the husband and the assassin? The first part of an answer goes back to the claim that "luck," like "chance," has question-begging implications in ordinary language that are not necessarily implications of "indeterminism" (which implies only the absence of deterministic causation). The core meaning of "he got lucky," which *is* implied by indeterminism, I suggest, is that "he succeeded *despite the probability or chance of failure*"; and this core meaning does not imply lack of responsibility, if he succeeds.

If "he got lucky" had further meanings in these contexts often associated with "luck" and "chance" in ordinary usage (e.g., the outcome was not his doing, or occurred by *mere* chance, or he was not responsible for it), the inference would not fail for the husband and assassin, as it clearly does. But the point is that these further meanings of "luck" and "chance" do not follow *from the mere presence of indeterminism*. Second, the inference "he got lucky, so he was not responsible" fails because *what* the assassin and husband succeeded in doing was what they were trying and wanting to do all along. Third, *when* they succeeded, their reaction was not "oh dear, that was a mistake, an accident—something that *happened* to me, not something I *did.*" Rather they *endorsed* the outcomes as something they were trying and wanting to do all along, that is to say, knowingly and purposefully, not by mistake or accident.

But these conditions are satisfied in the businesswoman's case as well, *either way* she chooses. If she succeeds in choosing to return to help the victim (or in choosing to go on to her meeting) (i) she will have "succeeded despite the probability or chance of failure," (ii) she will have succeeded in doing what she was trying and wanting to do all along (she wanted both outcomes very much, but for different reasons, and was trying to make those reasons prevail in both cases), and (iii) when she succeeded (in choosing to return to help) her reaction was not "oh dear, that was a mistake, an accident—something that happened to me, not something I did." Rather she endorsed the outcome as something she was trying and wanting to do all along; she recognized it as her resolution of the conflict in her will. And if she had chosen to go on to her meeting she would have endorsed that outcome, recognizing it as her resolution of the conflict in her will.

VI. The Luck Argument Revisited

With this in mind, let us return to the L*-version of the argument from (1)–(5). I said that Mele clearly intends this stronger L*-version of the argument, since the force of his argument depends on the fact that John's choice in his example is an SFA, like the businesswoman's, rather than being like the actions of the husband and assassin. But if this is so, then John's situation will also be like the businesswoman's on the account just given of SFAs. Since both of them are simultaneously trying to do *both* of the things they may do (choose to help or go on, overcome the temptation to arrive late or not), they will do either with intent or on purpose, as a result of wanting and trying to do it—i.e., intentionally and voluntarily. Thus, their "failing" to do one of the options will not be a mistake or accident, but a voluntary and intentional doing *of the other.*

Likewise, businesswoman* and John* are simultaneously trying to do both things in their respective worlds; and they will not "fail" to act on moral or weak-willed motives by mistake or accident, as the case may be, but by voluntarily and intentionally choosing to act on the opposing motives. The point is that in self-formation of these kinds (SFAs), failing is never *just* failing; it is always also a *succeeding* in doing something else we wanted and were trying to do. And we found that one can be responsible for succeeding in doing what one was trying to do, even in the presence of indeterminism. So even if we add the L* requirement of more-than-one-way voluntariness and intentionality to the argument of (1)–(5), the argument remains invalid for cases like the businesswoman's and other SFAs, like John's.

But one might argue further, as Mele does, that John and John* (and businesswoman and businesswoman*) not only had the same capacities, motives, characters, etc., prior to choice but they made exactly the same *efforts* as well. And this does seem to suggest that the success of one and failure of the other was a matter of mere luck or chance, so that John and the businesswoman were not responsible. But again the inference is too hasty. Note, first, that husband and husband* also made the same efforts (as well as having the same capacities, motives and characters) up to the very moment of breaking of the table. Yet it does not follow that the husband is not responsible when he succeeds. And *both* the businesswoman and businesswoman*, and John and John*, are in the position of the husband in their respective worlds, since both will have succeeded in doing what they were trying to do.

But one may still want to object: if the businesswoman and businesswoman*, and John and John*, make exactly the same efforts, how can it *not* be a matter of chance that one succeeds and the other does not, in a way that makes them not responsible? To which I reply: but if they both succeeded in doing what they were trying to do (because they were simultaneously trying to do both things), and then having succeeded, they both *endorsed* the outcomes of their respective efforts (i.e. their choices) as what they were trying to do, rather than disowning or disassociating from those choices, how then can we *not* hold them responsible? It just does not follow that, because they made exactly the same efforts, they chose *by* chance.

To say something was done "by chance" usually means (as in the assassin and husband cases when they fail), it was done "by mistake" or "accidentally," "inadvertently," "involuntarily," or "as an unintended fluke." But none of these things holds of the businesswoman and John either way they choose. Unlike husband*, businesswoman* and John do not fail to overcome temptation by mistake or accident, inadvertently or involuntarily. They consciously and willingly fail to overcome temptation *by* consciously and willingly choosing to act in selfish or weak-willed ways. So, just as it would have been a poor excuse for the husband to say to his wife when the table broke that "luck or chance did it, not me," it would be a poor excuse for businesswoman* and John to say "luck or chance did it, not me" when they failed to help the assault victim or failed to arrive on time.

Worth highlighting in this argument is the point that we cannot simply say the businesswoman and businesswoman* (or John and John*) made exactly the same *effort* (in the singular) in their respective possible worlds and one succeeded while the other failed. We must say they made exactly the same *efforts* (plural) in their respective worlds. Mentioning only one effort prejudices the case, for it suggests that the failure of that effort in one of the worlds was a *mere* mistake or accident, when the fact is that both of the agents (P and P*) made *both* efforts in *both* worlds. In one world, one of the efforts issued in a choice and in the other world, a different effort issued in a different choice; but neither was merely accidental or inadvertent in either world. I would go even further and say that we may also doubt that the efforts they were both making really were exactly the same. Where events are indeterminate, as are the efforts they were making, there is no such thing as exact sameness or difference of events in different possible worlds. Their efforts were not exactly the same, nor were they exactly different, because they were not exact. They were simply unique.[25]

One might try another line: perhaps we are begging the question in assuming that the outcomes of the efforts of the businesswoman and her counterpart were *choices* at all. If they were not choices to begin with, they could not have been voluntary choices. One might argue this on the grounds that (A) "if an event is undetermined, it must be something that merely happens and cannot be somebody's choice"; and (B) "if an event is undetermined, it must be something that merely happens, it cannot be something an agent does (it cannot be an action)." But to see how question-begging these assumptions are, one has only to note that (A) and (B) imply respectively (A') "if an event is a choice, it must be determined" ("All choices are determined") and (B') "if an event is an action, it must be determined" ("All actions are determined"). Are these supposed to be a priori or analytic truths? If so, then long-standing issues about freedom and determinism would be settled by fiat. If an event were not determined, it could not be a choice or action necessarily or by definition.[26]

This explains the businesswoman's suspicions when she exited the neuroscientists' offices. They told her that when she "chose" to go back to help the assault victim the day before, there was some indeterminism in her neural processes prior to choice. She accepted this as a correct empirical finding. But she was suspicious when the neuroscientists tried to get her to make the further inference from those findings that she did not really *choose* to help the assault victim yesterday. She refused to accept that conclusion, and rightly so. For in drawing it, they were going beyond their empirical findings and trying to foist on her the a priori assumption that if an event was undetermined, it could not have been her choice or could not have been something she did. She rightly saw that there was nothing in the empirical evidence that required her to say that. To choose is to consciously and deliberately form an intention to do something; and she did that, despite the indeterminism in her neural processes (as did businesswoman* when she chose to go on to her meeting).

VII. Final Considerations: Control and Explanation

But it is one thing to say that she chose and another to say she chose *freely* and *responsibly*. This would require that she not only chose, but had voluntary *control* over her choice either way. We have not talked at length to this point about the matter of control (considerations (i) and (iii) of section 2) and must now do so. For this may be the reason why we may think the choices made by the businesswoman and businesswoman* (or John and John*) could not be responsible, if they were undetermined. We might deny that they had voluntary control over what they chose, where voluntary control means being able to bring about something in accordance with one's will or purposes (or, as we often say, the ability to bring something about "at will").

One thing does seem to be true about control that critics of indeterminist freedom have always maintained: indeterminism, wherever it appears, does seem to *diminish* rather than enhance agents' voluntary control (consideration (iii) of section 2). The assassin's voluntary control over whether or not the prime minister is killed (his ability to realize his purpose or what he is trying to do) is diminished by the undetermined impulses in his arm—and so also for the husband and his breaking the table. Moreover, this limitation is connected to another, which I think we must also grant—that indeterminism, wherever it occurs, functions as a *hindrance* or *obstacle* to our purposes that must be overcome by effort (consideration (iii)).

But recall that in the businesswoman's case (and for SFAs generally, like John's), the indeterminism that is admittedly diminishing her ability to overcome selfish temptation, and *is* indeed a hindrance to her doing so, is coming from her own will—from her desire and effort to do the opposite—since she is simultaneously trying to realize two conflicting purposes at once. Similarly, her ability to overcome moral qualms is diminished by the fact that she also simultaneously wants and is trying to act on moral reasons. If we could look at each of the two competing neural networks involved separately, abstracting from the other, the situation would look analogous to the situations of the husband and the assassin. The agent would be trying to do something while being hindered by indeterminism coming from an external source. But, in fact we cannot look at the two networks separately in this way because in reality they are connected and interacting. The indeterminism which is a hindrance to her fulfilling one is coming from its interactions with the other. The indeterminism therefore does not have an external source. It is internal to her will, and hence to her self, since she identifies with both networks and will identify with the choice reached by either of them as her choice.

The upshot is that, despite the businesswoman's diminished control over *each* option considered separately, due to a conflict in her will, she nonetheless has what I call "plural voluntary control" over the two options considered *as a set*.[27] Having plural voluntary control over a set of options means being able to bring about *whichever* of the options you will or most want, *when* you will to do so, for the reasons you will to do so, without being coerced or compelled in doing so. And the businesswoman (or John) has this power, because whichever of the options she chooses (to help the victim or go on to her meeting) will be *endorsed* by her as what she wills or most wants to do at the moment when she chooses it (though not necessarily beforehand); she will choose it for the reasons she most wants to act on then and there (moral or selfish reasons, as the case may be); she need not have been coerced by anyone else into choosing one rather than the other; and she will not be choosing either compulsively, since neither choice is such that she could not have chosen it then and there, even if she most wanted to.[28]

One must add, of course, that such plural voluntary control is not the same as what may be called "antecedent determining control"—the ability to determine or guarantee which of a set of options will occur *before* it occurs.[29] With respect to undetermined self-forming choices (SFAs), agents cannot determine or guarantee which choice outcome will occur *beforehand*. For that could only be done by predetermining the outcome. But it does not follow that, because one cannot determine which of a set of outcomes will occur before it occurs, one does not determine which of them occurs *when* it occurs. When the conditions of plural voluntary control are satisfied, agents exercise control over their present and future lives then and there by deciding.

But can we not at least say that, if indeterminism is involved, then *which* option is chosen is "arbitrary"? I grant that there is a sense in which this is true. An ultimate arbitrariness remains in all undetermined SFAs because there cannot in principle be sufficient or overriding *prior* reasons for making one set of competing reasons prevail over the other. But I argue that such arbitrariness relative to prior reasons tells us something important about free will. It tells us, as I have elsewhere expressed it, that every undetermined self-forming choice (SFA) "is the initiation of a 'value experiment' whose justification lies in the *future* and is not fully explained by the *past*. [Making such a choice], we say in effect, 'Let's try this. It is not required by my past, but is consistent with my past and is one branching pathway my life could now meaningfully take. I am willing to take responsibility for it one way or the other.'"[30] To initiate and take responsibility for such value experiments whose justification lies in the future, is to "take chances" without prior guarantees of success. Genuine self-formation requires this sort of risk-taking and indeterminism is a part of it. If there are persons who need to be certain in advance just exactly what is the best or right thing to do in every circumstance (perhaps to be told so by some human or divine authority), then free will is not for them.

This point also throws light on why the Luck Argument fails, even in the stronger L*-version, despite its initial plausibility. Consider the move from step (3)—the agents P and P* have the same powers, characters, motives, etc. prior to t in the two possible worlds—to step (4), which says it was a matter of luck or chance that P did A and P* did B at t. An important reason given for this move was that if both agents have all the same prior powers, characters, motives, etc. there can be no "explanation of the difference in choice" between the two agents in terms of their prior reasons or motives; and this is taken to imply that the difference in choices in the two worlds is a matter of luck or chance *in a way* that precludes responsibility.

But this move, like others discussed earlier, is too hasty. The absence of an explanation of the difference in choice in terms of prior reasons does not have the tight connection to issues of responsibility one might initially credit it with. For one thing, the absence of such an explanation does not imply (as I have been arguing throughout this paper) that businesswoman and businesswoman* (John and John*) (1) did not *choose* at all, nor does it imply that they did not both choose (2) *as a result of their efforts,* nor that they did not choose (3) *for reasons* (different reasons, of course) which (4) they most wanted to choose for *when* they chose, nor that they did not choose for those reasons (5) *knowingly* and (6) *on purpose* when they chose, and hence (7) *rationally*, (8) *voluntarily* and (9) *intentionally*. None of these conditions is precluded by the absence of an explanation of the difference of choice in terms of prior reasons. Yet these are precisely the kinds of conditions we look for when deciding whether or not persons are responsible.

I suggest that the reason why these conditions are not excluded is that the explanation of the difference of choice in the two possible worlds that is missing is an explanation in terms of *sufficient* or *conclusive* reasons—one that would render an alternative choice, given the same prior reasons, irrational or inexplicable. And, of course, *that* sort of explanation is not possible for undetermined SFAs, when there is conflict in the will and the agent has good (but not decisive or conclusive) prior reasons for going either way. But neither is that sort of explanation required to say that an agent acts as the result of her effort for reasons she most wants to act on then and there. In sum, *you can choose responsibly for prior reasons that were not conclusive or decisive prior to your choosing for them.*

I said a moment ago that such arbitrariness relative to prior reasons tells us something important about free will—that every self-forming choice is the initiation of a value experiment whose justification lies in the future and cannot be fully explained by the past. It is worth adding in this regard that the term "arbitrary" comes from the Latin *arbitrium*, which means "judgment"—as in *liberum arbitrium voluntatis* ("free judgment of the will")—the medieval designation for free will. Imagine a writer in the middle of a novel. The novel's heroine faces a crisis and the writer has not yet developed her character in sufficient detail to say exactly how she will react. The author must make a "judgment" (*arbitrium*) about how she will react that is not determined by the heroine's already formed past, which does not give unique direction. In this sense, the author's judgment of how she will act is "arbitrary," but not entirely so. It has input from the heroine's fictional past and in turn gives input to her projected future.

In a similar manner, agents who exercise free will are both authors of, and characters in, their own stories at once. By virtue of "self-forming" judgments of the will (*arbitria voluntatis*), they are "arbiters" of their own lives, taking responsibility for "making themselves" out of past that, if they are truly free, does not limit their future pathways to one. If someone should charge them with not having a sufficient or conclusive prior reason for choosing as they did, they may reply as follows: "Perhaps so. But that does not mean I did not *choose*; and it does not mean I did not choose for *good* reasons, which I stand by and take responsibility for. If I lacked sufficient or conclusive prior reasons, that is because, like the heroine of the novel, I was not a fully formed person before I chose—and still am not, for that matter.[31] Like the author of the novel, I am in the process of writing a story and forming a person (who, in my case, is myself). It is a heavy burden, but an eminently human one."

Notes

This paper was prompted by a recent objection made in various forms against my view and other incompatibilist views of freedom and responsibility by Galen Strawson, Alfred Mele, Bernard Berofsky, Bruce Waller, Richard Double, Mark Bernstein and Ishtiyaque Haji. (See footnote 10 for references.) The paper has benefitted from interchanges with the above persons and with participants at a conference on my work on free will at the University of Arkansas in September, 1997: Gary Watson, Barry Loewer, Timothy O'Connor, Randolph Clarke, Christopher Hill and Thomas Senor. It has also benefitted from interchanges in conferences or in correspondence with John Martin Fischer, William Rowe, Nicholas Nathan, David Hodgson, Saul Smilansky, Kevin Magill, Peter van Inwagen, Derk Pereboom, Laura Ekstrom, Hugh McCann and Ilya Prigogine. I'm especially grateful to Alfred Mele and Galen Strawson for pursuing me assiduously on these issues since the publication of my latest work, and for perceptive comments on the penultimate draft by Mele, Bernard Berofsky and George Graham.

1. *Culture and Value* (Oxford: Blackwell, 1980), p. 75.

2. *Elbow Room* (Cambridge: MIT, 1984), chapter 1 and pp. 32–34, 64–65, 119–20, 169–70.

3. See my *The Significance of Free Will* (Oxford and New York: Oxford, 1996), pp. 10–14, 33–37.

4. For example, physicist A. H. Compton, *The Freedom of Man* (New Haven: Yale, 1935) and neurophysiologist John Eccles *Facing Reality* (New York: Springer-Verlag, 1970).

5. See, for example, Galen Strawson, who argues that even if free will should be incompatible with determinism, indeterminism would be "no help" in enhancing either freedom or responsibility ("The Unhelpfulness of Indeterminism," forthcoming in *Philosophy and Phenomenological Research*).

6. *Essay on the Freedom of the Will* (Indianapolis: Bobbs-Merrill, 1960), p. 47.

7. This dilemma for incompatibilist accounts of freedom is nicely described by Thomas Nagel, *The View From Nowhere* (Oxford: Oxford, 1986), ch. 7.

8. Leibniz, *Selections* (New York: Scribner's, 1951), p. 435.

9. Stephen M. Cahn makes a persuasive case for their being such a role in "Random Choices," *Philosophy and Phenomenological Research*, 37 (1977): 549–51.

10. Strawson, "The Impossibility of Moral Responsibility," *Philosophical Studies*, 75 (1994): 5–24 and "The Unhelpfulness of Indeterminism," *op. cit.*; Mele, Review of R. Kane, *The Significance of Free Will, Journal of Philosophy* 95:1 (1998): 581–84, and "Luck and the Significance of Free Will," forthcoming in *Philosophical Explorations*; Berofsky, "Ultimate Responsibility in a Deterministic World," forthcoming in *Philosophy and Phenomenological Research*; Waller, "Free Will Gone Out of Control," *Behaviorism* 16 (1988): 149–67; Double, *The Non-re-*

ality of Free Will (Oxford: Oxford, 1991), p. 140; Bernstein, "Kanean Libertarianism," *Southwest Philosophy Review* 11 (1995): 151–57; Haji, "Indeterminism and Frankfurt-type Examples," forthcoming in *Philosophical Explorations*. Different, but related, concerns about indeterminism and agency are aired by Timothy O'Connor, "Indeterminism and Free Agency: Three Recent Views," *Philosophy and Phenomenological Research* 53 (1993): 499–526; and Randoph Clarke, "Free Choice, Effort and Wanting More," forthcoming in *Philosophical Explorations*.

11. Waller, *ibid*, p. 151.

12. Mele, *Journal of Philosophy, op. cit.*, p. 582–83.

13. I defend this point at length in *Free Will and Values* (Albany: SUNY, 1985), chs. 4 and 5. It is also defended by Peter van Inwagen, "When is the Will Free?" in J. Tomberlin, ed., *Philosophical Perspectives* 3 (Atascadero: Ridgeview, 1989): 399–422. John Martin Fischer has described the view that van Inwagen and I defend as "restricted libertarianism" and has criticized it in "When the Will is Free," in Tomberlin, ed., *Philosophical Perspectives* 6 (Atascadero: Ridgeview, 1992): 423–51. Another critic is Hugh McCann, "On When the Will is Free" in G. Holmstrom-Hintikka and R. Tuomela, eds., *Contemporary Action Theory* Vol. I (Netherlands: Kluwer, 1997), pp. 219–32. van Inwagen responds to Fischer in "When is the Will Not Free?" *Philosophical Studies* 75 (1994): 95–114; and I respond in *op. cit.*, 1996, pp. 32–43.

14. See my *op. cit*, 1996, pp. 74–78. SFAs are also in that work sometimes called "self-forming willings" or SFWs (pp. 125ff).

15. This, in broad outline, is the account developed in my *op. cit.*, 1996, chs. 8–10. In later sections of this paper I make important additions to it in response to criticisms.

16. See P. Huberman and G. Hogg, "Phase Transitions in Artificial Intelligence Systems," *Artificial Intelligence* 33 (1987): 155–72; C. Skarda and W. Freeman, "How Brains Make Chaos in Order to Make Sense of the World," *Behavior and Brain Sciences* 10 (1987): 161–95; A. Babloyantz and A. Destexhe, "Strange Attractors in the Human Cortex," in L. Rensing, ed., *Temporal Disorder in Human Oscillatory Systems* (New York: Springer-Verlag, 1985), pp. 132–43.

17. Important recent defenses of the claim that indeterminism does not necessarily undermine control and responsibility include Randolph Clarke, "Indeterminism and Control," *American Philosophical Quarterly* 32 (1995): 125–38; Carl Ginet, *On Action* (Cambridge: Cambridge, 1990), ch. 6; O'Connor, *op. cit.*; and Laura Ekstrom, *Free Will* (Boulder: Westview, 2000).

18. Austin, "Ifs and Cans," *Philosophical Papers* (Oxford: Oxford, 1961), pp. 153–80; Foot, "Free Will as Involving Determinism." In B. Berofsky, ed., *Free Will and Determinism* (New York: Harper and Row, 1966), pp. 95–108.

19. We must of course assume in both these examples that other (compatibilist) conditions for responsibility are in place—e.g., that, despite his anger, the husband was not acting compulsively and would have controlled himself, if he had wished; that he knew what he was doing and was doing it intentionally to anger his wife, etc. (and similarly for the assassin). But the point is that nothing in the facts of either case preclude these assumptions from also being satisfied.

20. Mele, *Journal of Philosophy, op. cit.*, p. 583. I have elsewhere denied that the pasts of the agents can be exactly the same, since, with indeterminist efforts, there cannot be exact sameness or difference (*op. cit.*, 1996, pp. 171–74). But Mele's argument is a response to that denial and is designed to work whether the denial of exact sameness is assumed or not.

21. See my *op. cit.*, 1996, pp. 112–14.

22. This further "doubling" move is consistent with the theory put forward in my *op. cit.*, 1996, and presupposes much of that theory, but is not made in that work. It is a further development especially provoked by Mele's argument discussed here as well as by criticisms of other persons since the book's publication, such as Galen Strawson, Bernard Berofsky, Nicholas Nathan, Gary Watson, Randolph Clarke, Timothy O'Connor, Richard Double and Ishitaque Haji.

23. In *op. cit.*, 1996, pp. 137–42, I account for this in terms of the notion of a "self-network," a more comprehensive network of neural connections representing the general motivational system in terms of which agents define themselves as agents and practical reasoners. For further discussion of such a notion, see Owen Flanagan, *Consciousness Reconsidered* (Cambridge: MIT, 1992), pp. 207 ff.

24. In response to the claim in my *op. cit.*, 1996 (p. 215) that "free willers [who engage in SFAs] are always trying to be better than they are by their own lights," by trying to overcome temptations of various sorts, Galen Strawson asks: but "can't they also try to be worse than they are?" ("The Unhelpfulness of Indeterminism" *op. cit.* forthcoming). He is right of course; they can. I should have added what I am saying here, that free willers can and do *also* try to be as bad or worse than they are by resisting efforts to be better. Strange creatures indeed.

25. See my *op. cit*, 1996, pp. 171–74.

26. *Ibid.*, pp. 183–86, for a fuller account of why indeterminism does not rule out action or choice.

27. *Ibid.*, pp. 134–43.

28. *Ibid.*, pp. 133–38, where a more detailed case is made for each of these claims.

29. *Ibid.*, p. 144.

30. *Ibid.*, pp. 145–46.

31. Jan Branson (in "Alternatives of Oneself," forthcoming in *Philosophy and Phenomenological Research)* has made an important distinction that is relevant here—between choosing "alternatives *for* oneself" and choosing "alternatives *of* oneself." Branson notes that some choices in life are for different courses of action that will make a difference in what sort of person the chooser will become in future. In such cases, agents are not merely choosing alternatives for themselves but are choosing alternatives of themselves. Most SFAs, as I understand them, would be of this kind.

Part III

Free Will and Moral Responsibility

11

Freedom and Resentment

PETER STRAWSON

I

Some philosophers say they do not know what the thesis of determinism is. Others say, or imply, that they do know what it is. Of these, some—the pessimists perhaps—hold that if the thesis is true, then the concepts of moral obligation and responsibility really have no application, and the practices of punishing and blaming, of expressing moral condemnation and approval, are really unjustified. Others—the optimists perhaps—hold that these concepts and practices in no way lose their *raison d'etre* if the thesis of determinism is true. Some hold even that the justification of these concepts and practices requires the truth of the thesis. There is another opinion which is less frequently voiced: the opinion, it might be said, of the genuine moral sceptic. This is that the notions of moral guilt, of blame, of moral responsibility are inherently confused and that we can see this to be so if we consider the consequences either of the truth of determinism or of its falsity. The holders of this opinion agree with the pessimists that these notions lack application if determinism is true, and add simply that they also lack it if determinism is false. If I am asked which of these parties I belong to, I must say it is the first of all, the party of those who do not know what the thesis of determinism is. But this does not stop me from having some sympathy with the others, and a wish to reconcile them. Should not ignorance, rationally, inhibit such sympathies? Well, of course, though darkling, one has some inkling—some notion of what sort of thing is being talked about. This lecture is intended as a move towards reconciliation; so is likely to seem wrongheaded to everyone.

But can there be any possibility of reconciliation between such clearly opposed positions as those of pessimists and optimists about determinism? Well, there might be a formal withdrawal on one side in return for a substantial concession on the other. Thus, suppose the optimist's position were put like this: (1) the facts as we know them do not show determinism to be false; (2) the facts as we know them supply an adequate basis for the concepts and practices which the pessimist feels to be imperilled by the possibility of determinism's truth. Now it might be that the optimist is right in this, but is apt to give an inadequate account of the facts as we know them, and of how they constitute an adequate basis for the problematic concepts and practices; that the reasons he gives for the adequacy of the basis are themselves inadequate and leave out something vital. It might be that the pessimist is rightly anxious to get this vital thing back and, in the grip of his anxiety, feels he has to go beyond the facts as we know them; feels that the vital thing can be secure only if, beyond the facts as we know them, there is the further fact that determinism is false. Might *he* not be brought to make a formal withdrawal in return for a vital concession?

II

Let me enlarge very briefly on this, by way of preliminary only. Some optimists about determinism point to the efficacy of the practices of punishment, and of moral condemnation and approval, in regulating behaviour in socially desirable ways.[1] In the fact of their efficacy, they suggest, is an adequate basis for these practices, and this fact certainly does not show determinism to be false. To this the pessimists reply, all in a rush, that *just* punishment and *moral* condemnation imply moral guilt and guilt implies moral responsibility and moral responsibility implies freedom and freedom implies the falsity of determinism. And to this the optimists are wont to reply in turn that it is true that these practices require freedom in a sense, and the existence of freedom in this sense is one of the facts as we know them. But what 'freedom' means here is nothing but the absence of certain conditions the presence of which would make moral condemnation or punishment inappropriate. They have in mind conditions like compulsion by another, or innate incapacity, or insanity, or other less extreme forms of psychological disorder, or the existence of circumstances in which the making of any other choice would be morally inadmissible or would be too much to expect of any man. To this list they are constrained to add other factors which, without exactly being limitations of freedom, may also make moral condemnation or punishment inappropriate or mitigate their force: as some forms of ignorance, mistake, or accident. And the general reason why moral condemnation or punishment are inappropriate when these factors or conditions are present is held to be that the practices in question will be generally efficacious means of regulating behaviour in desirable ways only in cases where these factors are not present. Now the pessimist admits that the facts as we know them include the existence of freedom, the occurrence of cases of free action, in the negative sense which the optimist concedes, and admits, or rather insists, that the existence of freedom in this sense is compatible with the truth of determinism. Then what does the pessimist find missing? When he tries to answer this question, his language is apt to alternate between the very familiar and the very unfamiliar.[2] Thus he may say, familiarly enough, that the man who is the subject of justified punishment, blame or moral condemnation must really *deserve* it; and then add, perhaps, that, in the case at least where he is blamed for a positive act rather than an omission, the condition of his really deserving blame is something that goes beyond the negative freedoms that the optimist concedes. It is, say, a genuinely free identification of the will with the act. And this is the condition that is incompatible with the truth of determinism.

The conventional, but conciliatory, optimist need not give up yet. He may say: Well, people often decide to do things, really intend to do what they do, know just what they're doing in doing it, the reasons they think they have for doing what they do, often really are their reasons and not their rationalizations. These facts, too, are included in the facts as we know them. If this is what you mean by freedom—by the identification of the will with the act—then freedom may again be conceded. But again the concession is compatible with the truth of the determinist thesis. For it would not follow from that thesis that nobody decides to do anything, that nobody ever does anything intentionally; that it is false that people sometimes know perfectly well what they are doing. I tried to define freedom negatively. You want to give it a more positive look. But it comes to the same thing. Nobody denies freedom in this sense, or these senses, and nobody claims that the existence of freedom in these senses shows determinism to be false.

But it is here that the lacuna in the optimistic story can be made to show. For the pessimist may be supposed to ask: But *why* does freedom in this sense justify blame, etc.? You turn towards me first the negative, and then the positive, faces of a freedom which nobody challenges. But the only reason you have given for the practices of moral condemnation and punishment in cases where this freedom is present is the efficacy of these practices in regulating behaviour in socially desirable ways. But this is not a sufficient basis, it is not even the right *sort* of basis, for these practices as we understand them.

Now my optimist, being the sort of man he is, is not likely to invoke an intuition of fittingness at this point. So he really has no more to say. And my pessimist, being the sort of man he is, has only one more thing to say; and that is that the admissibility of these practices, as we understand them, demands another kind of freedom, the kind that in turn demands the falsity of the thesis of determinism. But might we not induce the pessimist to give up saying this by giving the optimist something more to say?

III

I have mentioned punishing and moral condemnation and approval; and it is in connection with these practices or attitudes that the issue between optimists and pessimists—or, if one is a pessimist, the issue between determinists and libertarians—is felt to be particularly important. But it is not of these practices and attitudes that I propose, at first, to speak. These practices or attitudes permit, where they do not imply, a certain detachment from the actions or agents which are their objects. I want to speak, at least at first, of something else: of the non-detached attitudes and reactions of people directly involved in transactions with each other; of the attitudes and reactions of offended parties and beneficiaries; of such things as gratitude, resentment, forgiveness, love, and hurt feelings. Perhaps something like the issue between optimists and pessimists arises in this neighbouring field too; and since this field is less crowded with disputants, the issue might here be easier to settle; and if it is settled here, then it might become easier to settle it in the disputant-crowded field.

What I have to say consists largely of commonplaces. So my language, like that of commonplace generally, will be quite unscientific and imprecise. The central commonplace that I want to insist on is the very great importance that we attach to the attitudes and intentions towards us *of* other human beings, and the great extent to which our personal feelings and reactions depend upon, or involve, our beliefs about these attitudes and intentions. I can give no simple description of the field of phenomena at the centre of which stands this commonplace truth; for the field is too complex. Much imaginative literature is devoted to exploring its complexities; and we have a large vocabulary for the purpose. There are simplifying styles of handling it in a general way. Thus we may, like La Rochefoucauld, put self-love or self-esteem or vanity at the centre of the picture and point out how it may be caressed by the esteem, or wounded by the indifference or contempt, of others. We might speak, in another jargon, of the need for love, and the loss of security which results from its withdrawal; or, in another, of human self-respect and its connection with the recognition of the individual's dignity. These simplifications are of use to me only if they help to emphasize how much we actually mind, how much it matters to us, whether the actions of other people—and particularly of *some* other people—reflect attitudes towards us of goodwill, affection, or esteem on the one hand or contempt, indifference, or malevolence on the other. If someone treads on my hand accidentally, while trying to help me, the pain may be no less acute than if he treads on it in contemptuous disregard of my existence or with a malevolent wish to injure me. But I shall generally feel in the second case a kind and degree of resentment that I shall not feel in the first. If someone's actions help me to some benefit I desire, than I am benefited in any case; but if he intended them so to benefit me because of his general goodwill towards me, I shall reasonably feel a gratitude which I should not feel at all if the benefit was an incidental consequence, unintended or even regretted by him, of some plan of action with a different aim.

These examples are of actions which confer benefits or inflict injuries over and above any conferred or inflicted by the mere manifestation of attitude and intention themselves. We should consider also in how much of our behaviour the benefit or injury resides mainly or entirely in the manifestation of attitude itself. So it is with good manners, and much of what we call kindness, on the one hand; with deliberate rudeness, studied indifference, or insult on the other.

Besides resentment and gratitude, I mentioned just now forgiveness. This is a rather unfashionable subject in moral philosophy at present; but to be forgiven is something we sometimes ask, and forgiving is something we sometimes say we do. To ask to be forgiven is in part to acknowledge that the attitude displayed in our actions was such as might properly be resented and in part to repudiate that attitude for the future (or at least for the immediate future); and to forgive is to accept the repudiation and to forswear the resentment.

We should think of the many different kinds of relationship which we can have with other people—as sharers of a common interest; as members of the same family; as colleagues; as friends; as lovers; as chance parties to an enormous range of transactions and encounters. Then we should think, in each of these connections in turn, and in others, of the kind of importance we attach to the attitudes and intentions towards us of those who stand in these relationships to us, and of the kinds of *reactive* attitudes and feelings to which we ourselves are prone. In general, we demand some degree of goodwill or regard on the part of those who stand in these relationships to us, though the forms we require it to take vary widely in different connections. The range and intensity of our *reactive* attitudes towards goodwill, its absence or its opposite vary no less widely. I have mentioned, specifically, resentment and gratitude; and they are a usefully opposed pair. But, of course, there is a whole continuum of reactive attitude and feeling stretching on both sides of these and—the most comfortable area—in between them.

The object of these commonplaces is to try to keep before our minds something it is easy to forget when we are engaged in philosophy, especially in our cool, contemporary style, viz. what it is actually like to be involved in ordinary inter-personal relationships, ranging from the most intimate to the most casual.

IV

It is one thing to ask about the general causes of these reactive attitudes I have alluded to; it is another to ask about the variations to which they are subject, the particular conditions in which they do or do not seem natural or reasonable or appropriate; and it is a third thing to ask what it would be like, what it *is* like, not to suffer them. I am not much concerned with the first question; but I am with the second; and perhaps even more with the third.

Let us consider, then, occasions for resentment: situations in which one person is offended or injured by the action of another and in which—in the absence of special considerations—the offended person might naturally or normally be expected to feel resentment. Then let us consider what sorts of special considerations might be expected to modify or mollify this feeling or remove it altogether. It needs no saying now how multifarious these considerations are. But, for my purpose, I think they can be roughly divided into two kinds. To the first group belong all those which might give occasion for the employment of such expressions as 'He didn't mean to', 'He hadn't realized', 'He didn't know'; and also all those which might give occasion for the use of the phrase 'He couldn't help it', when this is supported by such phrases as 'He was pushed', 'He had to do it', 'It was the only way', 'They left him no alternative', etc. Obviously these various pleas, and the kinds of situations in which they would be appropriate, differ from each other in striking and important ways. But for my present purpose they have something still more important in common. None of them invites us to suspend towards the agent, either at the time of his action or in general, our ordinary reactive attitudes. They do not invite us to view the *agent* as one in respect of whom these attitudes are in any way inappropriate. They invite us to view the *injury* as one in respect of which a particular one of these attitudes is inappropriate. They do not invite us to see the *agent* as other than a fully responsible agent. They invite us to see the *injury* as one for which he was not fully, or at all, responsible. They do not suggest that the agent is in any way an inappropriate object of that kind of demand for goodwill or regard which is reflected in our ordinary reactive attitudes.

They suggest instead that the fact of injury was not in this case incompatible with that demand's being fulfilled, that the fact of injury was quite consistent with the agent's attitude and intentions being just what we demand they should be.[3] The agent was just ignorant of the injury he was causing, or had lost his balance through being pushed or had reluctantly to cause the injury for reasons which acceptably override his reluctance. The offering of such pleas by the agent and their acceptance by the sufferer is something in no way opposed to, or outside the context of, ordinary inter-personal relationships and the manifestation of ordinary reactive attitudes. Since things go wrong and situations are complicated, it is an essential and integral element in the transactions which are the life of these relationships.

The second group of considerations is very different. I shall take them in two sub-groups of which the first is far less important than the second. In connection with the first sub-group we may think of such statements as 'He wasn't himself', 'He has been under very great strain recently', 'He was acting under post-hypnotic suggestion'; in connection with the second, we may think of 'He's only a child', 'He's a hopeless schizophrenic', 'His mind has been systematically perverted', 'That's purely compulsive behaviour on his part'. Such pleas as these do, as pleas of my first general group do not, invite us to suspend our ordinary reactive attitudes towards the agent, either at the time of his action or all the time. They do not invite us to see the agent's action in a way consistent with the full retention of ordinary inter-personal attitudes and merely inconsistent with one particular attitude. They invite us to view the agent himself in a different light from the light in which we should normally view one who has acted as he has acted. I shall not linger over the first subgroup of cases. Though they perhaps raise, in the short term, questions akin to those raised, in the long term, by the second subgroup, we may dismiss them without considering those questions by taking that admirably suggestive phrase, 'He wasn't himself', with the seriousness that—for all its being logically comic—it deserves. We shall not feel resentment against the man he is for the action done by the man he is not; or at least we shall feel less. We normally have to deal with him under normal stresses; so we shall not feel towards him, when he acts as he does under abnormal stresses, as we should have felt towards him had he acted as he did under normal stresses.

The second and more important subgroup of cases allows that the circumstances were normal, but presents the agent as psychologically abnormal—or as morally undeveloped. The agent was himself; but he is warped or deranged, neurotic or just a child. When we see someone in such a light as this, all our reactive attitudes tend to be profoundly modified. I must deal here in crude dichotomies and ignore the ever-interesting and ever-illuminating varieties of case. What I want to contrast is the attitude (or range of attitudes) of involvement or participation in a human relationship, on the one hand, and what might be called the objective attitude (or range of attitudes) to another human being, on the other. Even in the same situation, I must add, they are not altogether *exclusive* of each other; but they are, profoundly, *opposed* to each other. To adopt the objective attitude to another human being to see him, perhaps, as an object of social policy, as a subject for what, in a wide range of sense, might be called treatment; as something certainly to be taken account, perhaps precautionary account, of; to be managed or handled or cured or trained; perhaps simply to be avoided, though *this* gerundive is not peculiar to cases of objectivity of attitude. The objective attitude may be emotionally toned in many ways, but not in all ways: it may include repulsion or fear, it may include pity or even love, though not all kinds of love. But it cannot include the range of reactive feelings and attitudes which belong to involvement or participation with others in inter-personal human relationships; it cannot include resentment, gratitude, forgiveness, anger, or the sort of love which two adults can sometimes be said to feel reciprocally, for each other. If your attitude towards someone is wholly objective, then though you may fight him, you cannot quarrel with him, and though you may talk to him, even negotiate with him, you cannot reason with him. You can at most pretend to quarrel, or to reason, with him.

Seeing someone, then, as warped or deranged or compulsive in behaviour or peculiarly unfortunate in his formative circumstances—seeing someone so tends, at least to some extent, to set him apart from normal participant reactive attitudes on the part of one who sees him, tends to promote, at least in the civilized, objective attitudes. But there is something curious to add to this. The objective attitude is not only something we naturally tend to fall into in cases like these, where participant attitudes are partially or wholly inhibited by abnormalities or by immaturity. It is also something which is available as a resource in other cases too. We look with an objective eye on the compulsive behaviour of the neurotic or the tiresome behaviour of a very young child, thinking in terms of treatment or training. But we *can* sometimes look with something like the same eye on the behaviour of the normal and the mature. We *have* this resource and can sometimes use it: as a refuge, say, from the strains of involvement; or as an aid to policy; or simply out of intellectual curiosity. Being human, we cannot, in the normal case, do this for long, or altogether. If the strains of involvement, say, continue to be too great, then we have to do something else—like severing a relationship. But what is above all interesting is the tension there is, in us, between the participant attitude and the objective attitude. One is tempted to say: between our humanity and our intelligence. But to say this would be to distort both notions.

What I have called the participant reactive attitudes are essentially natural human reactions to the good or ill will or indifference of others towards us, as displayed in *their* attitudes and actions. The question we have to ask is: What effect would, or should, the acceptance of the truth of a general thesis of determinism have upon these reactive attitudes? More specifically, would, or should, the acceptance of the truth of the thesis lead to the decay or the repudiation of all such attitudes? Would, or should, it mean the end of gratitude, resentment, and forgiveness; of all reciprocated adult loves; of all the essentially *personal* anatgonisms ?

But how can I answer, or even pose, this question without knowing *exactly* what the thesis of determinism is? Well, there is one thing we do know: that if there is a coherent thesis of determinism, then there must be a sense of 'determined' such that, if that thesis is true, then all behaviour whatever is determined in that sense. Remembering this, we can consider at least what possibilities lie formally open; and perhaps we shall see that the question can be answered *without* knowing exactly what the thesis of determinism is. We can consider what possibilities lie open because we have already before us an account of the ways in which particular reactive attitudes, or reactive attitudes in general, may be, and, sometimes, we judge, should be, inhibited. Thus I considered earlier a group of considerations which tend to inhibit, and, we judge, should inhibit, resentment, in particular cases of an agent causing an injury, without inhibiting reactive attitudes in general towards that agent. Obviously this group of considerations cannot strictly bear upon our question; for that question concerns reactive attitudes in general. But resentment has a particular interest; so it is worth adding that it has never been claimed as a consequence of the truth of determinism that one or another of *these* considerations was operative in every case of an injury being caused by an agent; that it would follow from the truth of determinism that anyone who caused an injury *either* was quite simply ignorant of causing it *or* had acceptably overriding reasons for acquiescing reluctantly in causing it *or* ..., etc. The prevalence of this happy state of affairs would not be a consequence of the reign of universal determinism, but of the reign of universal goodwill. We cannot, then, find here the possibility of an affirmative answer to our question, even for the particular case of resentment.

Next, I remarked that the participant attitude, and the personal reactive attitudes in general, tend to give place, and, it is judged by the civilized, should give place, to objective attitudes, just in so far as the agent is seen as excluded from ordinary adult human relationships by deep-rooted psychological abnormality—or simply by being a child. But it cannot be a consequence of any thesis which is not itself self-contradictory that abnormality is the universal condition.

Now this dismissal might seem altogether too facile; and so, in a sense, it is. But whatever is too quickly dismissed in this dismissal is allowed for in the only possible form of affirmative answer that remains. We can sometimes, and in part, I have remarked, look on the normal (those we rate as 'normal') in the objective way in which we have learned to look on certain classified cases of abnormality. And our question reduces to this: could, or should, the acceptance of the determinist thesis lead us always to look on everyone exclusively in this way? For this is the only condition worth considering under which the acceptance of determinism could lead to the decay or repudiation of participant reactive attitudes.

It does not seem to be self-contradictory to suppose that this might happen. So I suppose we must say that it is not absolutely inconceivable that it should happen. But I am strongly inclined to think that it is, for us as we are, practically inconceivable. The human commitment to participation in ordinary inter-personal relationships is, I think, too thoroughgoing and deeply rooted for us to take seriously the thought that a general theoretical conviction might so change our world that, in it, there were no longer any such things as inter-personal relationships as we normally understand them; and being involved in inter-personal relationships as we normally understand them precisely is being exposed to the range of reactive attitudes and feelings that is in question.

This, then, is a part of the reply to our question. A sustained objectivity of inter-personal attitude, and the human isolation which that would entail, does not seem to be something of which human beings would be capable, even if some general truth were a theoretical ground for it. But this is not all. There is a further point, implicit in the foregoing, which must be made explicit. Exceptionally, I have said, we can have direct dealings with human beings without any degree of personal involvement, treating them simply as creatures to be handled in our own interests, or our side's, or society's—or even theirs. In the extreme case of the mentally deranged, it is easy to see the connection between the possibility of a wholly objective attitude and the impossibility of what we understand by ordinary inter-personal relationships. Given this latter impossibility, no other civilized attitude is available than that of viewing the deranged person simply as something to be understood and controlled in the most desirable fashion. To view him as outside the reach of personal relationships is already, for the civilized, to view him in this way. For reasons of policy or self-protection we may have occasion, perhaps temporary, to adopt a fundamentally similar attitude to a 'normal' human being; to concentrate, that is, on understanding 'how he works', with a view to determining our policy accordingly or to finding in that very understanding a relief from the strains of involvement. Now it is certainly true that in the case of the abnormal, though not in the case of the normal, our adoption of the objective attitude is a consequence of our viewing the agent as incapacitated in some or all respects for ordinary inter-personal relationships. He is thus incapacitated, perhaps, by the fact that his picture of reality is pure fantasy, that he does not, in a sense, live in the real world at all; or by the fact that his behaviour is, in part, an unrealistic acting out of unconscious purposes; or by the fact that he is an idiot, or a moral idiot. But there is something else which, *because* this is true, is equally certainly *not* true. And that is that there is a sense of 'determined' such that (1) if determinism is true, all behaviour is determined in this sense, and (2) determinism might be true, i.e. it is not inconsistent with the facts as we know them to suppose that all behaviour might be determined in this sense, and (3) our adoption of the objective attitude towards the abnormal is the result of prior embracing of the belief that the behaviour, or the relevant stretch of behaviour, of the human being in question *is* determined in this sense. Neither in the case of the normal, then, nor in the case of the abnormal is it true that, when we adopt an objective attitude, we do so *because* we hold such a belief. So my answer has two parts. The first is that we cannot, as we are, seriously envisage ourselves adopting a thoroughgoing objectivity of attitude to others as a result of theoretical conviction of the truth of determinism, and the second is that when we do in fact adopt such an attitude in a particular case, our doing so is not the consequence of a theoretical conviction which might be expressed as 'Determinism in this case', but is a consequence of our abandoning, for different reasons in different cases, the ordinary inter-personal attitudes.

It might be said that all this leaves the real question unanswered, and that we cannot hope to answer it without knowing exactly what the thesis of determinism is. For the real question is not a question about what we actually do, or why we do it. It is not even a question about what we would *in fact* do if a certain theoretical conviction gained general acceptance. It is a question about what it would be *rational* to do if determinism were true, a question about the rational justification of ordinary inter-personal attitudes in general. To this I shall reply, first, that such a question could seem real only to one who had utterly failed to grasp the purport of the preceding answer, the fact of our natural human commitment to ordinary interpersonal attitudes. This commitment is part of the general framework of human life, not something that can come up for review as particular cases can come up for review within this general framework. And I shall reply, second, that if we could imagine what we cannot have, viz. a choice in this matter, then we could choose rationally only in the light of an assessment of the gains and losses to human life, its enrichment or impoverishment; and the truth or falsity of a general thesis of determinism would not bear on the rationality of *this* choice.[4]

V

The point of this discussion of the reactive attitudes in their relation—or lack of it—to the thesis of determinism was to bring us, if possible, nearer to a position of compromise in a more usual area of debate. We are not now to discuss reactive attitudes which are essentially those of offended parties or beneficiaries. We are to discuss reactive attitudes which are essentially not those, or only incidentally are those, of offended parties or beneficiaries, but are nevertheless, I shall claim, kindred attitudes to those I have discussed. I put resentment in the centre of the previous discussion. I shall put moral indignation—or, more weakly, moral disapprobation—in the centre of this one.

The reactive attitudes I have so far discussed are essentially reactions to the quality of others' wills towards us, as manifested in their behaviour: to their good or ill will or indifference or lack of concern. Thus resentment, or what I have called resentment, is a reaction to injury or indifference. The reactive attitudes I have now to discuss might be described as the sympathetic or vicarious or impersonal or disinterested or generalized analogues of the reactive attitudes I have already discussed. They are reactions to the qualities of others' wills, not towards ourselves, but towards others. Because of this impersonal or vicarious character, we give them different names. Thus one who experiences the vicarious analogue of resentment is said to be indignant or disapproving, or morally indignant or disapproving. What we have here is, as it were, resentment on behalf of another, where one's own interest and dignity are not involved; and it is this impersonal or vicarious character of the attitude, added to its others, which entitle it to the qualification 'moral'. Both my description of, and my name for, these attitudes are, in one important respect, a little misleading. It is not that these attitudes are essentially vicarious—one can feel indignation on one's own account—but that they are essentially capable of being vicarious. But I shall retain the name for the sake of its suggestiveness; and I hope that what is misleading about it will be corrected in what follows.

The personal reactive attitudes rest on, and reflect, an expectation of, and demand for, the manifestation of a certain degree of goodwill or regard on the part of other human beings towards ourselves; or at least on the expectation of, and demand for, an absence of the manifestation of active ill will or indifferent disregard. (What will, in particular cases, *count as* manifestations of good or ill will or disregard will vary in accordance with the particular relationship in which we stand to another human being.) The generalized or vicarious analogues of the personal reactive attitudes rest on, and reflect, exactly the same expectation or demand in a generalized form; they rest on, or reflect, that is, the demand for the manifestation of a reasonable degree of goodwill or regard, on the part of others, not simply towards oneself, but towards all those on whose behalf moral indignation may be felt, i.e. as we now think, towards all men. The generalized and nongeneralized forms of demand, and the vicarious and personal reactive attitudes which rest upon, and reflect, them are connected not merely logically. They are connected humanly; and not merely with each other. They are connected also with yet another set of attitudes which I must mention now in order to complete the picture. I have considered from two points of view the demands we make on others and our reactions to their possibly injurious actions. These were the points of view of one whose interest was directly involved (who suffers, say, the injury) and of others whose interest was not directly involved (who do not themselves suffer the injury). Thus I have spoken of personal reactive attitudes in the first connection and of their vicarious analogues in the second. But the picture is not complete unless we consider also the correlates of these attitudes on the part of those on whom the demands are made, on the part of the agents. Just as there are personal and vicarious reactive attitudes associated with demands on others for oneself and demands on others for others, so there are self-reactive attitudes associated with demands on oneself for others. And here we have to mention such phenomena as feeling bound or obliged (the 'sense of obligation'), feeling compunction; feeling guilty or remorseful or at least responsible, and the more complicated phenomenon of shame.

All these three types of attitude are humanly connected. One who manifested the personal reactive attitudes in a high degree but showed no inclination at all to their vicarious analogues would appear as an abnormal case of moral egocentricity, as a kind of moral solipsist. Let him be supposed fully to acknowledge the claims to regard that others had on him, to be susceptible of the whole range of self-reactive attitudes. He would then see himself as unique both as one *(the* one) who had a general claim on human regard and as one *(the* one) on whom human beings in general had such a claim. This would be a kind of moral solipsism. But it is barely more than a conceptual possibility, if it is that. In general, though within varying limits, we demand of others for others, as well as of ourselves for others, something of the regard which we demand of others for ourselves. Can we imagine, besides that of the moral solipsist, any other case of one or two of these three types of attitude being fully developed, but quite unaccompanied by any trace, however slight, of the remaining two or one? If we can, then we imagine something far below or far above the level of our common humanity—a moral idiot or a saint. For all these types of attitude alike have common roots in our human nature and our membership of human communities.

Now, as of the personal reactive attitudes, so of their vicarious analogues, we must ask in what ways, and by what considerations, they tend to be inhibited. Both types of attitude involve, or express, a certain sort of demand for inter-personal regard. The fact of injury constitutes a prima-facie appearance of this demand's being flouted or unfulfilled. We saw, in the case of resentment, how one class of considerations may show this appearance to be mere appearance, and hence inhibit resentment, *without* inhibiting, or displacing, the sort of demand of which resentment can be an expression, without in any way tending to make us suspend our ordinary inter-personal attitudes to the agent. Considerations of this class operate in just the same way, for just the same reasons, in connection with moral disapprobation or indignation; they inhibit indignation without in any way inhibiting the sort of demand on the agent of which indignation can be an expression, the range of attitudes towards him to which it belongs. But in this connection we may express the facts with a new emphasis. We may say, stressing the moral, the generalized aspect of the demand, considerations of this group have no tendency to make us see the agent as other than a morally responsible agent; they simply make us see the injury as one for which he was not morally responsible. The offering and acceptance of such exculpatory pleas as are here in question in no way detracts in our eyes from the agent's status as a term of moral relationships. On the contrary, since things go wrong and situations are complicated, it is an essential part of the life of such relationships.

But suppose we see the agent in a different light: as one whose picture of the world is an insane delusion; or as one whose behaviour, or a part of whose behaviour, is unintelligible to us, perhaps even to him, in terms of conscious purposes, and intelligible only in terms of unconscious purposes; or even, perhaps, as one wholly impervious to the self-reactive attitudes I spoke of, wholly lacking, as we say, in moral sense. Seeing an agent in such a light as this tends, I said, to inhibit resentment in a wholly different way. It tends to inhibit resentment because it tends to inhibit ordinary interpersonal attitudes in general, and the kind of demand and expectation which those attitudes involve; and tends to promote instead the purely objective view of the agent as one posing problems simply of intellectual understanding, management, treatment, and control. Again the parallel holds for those generalized or moral attitudes towards the agent which we are now concerned with. The same abnormal light which shows the agent to us as one in respect of whom the personal attitudes, the personal demand, are to be suspended, shows him to us also as one in respect of whom the impersonal attitudes, the generalized demand, are to be suspended. Only, abstracting now from direct personal interest, we may express the facts with a new emphasis. We may say: to the extent to which the agent is seen in this light, he is not seen as one on whom demands and expectations lie in that particular way in which we think of them as lying when we speak of moral obligation; he is not, to that extent, seen as a morally responsible agent, as a term of moral relationships, as a member of the moral community.

I remarked also that the suspension of ordinary inter-personal attitudes and the cultivation of a purely objective view is sometimes possible even when we have no such reasons for it as I have just mentioned. Is this possible also in the case of the moral reactive attitudes? I think so; and perhaps it is easier. But the motives for a total suspension of moral reactive attitudes are fewer, and perhaps weaker: fewer, because only where there is antecedent personal involvement can there be the motive of seeking refuge from the strains of such involvement; perhaps weaker, because the tension between objectivity of view and the moral reactive attitudes is perhaps less than the tension between objectivity of view and the personal reactive attitudes, so that we can in the case of the moral reactive attitudes more easily secure the speculative or political gains of objectivity of view by a kind of setting on one side, rather than a total suspension, of those attitudes.

These last remarks are uncertain; but also, for the present purpose, unimportant. What concerns us now is to inquire, as previously in connection with the personal reactive attitudes, what relevance any general thesis of determinism might have to their vicarious analogues. The answers once more are parallel; though I shall take them in a slightly different order. First, we must note, as before, that when the suspension of such an attitude or such attitudes occurs in a particular case, it is *never* the consequence of the belief that the piece of behaviour in question was determined in a sense such that all behaviour *might be,* and, if determinism is true, all behaviour *is,* determined in that sense. For it is not a consequence of any general thesis of determinism which might be true that nobody knows what he's doing or that everybody's behaviour is unintelligible in terms of conscious purposes or that everybody lives in a world of delusion or that nobody has a moral sense, i.e. is susceptible of self-reactive attitudes, etc. In fact no such sense of 'determined' as would be required for a general thesis of determinism is ever relevant to our actual suspensions of moral reactive attitudes. Second, suppose it granted, as I have already argued, that we cannot take seriously the thought that theoretical conviction of such a general thesis would lead to the total decay of the personal reactive attitudes. Can we then take seriously the thought that such a conviction— a conviction, after all, that many have held or said they held—would nevertheless lead to the total decay or repudiation of the vicarious analogues of these attitudes? I think that the change in our social world which would leave us exposed to the personal reactive attitudes but not all to their vicarious analogues, the generalization of abnormal egocentricity which this would entail, is perhaps even harder for us to envisage as a real possibility than the decay of both kinds of attitude together. Though there are some necessary and some contingent differences between the ways and cases in which these two kinds of attitudes operate or are inhibited in their operation, yet, as general human capacities or pronenesses, they stand or lapse together. Finally, to the further question whether it would not be *rational,* given a general theoretical conviction of the truth of determinism, so to change our world that in it all these attitudes were wholly suspended, I must answer, as before, that one who presses this question has wholly failed to grasp the import of the preceding answer, the nature of the human commitment that is here involved: it is *useless* to ask whether it would not be rational for us to do what it is not in our nature to (be able to) do. To this I must add, as before, that if there were, say, for a moment open to us the possibility of such a godlike choice, the rationality of making or refusing it would be determined by quite other considerations than the truth or falsity of the general theoretical doctrine in question. The latter would be simply irrelevant; and this becomes ironically clear when we remember that for those convinced that the truth of determinism nevertheless really would make the one choice rational, there has always been the insuperable difficulty of explaining in intelligible terms how its falsity would make the opposite choice rational.

I am aware that in presenting the argument as I have done, neglecting the ever-interesting varieties of case, I have presented nothing more than a schema, using sometimes a crude opposition of phrase where we have a great intricacy of phenomena. In particular the simple opposition of objective attitudes on the one hand and the various contrasted attitudes which I have opposed to them must seem as grossly crude as it is central. Let me pause to mitigate this crudity a little, and also to strengthen one of my central contentions, by mentioning some things which straddle these contrasted kinds of attitude. Thus parents and others concerned with the care and upbringing of young children cannot have to their charges either kind of attitude in a pure or unqualified form. They are dealing with creatures who are potentially and increasingly capable both of holding, and being objects of, the full range of human and moral attitudes, but are not yet truly capable of either. The treatment of such creatures must therefore represent a kind of compromise, constantly shifting in one direction, between objectivity of attitude and developed human attitudes. Rehearsals insensibly modulate towards true performances. The punishment of a child is both like and unlike the punishment of an adult. Suppose we try to relate this progressive emergence of the child as a responsible being, as an object of non-objective attitudes, to that sense of 'determined' in which, if determinism is a possibly true thesis, all behaviour *may* be determined, and in which, if it is a true thesis, all behaviour *is* determined. What bearing *could* such a sense of 'determined' have upon the progressive modification of attitudes towards the child? Would it not be grotesque to think of the development of the child as a progressive or patchy emergence from an area in which its behaviour is in this sense determined into an area in which it isn't? Whatever sense of 'determined' is required for stating the thesis of determinism, it can scarcely be such as to allow of compromise, borderline-style answers to the question, 'Is this bit of behaviour determined or isn't it?' But in this matter of young children, it is essentially a borderline, penumbral area that we move in. Again, consider—a very different matter—the strain in the attitude of a psychoanalyst to his patient. *His* objectivity of attitude, *his* suspension of ordinary moral reactive attitudes, is profoundly modified by the fact that the aim of the enterprise is to make such suspension unnecessary or less necessary. Here we may and do naturally speak of restoring the agent's freedom. But here the restoring of freedom means bringing it about that the agent's behaviour shall be intelligible in terms of conscious purposes rather than in terms only of unconscious purposes. *This* is the object of the enterprise; and it is in so far as *this* object is attained that the suspension, or half-suspension, of ordinary moral attitudes is deemed no longer necessary or appropriate. And in this we see once again the *irrelevance* of that concept of 'being determined' which must be the central concept of determinism. For we cannot both agree that this object is attainable and that its attainment has this consequence and yet hold (1) that neurotic behaviour is determined in a sense in which, it may be, all behaviour is determined, and (2) that it is because neurotic behaviour is determined in this sense that objective attitudes are deemed appropriate to neurotic behaviour. Not, at least, without accusing ourselves of incoherence in our attitude to psychoanalytic treatment.

VI

And now we can try to fill in the lacuna which the pessimist finds in the optimist's account of the concept of moral responsibility, and of the bases of moral condemnation and punishment; and to fill it in from the facts as we know them. For, as I have already remarked, when the pessimist himself seeks to fill it in, he rushes beyond the facts as we know them and proclaims that it cannot be filled in at all unless determinism is false.

Yet a partial sense of the facts as we know them is certainly present to the pessimist's mind. When his opponent, the optimist, undertakes to show that the truth of determinism would not shake the foundations of the concept of moral responsibility and of the practices of moral condemnation and punishment, he typically refers, in a more or less elaborated way, to the efficacy of these practices in regulating behaviour in socially desirable ways. These practices are represented solely as instruments of policy, as methods of individual treatment and social control. The pessimist recoils from this picture; and in his recoil there is, typically, an element of emotional shock. He is apt to say, among much else, that the humanity of the offender himself is offended by *this* picture of his condemnation and punishment.

The reasons for this recoil—the explanation of the sense of an emotional, as well as a conceptual, shock—we have already before us. The picture painted by the optimists is painted in a style appropriate to a situation envisaged as wholly dominated by objectivity of attitude. The only operative notions invoked in this picture are such as those of policy, treatment, control. But a thoroughgoing objectivity of attitude, excluding as it does the moral reactive attitudes, excludes at the same time essential elements in the concepts of *moral* condemnation and *moral* responsibility. This is the reason for the conceptual shock. The deeper emotional shock is a reaction, not simply to an inadequate conceptual analysis, but to the suggestion of a change in our world. I have remarked that it is possible to cultivate an exclusive objectivity of attitude in some cases, and for some reasons, where the object of the attitude is not set aside from developed inter-personal and moral attitudes by immaturity or abnormality. And the suggestion which seems to be contained in the optimist's account is that such an attitude should be universally adopted to all offenders. This is shocking enough in the pessimist's eyes. But, sharpened by shock, his eyes see further. It would be hard to make *this* division in our natures. If to all offenders, then to all mankind. Moreover, to whom could this recommendation be, in any real sense, addressed? Only to the powerful, the authorities. So abysses seem to open.[5]

But we will confine our attention to the case of the offenders. The concepts we are concerned with are those of responsibility and guilt, qualified as 'moral', on the one hand—together with that of membership of a moral community; of demand, indignation, disapprobation and condemnation, qualified as 'moral', on the other hand—together with that of punishment. Indignation, disapprobation, like resentment, tend to inhibit or at least to limit our goodwill towards the object of these attitudes, tend to promote an at least partial and temporary withdrawal of goodwill; they do so in proportion as they are strong; and their strength is in general proportioned to what is felt to be the magnitude of the injury and to the degree to which the agent's will is identified with, or indifferent to, it. (These, of course, are not contingent connections.) But these attitudes of disapprobation and indignation are precisely the correlates of the moral demand in the case where the demand is felt to be disregarded. The making of the demand *is* the proneness to such attitudes. The holding of them does not, as the holding of objective attitudes does, involve as a part of itself viewing their object other than as a member of the moral community. The partial withdrawal of goodwill which *these* attitudes entail, the modification *they* entail of the general demand that another should, if possible, be spared suffering, is, rather, the consequence of *continuing* to view him as a member of the moral community; only as one who has offended against its demands. So the preparedness to acquiesce in that infliction of suffering on the offender which is an essential part of punishment is all of a piece with this whole range of attitudes of which I have been speaking. It is not only moral reactive attitudes towards the offender which are in question here. We must mention also the self-reactive attitudes of offenders themselves. Just as the other-reactive attitudes are associated with a readiness to acquiesce in the infliction of suffering on an offender, within the 'institution' of punishment, so the self-reactive attitudes are associated with a readiness on the part of the offender to acquiesce in such infliction *without* developing the reactions (e.g. of resentment) which he would normally develop to the infliction of injury upon him, i.e. with a readiness, as we say, to accept punishment[6] as 'his due' or as 'just'.

I am not in the least suggesting that these readinesses to acquiesce, either on the part of the offender himself or on the part of others, are always or commonly accompanied or preceded by indignant boilings or remorseful pangs; only that we have here a continuum of attitudes and feelings to which these readinesses to acquiesce themselves belong. Nor am I in the least suggesting that it belongs to this continuum of attitudes that we should be ready to acquiesce in the infliction of injury on offenders in a fashion which we saw to be quite indiscriminate or in accordance with procedures which we knew to be wholly useless. On the contrary, savage or civilized, we have some belief in the utility of practices of condemnation and punishment. But the social utility of these practices, on which the optimist lays such exclusive stress, is not what is now in question. What is in question is the pessimist's justified sense that to speak in terms of social utility alone is to leave out something vital in our conception of these practices. The vital thing can be restored by attending to that complicated web of attitudes and feelings which form an essential part of the moral life as we know it, and which are quite opposed to objectivity of attitude. Only by attending to this range of attitudes can we recover from the facts as we know them a sense of what we mean, i.e. of *all* we mean, when, speaking the language of morals, we speak of desert, responsibility, guilt, condemnation, and justice. But we *do* recover it from the facts as we know them. We do not have to go beyond them. Because the optimist neglects or misconstrues these attitudes, the pessimist rightly claims to find a lacuna in his account. We can fill the lacuna for him. But in return we must demand of the pessimist a surrender of his metaphysics.

Optimist and pessimist misconstrue the facts in very different styles. But in a profound sense there is something in common to their misunderstandings. Both seek, in different ways, to over-intellectualize the facts. Inside the general structure or web of human attitudes and feelings of which I have been speaking, there is endless room for modification, redirection, criticism, and justification. But questions of justification are internal to the structure or relate to modifications internal to it. The existence of the general framework of attitudes itself is something we are given with the fact of human society. As a whole, it neither calls for, nor permits, an external 'rational' justification. Pessimist and optimist alike show themselves, in different ways, unable to accept this.[7] The optimist's style of over-intellectualizing the facts is that of a characteristically incomplete empiricism, a one-eyed utilitarianism. He seeks to find an adequate basis for certain social practices in calculated consequences, and loses sight (perhaps wishes to lose sight) of the human attitudes of which these practices are, in part, the expression. The pessimist does not lose sight of these attitudes, but is unable to accept the fact that it is just these attitudes themselves which fill the gap in the optimist's account. Because of this, he thinks the gap can be filled only if some general metaphysical proposition is repeatedly verified, verified in all cases where it is appropriate to attribute moral responsibility. This proposition he finds it as difficult to state coherently and with intelligible relevance as its determinist contradictory. Even when a formula has been found ('contra-causal freedom' or something of the kind) there still seems to remain a gap between its applicability in particular cases and its supposed moral consequences. Sometimes he plugs this gap with an intuition of fittingness—a pitiful intellectualist trinket for a philosopher to wear as a charm against the recognition of his own humanity.

Even the moral sceptic is not immune from his own form of the wish to over-intellectualize such notions as those of moral responsibility, guilt, and blame. He sees that the optimist's account is inadequate and the pessimist's libertarian alternative inane; and finds no resource except to declare that the notions in question are inherently confused, that 'blame is metaphysical'. But the metaphysics was in the eye of the metaphysician. It is a pity that talk of the moral sentiments has fallen out of favour. The phrase would be quite a good name for that network of human attitudes in acknowledging the character and place of which we find, I suggest, the only possibility of reconciling these disputants to each other and the facts.

There are, at present, factors which add, in a slightly paradoxical way, to the difficulty of making this acknowledgement. These human attitudes themselves, in their development and in the variety of their manifestations, have to an increasing extent become objects of study in the social and psychological sciences; and this growth of human self-consciousness, which we might expect to reduce the difficulty of acceptance, in fact increases it in several ways. One factor of comparatively minor importance is an increased historical and anthropological awareness of the great variety of forms which these human attitudes may take at different times and in different cultures.

This makes one rightly chary of claiming as essential features of the concept of morality in general, forms of these attitudes which may have a local and temporary prominence. No doubt to some extent my own descriptions of human attitudes have reflected local and temporary features of our own culture. But an awareness of variety of forms should not prevent us from acknowledging also that in the absence of *any* forms of these attitudes it is doubtful whether we should have anything that *we* could find intelligible as a system of human relationships, as human society. A quite different factor of greater importance is that psychological studies have made us rightly mistrustful of many particular manifestations of the attitudes I have spoken of. They are a prime realm of self-deception, of the ambiguous and the shady, of guilt-transference, unconscious sadism and the rest. But it is an exaggerated horror, itself suspect, which would make us unable to acknowledge the facts because of the seamy side of the facts. Finally, perhaps the most important factor of all is the prestige of these theoretical studies themselves. That prestige is great, and is apt to make us forget that in philosophy, though it also is a theoretical study, we have to take account of the facts in *all* their bearings; we are not to suppose that we are required, or permitted, as philosophers, to regard ourselves, as human beings, as detached from the attitudes which, as scientists, we study with detachment. This is in no way to deny the possibility and desirability of redirection and modification of our human attitudes in the light of these studies. But we may reasonably think it unlikely that our progressively greater understanding of certain aspects of ourselves will lead to the total disappearance of those aspects. Perhaps it is not inconceivable that it should; and perhaps, then the dreams of some philosophers will be realized.

If we sufficiently, that is *radically*, modify the view of the optimist, his view is the right one. It is far from wrong to emphasize the efficacy of all those practices which express or manifest our moral attitudes, in regulating behaviour in ways considered desirable; or to add that when certain of our beliefs about the efficacy of some of these practices turns out to be false, then we may have good reason for dropping or modifying those practices. What *is* wrong is to forget that these practices, and their reception, the reactions to them, really *are* expressions of our moral attitudes and not merely devices we calculatingly employ for regulative purposes. Our practices do not merely exploit our natures, they express them. Indeed the very understanding of the kind of efficacy these expressions of our attitudes have turns on our remembering this. When we do remember this, and modify the optimist's position accordingly, we simultaneously correct its conceptual deficiencies and ward off the dangers it seems to entail, without recourse to the obscure and panicky metaphysics of libertarianism.

Notes

1. Cf. P. H. Nowell-Smith, 'Freewill and Moral Responsibility', *Mind*, 1948.
2. As Nowell-Smith pointed out in a later article: "Determinists and Libertarians," *Mind*, 1954.
3. Perhaps not in every case *just* what we demand they should be, but in any case *not* just what we demand they should not be. For my present purpose these differences do not matter.

4. The question, then, of the connection between rationality and the adoption of the objective attitude to others is misposed when it is made to seem dependent on the issue of determinism. But there is another question which should be raised, if only to distinguish it from the misposed question. Quite apart from the issue of determinism might it not be said that we should be nearer to being purely rational creatures in proportion as our relation to others was in fact dominated by the objective attitude? I think this might be said; only it would have to be added, once more, that if such a choice were possible, it would not necessarily be rational to choose to be more purely rational than we are.

5. See J. D. Mabbott's "Freewill and Punishment," in *Contemporary British Philosophy*, 3rd ser. (London: Allen & Unwin, 1956).

6. Of course not *any* punishment for *anything* deemed an offence.

7. Compare the question of the justification of induction. The human commitment to inductive belief-formation is original, natural, non-rational (not *irrational*), in no way something we choose or could give up. Yet rational criticism and reflection can refine standards and their application, supply 'rules for judging of cause and effect'. Ever since the facts were made clear by Hume, people have been resisting acceptance of them.

12

The Reason View

SUSAN WOLF

The ability to act autonomously can be confused with the ability to act in accordance with Reason. Once these abilities are distinguished, we see that the latter seems more relevant to our status as responsible agents than the former. For within the class of agents who share the ability to act in accordance with Reason, the difference between autonomous and nonautonomous agents consists in the former's having the ability to act in *dis*cordance with Reason, an ability that at best seems irrelevant to our status as responsible agents and at worst bespeaks a position directly incompatible with that status.[1] If one has the ability to act in accordance with Reason, in other words, it seems that one may be responsible even without being autonomous. We might also point out that if one lacks the ability to act in accordance with Reason, one cannot be responsible even if one is autonomous. For dogs and psychopaths might conceivably be autonomous in the sense that they might be ultimate sources of their own actions, able to act on no basis. But because they lack the ability to act on a basis—in particular, the basis of Reason—they are not responsible in the sense that would allow them to be deserving of deep praise and blame.

The purpose of this essay is to argue that the ability that is crucial to responsibility is in fact the ability to act in accordance with Reason, as opposed to both the ability to act in accordance with one's Real Self and the ability to act autonomously. A better understanding of this position will emerge from a comparison between this view and the Real Self and Autonomy views. I will argue that this view preserves the insights of each of these latter views while avoiding their respective failures. Finally, once the overall thrust and spirit of this view have been conveyed, its implications for specific cases and its ability to explain and accord with our intuitions regarding these cases will be examined.

I. The Reason View Compared with the Autonomy View

Let us begin by comparing the present view, that a responsible agent is one who has the ability to act in accordance with Reason, with the view that a responsible agent is an autonomous agent. The latter view we might redescribe as the view that a responsible agent must always be able to do one thing *or* another. The agent must not be necessitated by causes, Reason, or anything else, to take action along a particular path. To put it still another way, this view amounts to the position that no matter what action the agent actually does perform, the agent, if she is to be considered responsible, must have been able to do otherwise. The present view, in contrast, denies that responsibility rests on the availability to the agent of at least two options. What matters is rather the availability of one very particular option, namely, the option to act in accordance with Reason.[2] If, on this view, the agent exercises this option, then it is irrelevant whether the agent might *not* have exercised it. In other words, it is irrelevant whether the agent had the ability to act in *dis*cordance with Reason. If, on the other hand, the agent does *not* exercise this option, then the question of whether she *could have* exercised it is all-important.

From one perspective, the difference between these two views may seem great. For on the Autonomy View, the ability necessary for responsibility is, as it were, bidirectional—it is an ability to do one thing or another, an ability to do X or something other than X. On the Reason View, in contrast, the ability necessary for responsibility is unidirectional—it is an ability to do one sort of thing, which is compatible with the *in*ability to do anything else.

From another perspective, however, the difference between these two views may seem very small. For with the exception of one very special type of case, the nominally different conditions of responsibility respectively entailed by the two views may be thought to amount to the same thing. Admittedly, regarding the case in which the agent actually does act in accordance with Reason—the case, that is, in which the agent does just what she ought to do for just the reasons that she ought to have—the Autonomy View requires that she have the ability to do otherwise while the Reason View does not. But when the agent fails to do what she ought to do, both views require that she could have done what she ought. And even when the agent does what she ought to do but not for the reasons that she ought to have, both views require that the agent could have acted in accordance with (and on the basis of) those reasons.

In other words, except in cases where the agent does the right thing for the right reasons, both views require that the responsible agent have the ability to do otherwise. Only in those cases in which the agent does do the right thing for the right reasons do the two views differ. And even there, it might be argued, the views differ in letter but not in spirit. For the spirit of the Autonomy View, it might be said, is to deny that responsibility is compatible with being fated to live one's life along a preordained track. The Autonomy View insists that the responsible agent be flexible, that she be able to choose and act in a way that is not forced upon her by the uncontrollable features and events of her past. But the Reason View might be thought to have the relevant kind of flexibility built into it. For the Reason View requires that the agent be able to act in accordance with Reason, and part of what it is to act in accordance with Reason is to be sensitive and responsive to relevant changes in one's situation and environment—that is, to be flexible.

Perhaps the proponent of the Autonomy View was a proponent of that view simply because she thought that the ability to do otherwise was necessary if an agent was to be sensitive and responsive to changes in the environment in rational ways. Perhaps she thought that if an agent could not act otherwise in a given situation, then it would have to be the case that the agent was acting blindly or rigidly, according to a rule that she was incapable of questioning. Perhaps it simply had not occurred to the proponent of autonomy that one explanation for why an agent might not be able to do otherwise is that it is so obviously rational to do what she plans to do and the agent is too rational to ignore that fact. Once this does occur to the proponent of autonomy, she may simply give up the Autonomy View and accept the Reason View as the view she was confusedly after all along.

Even if the Reason View may in this way appear as a mere refinement of the Autonomy View, the significance of the shift from autonomy to reason should not be underestimated. For the suggestion that autonomy is required for free will and responsibility involves the suggestion that the problems of free will and responsibility are, at the most fundamental level, purely metaphysical problems. The question we must answer, if we are to know whether we are free and responsible beings, concerns what metaphysical kinds of beings we are. In particular, we must know whether we are metaphysically integrated with other parts of nature; whether we are part of the same causal network as the rest of nature; whether we are subject, and wholly subject, to the same sorts of psychological and physical forces as other animals and things. If we are so subject, the Autonomy View suggests, that necessarily excludes us from the realm of free and responsible beings. For then our choices and the actions that flow from them are not ultimately up to us, but are rather consequences of the same combination of chance and determination that accounts for the flow of events that constitute the rest of the world. In order to be free and responsible beings, we must, on the contrary, be metaphysically distinctive, endowed with contracausal powers, or perhaps with our own peculiar and irreducible kind of causality.[3]

The Reason View locates the essence of the problems of free will and responsibility elsewhere. According to the Reason View, what we need to know if we are to find out whether we are free and responsible beings is whether we possess the ability to act in accordance with Reason. Since Reason is here understood to refer to the highest faculty or set of faculties there is, the faculty or set of faculties that, in most circumstances, will help us form true beliefs and good values, this amounts to the suggestion that we need to know whether we have the ability to think—and on the basis of our thought, to act—well rather than badly. That is, we need to know whether we have the ability to choose and to act on the basis of the right reasons for choosing and acting. And since we can assume that if one acts according to the right reasons one will perform the right action, the ability we are concerned with might be described as the ability to do the right thing for the right reasons. The question of whether we have this ability is not so much a metaphysical as a metaethical, and perhaps also an ethical, one. For we cannot answer it unless we know what counts as doing the right thing and having the right reasons.

To shift from the Autonomy View to the Reason View, then, is to shift from a view that takes the problems of responsibility and free will to be purely metaphysical problems, the solutions to which can be found independently of any metaethical commitments, to a view that takes these problems to be inextricably bound to metaethical, and perhaps also ethical, commitments. According to the Autonomy View, having the status of a responsible being depends on having a distinctive metaphysical power, the power to choose one path of action or another independently of any forces that would push one in one direction or the other. According to the Reason View, having responsible status depends rather on a distinctive intellectual power, the power to exercise right Reason and to govern one's actions accordingly. Since, again, right Reason refers to those faculties which will, in most circumstances, lead one to form true beliefs and good values, the power to exercise right Reason may be redescribed as the power to recognize the True and the Good. The ability to act in accordance with Reason might then be redescribed as the ability to act in accordance with, and on the basis of, the True and the Good.

If the Reason View is right, then proponents of autonomy are mistaken in regarding the problem of responsibility as a fundamentally metaphysical problem. They are mistaken in thinking that being responsible essentially requires being free of all external physical and psychological forces. But it is easy to see how the mistake could be made. For if the Reason View is right, then what responsibility really requires is the ability to act in accordance with and on the basis of the True and the Good, and it is easy to see how a person who is dimly in search of this ability might confusedly think that only beings who are free of all external physical or psychological forces could have it.

In particular, one can see how a person might think that if someone is governed by the True and the Good then she cannot be governed by one's garden variety of causes. To be governed by the True and the Good is not, after all, to be governed by the Past, and to do something because it is the right thing to do is not to do it because one has been taught to do it. One might think, then, that one can only be governed by one thing or the other. For if one is going to do whatever it is right to do, then it seems one will do it whether or not one has been so taught. And if one is going to do whatever one has been taught to do, then it seems one will do it whether or not it is right.

But such reasoning is mistaken. These two explanations do not compete, for they are explanations of different kinds. Perhaps an example or two will help to make this clear. Consider the following situation: You ask me to name the capital of Nevada, and I reply "Carson City." We can explain why I give this answer in either of the following ways: First, we can point out that when I was in the fifth grade I had to memorize the capitals of the states. I was taught to believe that Carson City was the capital of Nevada, and was subsequently positively reinforced for believing so. Second, we can point out that Carson City is the capital of Nevada, and that this was, after all, what you wanted to know. So, on the one hand, I gave my answer because I was taught. And, on the other, I gave my answer because it was right.

Presumably, these explanations are not unrelated. For if Carson City were not the capital of Nevada, I would not have been taught that it was. And if I hadn't been taught that Carson City was the capital of Nevada, I wouldn't have known that it was. Indeed, one might think that if the answer I gave weren't right, I *couldn't* have given it because I was taught. For no school board would have hired a teacher who got such facts wrong. And if I hadn't been taught that Carson City was the capital of Nevada, perhaps I couldn't have given this answer because it was right. For that Carson City is the capital of Nevada is not something that can be known *a priori*.

Similarly, we can explain why a person acts justly in either of the following ways: First, we can point out that she was taught to act justly, and was subsequently positively reinforced for doing so. Second, we can point out that it is right to act justly, and go on to say why she knows this is so. Again, these explanations are likely to be related. For it if weren't right to act justly, the person might well not have been taught that it was. And if the person hadn't been taught that she ought to act justly, the person might not have discovered this on her own. Of course, the explanations of both kinds in this case will be more complex than the explanations in the previous case. But what is relevant here is that these explanations are compatible: that one can be determined by the Good *and* determined by the Past.

The Reason View thus offers an explanation for the attractiveness of the Autonomy View. Once one sees what is really involved in being a free and responsible being—namely, having the ability to act in accordance with the True and the Good—then one can understand how it might have seemed that what was involved was a metaphysical property, namely, autonomy. For one can understand how having the ability to act in accordance with the True and the Good can seem to be incompatible with being metaphysically ordinary, with being subject, and wholly subject, to the same causal forces as those which govern the behavior of other animals and objects. Once we have identified the ability that this radical metaphysical independence seemed necessary to be secure, however, we can see, first, that metaphysical independence is not necessary after all and, second, that we can state the condition of freedom and responsibility more directly by referring outright to the ability to act in accordance with (and on the basis of) the True and the Good.

II. The Reason View Compared with the Real Self View

In form, this response to autonomists is similar to a response that proponents of the Real Self View might make (and, indeed, it has something in common with Hume's own response). For like the proponents of the Reason View, the proponents of the Real Self View believe they know what really matters for free will and responsibility. On their view, what really matters is the ability to act in accordance with one's valuational system, that is, the ability to act from one's Real Self. And though, they may point out, this ability may *seem* to require a peculiar metaphysical independence from causes, on closer examination we can see that in fact no such metaphysical status is necessary.

Proponents of the Reason View and proponents of the Real Self View share the belief that the ability or freedom crucial to responsibility is unidirectional, that being responsible involves having the ability *to* act in one sort of way or on one sort of basis, but does not involve the ability *not* to act in that way or on that basis. Moreover, both views agree that having the requisite unidirectional ability is compatible with being metaphysically ordinary. Thus proponents of both views believe that, in cases in which agents seem not sufficiently free to be responsible, the problems lie not in whether but in how the actions of these agents are caused. To put it another way, they believe that the problems in these cases have to do not with the ultimacy but with the type of the agents' control of their behavior.

Just as other considerations promoted a perspective from which the difference between the Autonomy View and the Reason View seemed very slight, these considerations encourage us to see the Real Self View and the Reason View as very similar. For the Reason View and the Real Self View both suggest that what is of fundamental importance to freedom and responsibility is not the quantity but the quality of the option(s) available. These views differ simply with respect to *which* quality they take to be so important. According to the Real Self View, it is the ability to act in accordance with one's Real Self; according to the Reason View, it is the ability to act in accordance with Reason. But these two abilities may themselves be seen as very similar. For the Real Self View, by emphasizing the importance of the ability to act in accordance with one's values, stresses the fact that a responsible being must be able to choose her actions for herself, rather than let her actions be chosen for her by another person or even by a compulsive desire or habit with which she does not identify. The Reason View seems to make the same point—for, after all, the claim that a responsible being must be able to act in accordance with Reason is to be understood as insisting that the responsible being be able to act in accordance with her own Reason, that is, that she be able to exercise the faculties that will lead her to the True and the Good herself, and be able to govern her actions on that basis. Both views, then, seem primarily concerned to stress that a responsible being must be able to act on the basis of her own most deeply held thoughts and feelings. The Reason View is simply more restrictive than the Real Self View, insisting that the agent be able to identify her most deeply held thoughts and feelings with the thoughts and feelings that arise out of, or, at any rate, are capable of coexisting comfortably with, her exercise of Reason.

The way in which Reason is defined, however, makes this restriction more significant than it might at first seem, and thus makes the difference between the Reason View and the Real Self View considerable. For the difference between an agent who has the ability to act in accordance with Reason and an agent who lacks this ability is not essentially the difference between an agent who can form her values according to more intellectual, self-consciously deliberative means and an agent who forms her values in a less articulable and cognitive manner. Rather, the difference referred to is that between an agent who can form (and act on) right values because they are right—that is, an agent who is able to "track" the True and Good in her value judgments—and an agent who cannot.[4]

Thus, the difference between the Real Self View and the Reason View might be stated in the following way: According to the Real Self View, an individual is responsible if and only if she is able to form her actions on the basis of her values. The Reason View insists that responsibility requires something more. According to the Reason View, an individual is responsible if and only if she is able to form her actions on the basis of her values *and* she is able to form her values on the basis of what is True and Good.

Whether an agent is able to form her values on the basis of the True and the Good, however, is not solely a matter of the agent's intelligence, alertness, and psychological complexity. Two agents alike in these respects may nonetheless differ in their capacity to recognize the True and the Good. A victim of a deprived (or depraved) childhood, for example, may be as smart as a person raised in a more normal environment, but, because of a regrettably skewed set of experiences, her values may be distorted. She is able to reason, as it were, but not able to act in accordance with Reason. Having been exposed to an unfortuitous collection of data, *her* reason will not reach its goal.

This marks a fairly dramatic difference between the Reason View and the Real Self View. For where the Real Self View claims that the freedom to govern one's actions according to one's real self is all the freedom it is intelligible or at any rate necessary for a person to hope for, the Reason View insists that this is not enough. According to the Reason View, some real selves may be responsible while others may not, and individuals may be responsible for some actions that arise out of their real selves but not be responsible for others. In this respect, the Reason View is more like the Autonomy View. But we have already seen that while the Autonomy View takes the extra condition to be a purely metaphysical property, the property with which the Reason View is concerned is explicitly normative.

III. The Reason View as an Intermediary Between the Other Views

In focusing on a feature of agents that is explicitly normative, the Reason View differs from both the Autonomy View and the Real Self View. For both these other views, the problems of free will and responsibility are understood to be purely metaphysical problems. The debate between the proponents of the last two views centers on the question of how much metaphysical freedom and power a responsible being is required to have. I have already mentioned that proponents of the Real Self View think that the freedom and power to govern one's actions according to one's real self are all the freedom and power it is intelligible or at any rate necessary for a person to hope for. Proponents of the Autonomy View claim that this is not sufficient. To be responsible, they say, an agent not only must be able to govern her actions by her real self, she also must be able to ensure that her real self is not in turn governed by anything else. Proponents of autonomy criticize their opponents for being unable to explain why being able to govern one's actions by one's real self should make a person responsible given that the person's real self may itself be the inevitable product of external forces. Proponents of the Real Self View question in return how it can make any difference whether the real self is an inevitable product of external forces or instead an arbitrary existent emerging inexplicably from the void.

From the perspective of the Reason View, both the criticisms these other views respectively level against the other are correct: The ability to act in accordance with one's real self is *not* sufficient to explain responsibility, but the real self's metaphysical independence from all other things will not explain it either. Both views, by searching for a property that can be stated in a way that is not implicitly value-laden, miss the crucial feature that distinguishes responsible beings from others.

This feature, according to the Reason View, is the ability to be in touch with the True and the Good. In other words, what makes responsible beings special is their ability to recognize good values as opposed to bad ones and to act in a way that expresses appreciation of this recognition. The freedom and power necessary for responsibility, then, are the freedom and power to *be* good, that is, the freedom and power to do the right thing for the right reasons. Having the ability to govern one's actions in accordance with one's real self does not necessarily guarantee this sort of freedom and power (remember the victim of the deprived childhood), but neither does the metaphysical independence of autonomous agency. Moreover, one may have this sort of freedom and power without metaphysical independence: One's ability to be good may *arise from* one's experiences; it need not exist *despite* them.

We might capture the difference between a nonresponsible being and a responsible one, then, by pointing out that the latter, unlike the former, is capable of recognizing things she might be responsible for. The responsible being is capable of recognizing that some actions, characters, and lives are better than others, of seeing which ones are better than others, and of controlling her behavior so as to make her actions, character, and life better rather than worse. That is why, if she does something good, she deserves a special kind of credit for it—the responsible being, and only the responsible being, knows what she is doing in the relevant sense, and does it on purpose. And that is why, if she does something wrong, she deserves a special kind of blame for it—the responsible being, and only the responsible being, could have and should have known better.

The proponents of the Autonomy View were right, then (and those of the Real Self View wrong), to insist that the ability to act in accordance with one's real self is insufficient for responsibility. The ability to ensure that one's actions are really one's own, will not make one responsible unless one is oneself an appropriately special kind of being. The proponents of autonomy were wrong, though, (and those of the Real Self View right) to think that being appropriately special involves being metaphysically independent—that is, being ungoverned by anything else.

Certainly, there are some things that might govern a real self that would render it incapable of responsibility. But the problem is not *that* the real self is governed, but *by what*. A real self is incapable of responsibility if it is incapable of acting in accordance with and on the basis of the True and the Good, and this implies that a real self is incapable of responsibility if it is governed by something that prevents the agent from being able to recognize and appreciate the True and the Good. Presumably, certain traumatic experiences, bad role models, or neurological pathologies may exemplify such barriers to responsibility. But just as a real self is not responsible if it is governed by the wrong things, a real self is responsible if it is governed by the right, even if it is irresistibly governed by the right. For it may be that the reason one is able to recognize and appreciate the True and the Good is that one has been shaped, at the deepest level, by things that *make* one sensitive and responsive to good values. One has had a good moral education, perhaps, a good set of role models, and an environment that has developed in one dispositions of attention, sympathy, understanding, and sound reasoning.

In light of the above remarks, one might see the Reason View as an intermediary, though not a compromise, between the Real Self View and the Autonomy View. For the above remarks suggest a perspective from which the conditions of responsibility offered by the Real Self View are too weak, and from which the conditions offered by the Autonomy View are too strong. This shows itself in a somewhat startling way if one poses the question of how the Reason View compares to the other two alternatives with respect to the issue of whether responsibility is compatible with psychological determinism.

IV. The Asymmetry of the Reason View

The Real Self View is naturally associated with compatibilism, for one may be determined to have a particular real self and one may be determined to act in accordance with it. From the point of view of a proponent of the Real Self View, then, the fact that an agent's action is determined is always compatible with her being responsible for it. The Autonomy View, on the other hand, is naturally associated with incompatibilism, for if one is determined to act in accordance with one's values, and one's values are determined by something external to oneself, then one's choices are not independent of external forces. From the point of view of a proponent of the

Autonomy View, then, the fact that an agent's action is determined is always incompatible with her being responsible for it.

According to the Reason View, however, responsibility depends on the ability to act in accordance with the True and the Good. If one is psychologically determined to do the right thing for the right reasons, this is compatible with having the requisite ability. (Indeed, it would seem to be absolute proof that one has it.) But if one is psychologically determined to do the wrong thing, for whatever reason, this seems to constitute a denial of that ability. For if one *has* to do the wrong thing, then one *cannot* do the right, and so one lacks the ability to act in accordance with the True and the Good. The Reason View is thus committed to the curious claim that being psychologically determined to perform good actions is compatible with deserving praise for them, but that being psychologically determined to perform bad actions is not compatible with deserving blame.[5]

This claim sounds paradoxical so long as one continues to think of the problems of freedom and responsibility as purely metaphysical and nonnormative problems. For, metaphysically speaking, the person who is psychologically determined to perform a bad action may have no less control over her actions than the person who is psychologically determined to perform a good one, and the person who is determined to act rightly is no more free than the person who is determined to act wrongly. From a purely metaphysical perspective, then, it seems that either both determined agents must be responsible or neither can be. If the Reason View is right, however, then the purely metaphysical perspective common to the Real Self View and the Autonomy View is mistaken. Though the two agents we are considering may have the same amount of freedom, they have freedom to do different things, and though the two agents may have the same degree of control, their control differs with respect to its value.

If we suspend our tendency to think of responsibility as a wholly metaphysical issue and examine our intuitions regarding particular cases, the air of paradox surrounding the asymmetry between good actions and bad ones disappears. For if phrases like "I couldn't help it," "he had no choice," "she couldn't resist" typically count as excuses intended to exempt the agent from blame for an action, they do not ordinarily serve as grounds for withholding praise. "I cannot tell a lie," "he couldn't hurt a fly" are not exemptions from praiseworthiness but testimonies to it. If a friend presents you with a gift and says she "couldn't resist," this suggests the strength of her friendship and not the weakness of her will. If one feels one "has no choice" but to speak out against injustice, one ought not to be upset about the depth of one's commitment. And one has reason to be grateful if, during times of trouble, one's family "cannot help" coming to one's aid.

Of course, these phrases must be given an appropriate interpretation if they are to indicate that the agent is deserving of praise. "He couldn't hurt a fly" must allude to someone's gentleness—it would be perverse to say this of someone who was in an iron lung. It is not admirable in George Washington that he cannot tell a lie, if it is because he has a tendency to stutter that inhibits his attempts. "He could not have done otherwise" as it is used in the context of praise, then, must be taken to imply something like "because he was too good." An action is praiseworthy only if it is done for the right reasons. So it must be only in light of and because of these reasons that the praiseworthy agent "could not help" doing the right thing.

If an agent "cannot help" doing the wrong thing, however, then the agent patently lacks the ability to do the right. Perhaps she can recognize the right thing but cannot execute it—consider the kleptomaniac who does not want to steal but must. Or perhaps she can perform whatever action she thinks right, but her judgments about what is right are inevitably incorrect. Again, we can consider the victim of the deprived childhood, but also the victim of deception, or even a person raised in a society in which false values are too effectively reinforced. Whatever the explanation that prevents the agent from being able to do the right thing for the right reasons, our intuitions seem to support the claim that the agent does not deserve blame. If an agent is incapable of doing the right thing for the right reasons, then it is not her fault that she stumbles into doing something wrong.

V. The Reason View Applied

Let us look more closely at the implications of the Reason View for specific cases. Let us see what the claim that an agent is responsible—if and only if the agent can do the right thing for the right reasons entails.

We have already seen that it does not entail that the agent have the unconditional ability to do otherwise. For it is possible that the agent who can do the right thing for the right reasons cannot do anything *but* that. In particular, an agent's vision may be so clear that she cannot help seeing which action is "the right thing" and her virtue may be so sure that, knowing which action is right, she cannot help performing it. It is important to stress, though, that the agent who can do the right thing for the right reasons need not be like the agent just characterized. A person who does the right thing for the right reasons may be perfectly capable of doing something else. Moreover, an agent who actually does something else may yet have been capable of acting rightly. According to the Reason View, all three types of agents would be responsible beings, since it is only the ability to do the right thing for the right reasons, and not its inevitable exercise, that is required for responsibility.

With regard to agents who do the right thing and do so for the right reasons, then, the Reason View claims that it makes no difference whether they could have done anything else. In this respect, the Reason View is different from and more plausible than the Autonomy View. To see this, consider the cases of two lifesavers: Two persons, of equal swimming ability, stand on equally uncrowded beaches. Each sees an unknown child struggling in the water in the distance. Each thinks "The child needs my help" and directly swims out to save him. In each case, we assume that the agent reasons correctly—the child does need her help—and that, in swimming out to save him, the agent does the right thing. We further assume that in one of these cases, the agent has the ability to do otherwise, and in the other case not. According to the Autonomy View, only the first of these agents is then responsible. But it may be that the second agent lacks the ability to do otherwise simply because her understanding of the situation is so good and her moral commitment so strong. And even if this is not the explanation—if, in particular, the difference between the two agents is a metaphysical fact with no psychological implications—this hardly seems grounds for withholding praise from the second agent while giving it to the first. For there seems to be nothing of value that the first agent has but the second agent lacks. Both examples are examples of agents' thinking and doing exactly what we want agents to think and to do. Just as it would be absurd for the strength of one's commitment to exclude one from praiseworthiness, so would it be absurd to insist, for example, that one's moral character be perfect. Neither the fact that one is determined to do the right thing for the right reasons nor the fact that one is not so determined make one any less praiseworthy, so long as one actually does the right thing, and does it for the right reasons.

We must remember, however, that "doing the right thing for the right reasons" names a much narrower category than simply "doing the right thing." Only if a person acts for the right reasons does she deserve praise, and only if she is capable of so acting is she a responsible being. We all have our favorite examples of the person who helps others out of self-interested motives—the shopkeeper who gives children correct change because the policy is good for business, the philanthropist who gives away millions in order to impress her friends or to write it off on her taxes. But for the purpose of understanding the problem of responsibility, it is more illuminating to focus on a gap between "doing the right thing" and "doing it for the right reasons" that is less commonly noticed. In addition to the contrast between the agent who acts out of unselfish or moral motives and the agent who acts out of selfish or amoral ones, we should attend to the difference between the agent who is governed by intelligent and perceptive reasons and the agent who is governed by unintelligent or neurotic ones.

A person may, for example, act according to a good moral precept without ever having stopped to think whether or why it is good. Much of the time we simply do whatever our family or friends do, whatever our society

218 • *Susan Wolf*

encourages. If our familial and social circles happen to have good patterns of behavior, then our behavior will be good as well. We do the right thing, in these cases, not for the wrong reasons, but not for the right reasons either. Rather, we do it unthinkingly, blindly, by rote.

A different sort of case arises when a person's appreciation of one virtue is out of proportion to her appreciation of others. A person can get "hung up" on honesty, or be obsessed by the need to be generous or courageous. People sometimes take the value of loyalty too far; others, focusing too narrowly on the importance of impartiality, may not take loyalty far enough. When a person's devotion to a virtue is obsessive, her exhibitions of that virtue may not deserve praise. Thus, we may distinguish between a healthy form of patriotism and an unhealthy one. Either form may motivate the same desirable act, but we may think that the healthy patriot acts for the right reason and that the unhealthy patriot does not.

The importance of emphasizing the narrow scope of doing the right thing for the right reasons lies not in preventing the possibility of being too generous with one's praise but in avoiding the danger of being too lenient about the conditions of responsibility. For, according to the Reason View, the agent who does the right thing for the right reasons is responsible even if she cannot help doing that. It is important to see, then, that the person who cannot help doing the right thing for the right reasons is not the same person as the one who cannot help doing the right thing because everyone else in her society does it, nor is she the same as the person who cannot help doing the right thing because she has some sort of morality complex.

To return to examples, let us consider the woman who buys a gift for her friend claiming that she could not resist. Walking past a shop window, she sees a book that she knows her friend has been searching for for ages. It is only ten dollars, and so, imagining the delight on her friend's face when she delivers the book, she walks into the shop and buys it. Now there is nothing in this story that tells us whether the woman could have refrained from buying the book, and when she says to her friend, "I couldn't resist," there is no reason to think that she means this phrase literally. After all, the woman didn't *try* to resist—how should she know whether she could have? Still, according to the Reason View, even if the woman's remark, taken literally, were true, this would not prevent her from being a responsible agent. Assuming that she did the right thing for the right reasons (in this case, it would be more natural to say "assuming that she acted well, on noble motives"), the woman was responsible, and so deserves praise for her act of generosity whether she literally could have resisted performing it or not.

But to assume that she did the right thing for the right reasons is to assume quite a lot. It implies not only that she acted for her friend's sake and not for her own but also that her interest in her friend was healthy and in sound proportion to her interest in other people and things. In this context, the claim that the woman could not resist does not mean that the woman would have bought her friend the book no matter how much it cost or no matter how much she may have needed the money for other purposes. The assumption that she acted for the right reasons actually excludes these possibilities, for it implies that she acted out of a reasonable and desirable generosity and not out of an obsessive or foolish one. The claim that the agent could not have helped doing the right thing for the right reasons, then, actually implies that if the situation had been relevantly different, the agent could have done something else.

According to the Reason View, the praiseworthiness of the agent depends on her doing the right thing, and on her doing it for the right reasons. In other words, her praiseworthiness depends on her act's being an exhibition of her ability to govern her actions in accordance with the True and the Good. Moreover, this is all her praiseworthiness depends on. Once we know that her act was one of admirable generosity in the context of a healthy and rewarding form of friendship, we know all we need to know to justify our praise. The answer to the question of whether she could have been a less generous friend simply does not matter.

If, on the other hand, the woman had not bought the book and had thus acted in a disappointingly ungenerous manner, then the question of whether she could have been a more generous friend would matter. For it may be that the woman was twenty minutes late for an important appointment at the time she passed the bookstore. Or perhaps she was too distracted by thoughts of her job or her children or the Middle East situation to notice the titles of books in the shop window. Less obviously, she may have been able to notice the titles of books, but her preoccupations may have prevented her from connecting the relevant title with her friend. If, for any of these reasons, the woman could not have performed the generous act, then she may not be responsible for her failure.

VI. Blameworthiness According to the Reason View

So far the implications of the Reason View for specific cases seem to match the conclusion of the Real Self View. For whenever the agent is able to do the right thing for the right reasons, she is also able to act in accordance with her values, and so express her real self. (If she has the right reasons, they are presumed to be among her values.) And the examples above would suggest that whenever an agent is not able to do the right thing for the right reasons, she is also not able to act in accordance with her values. Another example, however, will bring out the difference between the Reason View and the Real Self View.

Imagine that the woman did not and could not have stopped to buy the book for her friend, but that the explanation for this does not lie in the distractions or the demands of her immediate circumstances. Rather, imagine that the explanation has to do with the woman's personality and the history of her social development. Perhaps she is too self-centered for the thought "My friend would like this book" to occur to her, or perhaps she is so unfamiliar with examples of sincere, noninstrumental friendships that the thought "I should buy this book, just to make my friend happy" cannot help appearing irrational to her. Assuming that the person does not mind being the kind of person she is—she thinks it is quite a reasonable, perhaps the only reasonable way to be—then, in not buying the book, she acts in accordance with her values and expresses her real self. According to the Real Self View, this person is responsible for her failure in friendship. According to the Reason View, however, she is not. For by hypothesis the person in question is *unable* to have different and better values—she is unable to change her real self in accordance with the True and the Good. With respect to the difference between the Real Self View and the Reason View in this case, the Reason View seems more plausible. For what we are here imagining is a person incapable of friendship, and it seems obvious that a person incapable of friendship is to be pitied rather than blamed.

Of course, the question of whether a person is truly incapable of friendship, or, for that matter, incapable of good temper, punctuality, or any other socially desirable trait, is apt to be controversial. The fact that a person *is* consistently self-centered does not imply that she *has* to be. Yet, according to the Reason View, an agent's responsibility turns on the truth or falsity of the latter claim. A person who acts badly, whether routinely or in an individual case, deserves blame for doing so if that person is capable of understanding that she acts badly and is able to use this understanding to act differently. A person who acts badly does not deserve blame if she is not in a position to understand that her action is bad, or if, understanding it to be bad, she remains unable to govern her actions accordingly. But it is hard to know whether a person who acts badly could have acted less badly, particularly if her action fits a consistent pattern of behavior. How are we to decide whether a person regularly fails to exercise an ability to reason and act better than she does or whether she simply lacks the ability altogether?

Typically, we base such decisions on evidence involving a more thorough knowledge of the individual or on comparisons between that individual and others who seem relevantly similar. If persons with a similar history all fail to develop a particular desirable trait, we tend to conclude that their history renders them incapable of developing it. If, on the other hand, some persons develop well while others develop badly and no apparently relevant differences are found in the heredities and environments of the two groups, then we are likely to conclude that the persons in question all have the ability to act well, but that some of them exercise this ability and others do not.

It is misleading to speak as if our judgments about persons' abilities to do things are an all-or-nothing matter. We are more likely to judge that it would be very unlikely for a person of a certain background to develop a certain trait than we are to judge that it would be literally impossible for that to happen. Though one may interpret this to mean that it is statistically improbable that such a person will have the all-or-nothing ability to develop that way, more often, I think, it expresses the view that it would be difficult for such a person to develop that way. We might even say that such a person is *less* able to develop that way than others, meaning that it would take more ingenuity or effort on her part. It is not unnatural that we make such judgments, given the statistical nature of our evidence. Since a larger percentage of people quit smoking than break heroin addictions, we conclude that heroin addiction is stronger, that is, more difficult to break, than nicotine addiction. Accordingly, we blame smokers for continuing to smoke (insofar as we are inclined to blame them) more strongly than we blame heroin addicts for continuing to be addicts.

The Reason View can easily accommodate the notion that ability is a matter of degree. If we think that some people are less able than others to act in accordance with the True and the Good, then the Reason View allows, as do our intuitions, that they will be less responsible, and so less blameworthy for failing to so act. It may be pointed out, however, that our evidence for these judgments if far from perfect. Most of the time we judge whether persons are able to do things on the basis of very small and unscientific comparative samples. And even if we observed a large number of people with similar backgrounds none of whom exhibited a particular character trait, this would not prove beyond a shadow of a doubt that they were all unable to develop that trait. Conversely, even if nine people out of ten quit smoking when they embarked on a particular program, that would not prove that the remaining ten percent could have stopped smoking but didn't. The conclusion to be drawn from this is that many of the judgments we make about whether people could have done things that they failed to do are uncertain, and so attributions about responsibility that rely on such judgments must be uncertain as well. Since, according to the Reason View, responsibility for bad action does depend on such judgments, the Reason View implies that we are not always in a position to know whether an agent is responsible and blameworthy. But this does not detract from the Reason View, for the view does not attempt to provide us with a way of knowing whether a person is responsible for an act. It only tells us what we would need to know if we wanted to discover this fact.

What we need to know in general is, to repeat, that the agent is able to do the right thing for the right reasons, that is, that the agent is able to act in accordance with the True and the Good. This ability may be roughly analyzed into two narrower abilities. The first is an ability of thought, the ability to *know* what is in accordance with the True and the Good; the second is an ability of execution, the ability to convert one's knowledge into action. With respect to a bad-acting agent, then, we need to know whether she could have known better and whether, knowing better, she could have acted better. The bad-acting agent, if she is responsible, must have been *able* to do both these things. Since she failed to do at least one of them, she must be guilty of at least one of two types of moral failure.

A person who is able to know, but fails to know, what is in accordance with the True and the Good is guilty of a kind of negligence, a certain laziness of the mind. A person who fails to ask herself whether it is all right to work for a nuclear arms manufacturer or who simply does not think about whether a portion of her salary ought to be given to charity might exemplify a failure of this kind. Exhibitions of thoughtlessness, carelessness, or inconsiderate behavior might also be forms of this type of fault. One simply forgets one's grandmother's birthday. The thought that at this time of night one's upstairs neighbors might be disturbed by the volume of one's stereo just does not cross one's mind. These failures are culpable only if the agents in question did not have to fail—if the agents, in other words, could have raised the right questions and could have come to the right conclusions, if they could have had the thoughts that they did not actually have. But given certain assumptions about the agents' cognitive abilities, past experiences, and present circumstances, this conclusion does not seem unreasonable. Consider, for example, a person of average intelligence and perceptiveness, who has been exposed to moral questioning and argument, and who occasionally receives solicitations from Oxfam, Amnesty International, and the like. Assuming that she is not overwhelmed by personal troubles, that she is not misinformed about these organizations' effectiveness, and so on, what reason is there to think that the person is not able to raise the question of charity on her own?[6]

Just as a person may be capable of knowing the right thing to do but fail to know it nonetheless, a person who knows the right thing to do may be capable of doing it but fail to do it nonetheless. This would be a failure of execution that is a form of weakness of the will. It is as easy to imagine this type of failure as it is to imagine the former type. One knows that one ought to visit one's friend in the hospital, but one goes to the movies instead. One knows that one ought to point out that the waitress has undercharged one, but it is easy to be silent and pay the smaller bill. Again, the agents in question will be culpable only if they could have acted on their knowledge. But again, assuming that transportation to the hospital is no less convenient than transportation to the movies, that the diner is not mute nor the waitress deaf, that neither agent is driven by neurotic compulsion or dire need—what reason is there for thinking that the agents could not have acted as they knew best?

Philosophical questions remain about the justification and meaning of the claim that an agent who actually does one thing could unconditionally be doing another. In ordinary discourse, however, we make and assume claims of this sort all the time, and it does not seem implausible that our judgments about responsibility should rely on them.

VII. The Unity and Spirit of the Reason View

According to the Reason View, our judgments about the responsibility of bad-acting agents do rely on claims of this sort. In this respect, I have argued, the Reason View is more plausible than the Real Self View. But the Reason View also denies that judgments about the responsibility of good-acting agents rely on claims of this sort. In this respect, I have argued, the Reason View is more plausible than the Autonomy View. Our intuitions about blame, both in general and with respect to individual cases, accord better with the Reason View than with the Real Self View. Our intuitions about praise, both in general and with respect to individual cases, accord better with the Reason View than with the Autonomy View. Thus, the Reason View seems to accord with and account for the whole set of our intuitions about responsibility better than either of the leading alternatives.

To draw this conclusion from these premises, however, is open to objection. For this inference assumes that the whole set of our intuitions about responsibility consists in the union of our intuitions about praise and our intuitions about blame. Against this assumption, it may be pointed out first that we think of responsibility as more unified than that—we understand responsibility to be a single feature of agents that makes them suitable objects of either praise or blame. Second, it may be noted that our concern with the issue of responsibility is not wholly tied to its connection with praise and blame. Our lives are not exclusively devoted to amassing credit and avoiding discredit, after all, and the goal of trying to make something of oneself, or even of trying to live above reproach, is hardly the highest goal on everyone's list. Though some people may want to be free and responsible beings because they want to be subject to deep evaluations, others may care about freedom and responsibility for what seem to be totally independent reasons. In particular, some may be concerned simply with their ability to govern their own actions, their ability to choose for themselves what to be and how to live. When we concentrate on this aspect of our interest in freedom and responsibility, the Reason View, with its emphasis on our connection to the True and the Good, may seem beside the point.

A further examination of the Reason View, however, yields answers to these objections. To the first objection, that the Reason View offers a segmented rather than a unified account of the concept of responsibility, we may reply that the appearance of disunity is an illusion, generated by the persistent tendency to see the problem of responsibility in fundamentally metaphysical terms and by the need to defend the view by comparing it to alternatives that encourage this tendency. From this purely metaphysical perspective, one may get the impression that the Reason View offers one set of conditions for being responsible for a good or desirable act and another set of conditions for being responsible for a bad or undesirable one. But in fact the Reason View proposes a single set of conditions for responsibility for any type of act: namely, that, at the time of performance, the agent possesses the ability to act in accordance with the True and the Good.[7] Whether the agent has this ability, and so whether the agent is responsible, is presumably independent of and prior to the question of whether she exercises it. The possession of this single and unified ability, then, underlies the agent's susceptibility to either praise or blame. If she deserves praise, it is for the exercise of her ability to act in accordance with the True and the Good. If she deserves blame, it is for the fact that she acted badly despite her ability to know and to do something better.

Indeed, the ability to act in accordance with the True and the Good is one the agent can be said to have or to lack at any time, including those times when the agent is doing nothing that one would want either to praise or to blame. Thus, the question of whether an agent is responsible for her actions can be answered even when the justification of praise or blame is not at issue. This is as it should be, since much of the time our actions are neither good nor bad and yet it seems intelligible to wonder whether we are responsible for them. I might wonder, for example, whether it is really up to me, in the relevant sense, to drink coffee, to exhibit a fondness for purple, to spend so much time doing philosophy. According to the Reason View, it is up to me if my decisions to do these things are made in the light of my knowledge or of my access to knowledge of the (true and good) reasons for doing and not doing them (assuming as well that my doing these things is dependent on my decisions to do them). For example, I am responsible for drinking coffee if in deciding whether to drink it, I am in a position to know, appreciate, and act on the reasons for and against drinking it. If, on the other hand, I am not in such a position—if perhaps I am hypnotized to drink coffee, or deceived about what is in my cup—then I am not responsible for drinking it.

This still leaves the second objection, however; that the conception of responsibility implicit in the Reason View is too exclusively tied to the issue of susceptibility to praise and blame to explain the various types of importance our status as responsible beings may have for us. According to the

Reason View, being responsible consists in being able to act in accordance with Reason, that is, in being able to do the right thing for the right reasons, that is, in being able to be and do good. But if that were what responsibility consisted in, the objection goes, it would seem that our only reason for caring about responsibility would be that we care more fundamentally about being rational and good. In fact, however, there are many people who do not care (much) about being rational and good, who, it is intelligible to suppose, may still care about being responsible beings. They may not care about whether their lives are good or bad or whether their conduct deserves praise or blame and yet be concerned that, whatever their lives are, they are that way by their own choice. It is not obvious that the ability to act in accordance with the True and the Good is necessary in order for one's life to be governable by one's choice. Indeed, it is not obvious that these two properties are even related.

But they *are* related. For when one speaks of the desire to make one's own choice, one implicitly assumes that one knows what one is choosing between. If people had to select their spouses or careers by picking names out of a hat, it would be a cruel joke to say they were choosing them for themselves. One wants to choose with one's eyes open, so to speak. Choosing blindly would not satisfy one's desire at all. In other words, one wants to be able to choose in light of the knowledge of one's options and in light of the comparative reasons for and against these options. To want this, however, is just to want to choose in light of the True and the Good.

It may be noted that wanting to choose *in light of* the True and the Good does not commit one to wanting to choose *in accordance with* the True and the Good. One might, I suppose, fully recognize that one action would be better and yet choose to perform another. But even if a person did not want or care about acting in accordance with the True and the Good, she would still have to want the ability to so act if she cared about governing her own actions. For, as mentioned earlier, the ability to act in accordance with the True and the Good is composed of the ability to know the True and the Good, that is, to form one's values and plans in light of them, and the ability to convert one's values and plans into action. If one lacked the first component, the choices one made would be blind. If one lacked the second, one's choices would be ineffective.

One might initially attempt to describe the freedom necessary for responsibility as the freedom to do whatever one wants or, alternatively, as the freedom to do whatever one chooses. When it is pointed out that this allows the possibility that one's wants or choices be themselves externally determined, one may revise one's original description by adding that one also needs the freedom to want whatever one wants to want[8] or, alternatively, the freedom to choose whatever one chooses to choose. Clearly, this attempt at revision will only lead to an infinitely embedded condition that cannot ultimately succeed. Yet some revision is certainly necessary. Implicit in the Reason View is the recognition that the freedom that is necessary in addition to the freedom to do whatever one wants or chooses is the freedom that one's wants and choices be freely formed, formed, that is, in the absence of delusion and compulsion, and in the presence of Reason and (metaphorical) light. The freedom necessary for responsibility, then, is not just the freedom that allows one's actions to be governed by one's reasons, but also a freedom that allows one's reasons to be governed by what reasons there are.

Our desire to be responsible for our actions is a desire for our actions to be our own, for our responses to the world to be of our own making. It is not, however, a desire that the world itself be of our own making. The freedom necessary for responsibility is a freedom *within* the world, not a freedom *from* it. The Reason View recognizes that freedom within the world requires the ability to see and appreciate the world for what it is.

Notes

1. I have in mind the possibility that in extreme cases, involving, for example, self-destructiveness or extraordinary evil, the ability to act in discord once with Reason may indicate some form of insanity.

2. This way of putting it is misleading insofar as it implicitly suggests that there will always be a *single* uniquely rational option. For stylistic purposes, I shall talk in this essay of "the"option to act in accordance with Reason, but it should be understood that when I say that someone has that option, I mean that she has *at least* one option to act in accordance with Reason and that she has that option because she recognizes it (at least) to be in accordance with Reason.

3. I have in mind the notion of immanent causation, also known as agent-causality, discussed, for example, by Roderick Chisholm.

4. The term is taken from Robert Nozick, *Philosophical Explanations* (Cambridge: Harvard University Press, 1981).

5. This point might also be made in terms of the Reason View's analysis of the phrase "he could have done otherwise" when that phrase is used to express the condition of freedom required for responsibility. For more on this see my "Asymmetrical Freedom," *Journal of Philosophy* 77 (March 1980): 151–66. (Portions of this essay are from that article.)

6. The question of whether a belief in neurophysiological or, for that matter, divine determinism might constitute a reason is discussed in Chapter 5 of my *Freedom Within Reason*.

7. I here leave aside questions about people who cannot help doing the wrong thing at the time of performance, but who could have kept themselves from getting into that position at some earlier time.

8. This is the suggestion of Harry Frankfurt in "Freedom of the Will and the Concept of a Person," *Journal of Philosophy* 68 (January 1971): 5–20.

13

Libertarianism and Frankfurt's Attack on the Principle of Alternative Possibilities

DAVID WIDERKER

Harry Frankfurt's well-known attack (Frankfurt 1969) on the principle of alternative possibilities,

(PAP) A person is morally responsible for performing a given act A only if he could have acted otherwise,

has received considerable attention in recent philosophical literature. Except for a few dissenters, it has on the whole gone unchallenged.[1] In this paper, I wish to take a fresh look at Frankfurt's attack on PAP from a libertarian viewpoint. I shall try to show that it does not succeed when applied to mental acts such as deciding, choosing, undertaking, forming an intention, that is, mental acts that for the libertarian constitute the basic *loci* of moral responsibility. If correct, this result will enable us to formulate a necessary condition for moral responsibility that is more adequate than PAP and not vulnerable to Frankfurt's criticism.

From *Philosophical Review* 104 (1995). Copyright 1995 Cornell University. Reprinted by permission of the publisher and the author.

At the outset, let me state a number of assumptions that I shall employ in the discussion to follow. First, the version of libertarianism I intend to defend is the view that an agent's decision (choice) is free in the sense of freedom required for moral responsibility only if (i) it is not causally determined, and (ii) in the circumstances in which the agent made that decision (choice), he could have avoided making it.[2] Second, I take 'a given act A' in PAP to refer to an action such that the agent was aware, at the time, that he was performing it (or was trying to perform it) and with regard to which he believed that he could have done otherwise.[3] Third, I shall adopt a fine-grained account of action individuation,[4] and shall thus treat 'A' in PAP as a variable for actions themselves, rather than actions under A-descriptions. I believe, however, that the conclusions I reach will also be acceptable, *mutatis mutandi*, to someone who individuates actions coarsely, such as, for example, Davidson.

I.

Frankfurt develops his attack on PAP in two steps. He first argues for the following thesis:

(IRR) There may be circumstances in which a person performs some action which although they make it impossible for him to avoid performing that action, they in no way bring it about that he performs it. (Frankfurt 1969, 830, 837)

Then he claims that an agent who was in a situation of the sort described in IRR (henceforth "IRR-situation") cannot in order to absolve himself of moral responsibility claim that he acted in circumstances that left him no alternative to doing what he did. For, by hypothesis, these circumstances had nothing to do with what he did. He would have acted the same even if those circumstances had not obtained. Hence, PAP is false (ibid., 836–37).

As we can see, the success of Frankfurt's case against PAP depends crucially upon his ability to convince us of the plausibility of IRR. It is, therefore, important to see whether he succeeds in this endeavor. To establish IRR, Frankfurt asks us to consider the following situation, which, he claims, is an example of an IRR-situation.

Suppose someone—Black, let us say—wants Jones to perform a certain action. Black is prepared to go to considerable lengths to get his way, but he prefers to avoid showing his hand unnecessarily. So he waits until Jones is about to make up his mind what to do, and he does nothing unless it is clear to him (Black is an excellent judge of such things) that Jones is going to decide something other than what he wants him to do. If it does become clear that Jones is going to decide something else, Black takes effective steps to ensure that Jones decides to do, and that he does do, what he wants him to do. Whatever Jones's initial preferences and inclinations, then, Black will have his way ... Now, suppose that Black never has to show his hand because Jones, for reasons of his own, decides to perform and does perform the very action Black wants him to perform. (ibid., 835)

To better grasp the scenario Frankfurt wishes us to consider, let us describe it in more concrete terms. Let us suppose that Jones is deliberating about whether to kill a certain person Smith at time t3. Suppose further that, unbeknownst to Jones, there is another person Black who for some reason wants it to be the case that Jones decides at t2 to kill Smith and then carries out this decision. Although Black can force Jones to act in the way he wants him to act, he prefers not to show his hand unnecessarily. Black can be sure that he will have his way in view of his knowing the following facts about Jones and himself:

(1) If Jones is blushing at t1, then, provided no one intervenes, Jones will decide at t2 to kill Smith.

(2) If Jones is not blushing at t1, then, provided no one intervenes, he will not decide at t2 to kill Smith.

(3) If Black sees that Jones shows signs that he will not decide at t2 to kill Smith, that is, sees that Jones is *not* blushing at t1, then Black forces Jones to decide at t2 to kill Smith; but if he sees that he is blushing at t1, then he does nothing.

Finally, suppose that Black does not have to show his hand, because

(4) Jones is blushing at t1, and decides at t2 to kill Smith for reasons of his own.

Given that the action in question is Jones's decision to kill Smith, has Frankfurt given us an example of an IRR-situation? Or to put it more precisely, has he succeeded in describing a situation in which a decision for which an agent is morally responsible is such that, though there is no causally sufficient condition for its occurrence, it nevertheless is unavoidable? If he has, then he has refuted libertarianism. For he will have shown that, contrary to what is implied by that position, a decision can be free in the sense of freedom pertinent to moral responsibility without being avoidable. Consequently, he will also have refuted PAP as applied to decisions. I wish to claim, however, that he has not established this result. To see this, let us examine (1) more closely. Note that the truth of (1) cannot be grounded in the fact that Jones's blushing at t1 is, in the circumstances, causally sufficient for his decision to kill Smith, or in the fact that it is indicative of a state that is causally sufficient for that decision, since such an assumption would be neither in accordance with IRR nor accepted by the libertarian. On the other hand, if (1) is not thus grounded, then the following two options are available to the libertarian to resist the contention that Jones's decision to kill Smith is unavoidable. He may either reject (1), claiming that the most that he would be prepared to allow is

(1a) If Jones is blushing at t1, then Jones will *probably* decide at t2 to kill Smith. (Adams 1977, 111)

But (1a) is compatible with Jones's having the power to decide not to kill Smith, since there is the possibility of Jones's acting out of character. Or the libertarian may construe (1) as a conditional of freedom in Plantinga's sense (Plantinga 1974, chap. 9), that is, as

(1b) If Jones is blushing at t1, then Jones will *freely* decide at t2 to kill Smith,[5]

in which case the libertarian may again claim that in the actual situation when Jones is blushing at t1, it is within his power to refrain from deciding to kill Smith at t2. To be sure, as things turned out Jones did not exercise that power, but this fact is irrelevant, claims the libertarian. Thus, in either case, Jones's power *not* to decide to kill Smith is preserved, and hence again we have not been given an example of an IRR-situation.

That Frankurt has failed to give us an example of an IRR-situation for decisions can be argued for in another way. We know that if Jones were *not* to blush at t1, then he would be forced to decide at t2 to kill Smith. But this fact by itself does not imply that in the actual scenario, where he was blushing at t1, Jones did not have it within his power at t1 to refrain from deciding to kill Smith. After all, he could have exercised this power immediately after blushing at t1. *Nothing* in the assumptions cited above rules out this possibility.[6] To put it in terms of possible worlds, nothing in the assumptions cited above rules out the possibility that the causally possible worlds, relative to t1, in which Jones can be said to exercise his power of not deciding at t2 to kill Smith are such that in some of them he is blushing at t1. To rule out this possibility, we must assume that Jones's *not* blushing at t1 is a causally necessary condition for his *not* deciding at t2 to kill Smith. But this means that his blushing at t1 is causally sufficient for his decision to kill Smith. For if p is a causally necessary condition for q, then the absence of p is a causally sufficient condition for the absence of q. But if so, then, as argued above, what we have is not an IRR-situation.[7]

My strategy, then, of resisting Frankfurt's argument for IRR is to put before Frankfurt the following dilemma: Either the truth of (1) is grounded in some fact that is causally sufficient (in the circumstances) for Jones's decision at t2 to kill Smith, or it is not. If it is, then the situation described by Frankfurt is not an IRR-situation, since the factor that makes it impossible for Jones to avoid his decision to kill Smith *does* bring about that decision. On the other hand, if the truth of (1) is not thus grounded, it is hard to see how Jones's decision is unavoidable.[8] In either case the truth of IRR has not been established. In view of these considerations, I conclude that Frankfurt's attack on PAP as applied to decisions fails.

At this point a defender of Frankfurt might make the following move. First, he might ask us to consider a situation in which the sign that Black uses as an indication of whether Jones is going to decide to kill Smith is Jones's inclination to act so.[9] (If immediately after the deliberation process, Jones shows an inclination to decide to kill Smith, Black does nothing. On the other hand, if Jones shows an inclination to the contrary, Black intervenes and forces Jones to decide to kill Smith.) He might then claim that my rebuttal of Frankfurt rests on a mistaken assumption as to the relation between an agent's decision to perform some act and his inclination to decide to perform it. The latter, he might claim, does not precede the decision, but is rather a part of it. That is, a decision to do A, on this view, is a temporal process that begins with an inclination to decide to do A, and is then followed by some appropriate set of mental events that taken together make up the decision. This being the case, Frankfurt's point remains intact, since the sort of dilemma that I developed earlier does not arise. Frankfurt might agree that Jones's showing an inclination to decide to kill Smith is not a causally sufficient condition of his actual decision to kill Smith, but still insist that Jones lacks the power to decide otherwise. For to be able to exercise that power, Jones would first have to show an inclination for deciding not to kill Smith. But then Black would intervene, and would force him to decide to kill Smith nevertheless.[10]

However, this attempt to rescue Frankfurt's argument is unconvincing for two reasons. First, it only pushes the debate between Frankfurt and the libertarian back one step. Instead of claiming that a free agent has it within his power to decide otherwise, the libertarian might now insist that such an agent has it within his power to form an inclination to decide otherwise. Second, and more importantly, the libertarian might reject the objector's conception of a decision. He might claim that a decision, being the forming of an intention, is a *simple* mental action[11] that does not exhibit the sort of complex structure assumed by the objector. This point, he might stress, is also borne out by our everyday talk about decisions. Thus, it would be conceptually wrong for one to describe what Jones is doing at a given moment by saying that he is in the *process* of deciding to kill Smith, or that he has not yet finished deciding to kill Smith. Jones, to be sure, can be said to be in the process of *trying to reach a decision* about whether to kill Smith. But that process and the event of deciding to kill Smith are two different things. To reject this libertarian reply, Frankfurt's defender would have to refute the conception of decision underlying it. And as long he has not done so, the libertarian position is immune to Frankfurt's attack on PAP.

II.

So far I have argued that Frankfurt's attack on the principle of alternative possibilities does not work for decisions. But how about actions other than deciding, for example, killing, stealing, voting, insulting, intentional omission such as an agent's intentionally not obeying an order, etc.? Frankfurt seems to be right in rejecting PAP when applied to this latter type of act. For example, assuming that Jones kills Smith for reasons of his own, the passive presence of a counterfactual intervener who, if he were to detect in Jones a pro-attitude or inclination not to kill Smith, would prevent Jones from acting so, would be sufficient to rob Jones of his freedom to act otherwise, without in any way forcing him to act as he actually did. What we want to understand is what accounts for this difference between the two sorts of cases. Our previous remarks on the nature of decisions suggest an answer to this question. Note that, unlike a decision, an act such as Jones's act of intentionally not killing Smith (which in this case may count as Jones's acting otherwise) is a *complex* act. It is a complex act in the sense that it requires both an intention on Jones's part not to kill Smith, as well as his being later, at t3, in the state of not killing Smith. The performance of such an act, could, therefore, be prevented by a powerful enough counterfactual intervener, who being able to detect the said intention in Jones, is in a position to prevent him from being in that state (the state of not killing Smith). The same, however, cannot be said in the case of Jones's decision to kill Smith. To act otherwise in this case, it is sufficient for Jones to decide not to kill Smith, which is a decision that Jones can make without (necessarily) having to form a *prior* intention not to decide to kill Smith, and which does not depend for its occurrence on the occurrence of any later events. Hence, the sort of way in which a counterfactual intervener can prevent an agent from acting otherwise in the case of an act like killing is not available to the intervener in the case of a decision.

This asymmetry between a complex action such as killing and the act of deciding can be also brought out by the following consideration. Suppose again that Jones kills Smith at t3, and consider what is known as the conditional analysis of 'could have done otherwise' as applied to this act, namely,

(5C) Had Jones chosen at t2 not to kill Smith at t3, he would have succeeded in doing so.

It seems intuitive to view (5C) as a necessary condition of

(5) Jones could have acted otherwise; that is, Jones could have performed the act of not killing Smith.

This fact also explains why the presence of a Frankfurt-type counterfactual intervener like Black would deprive Jones of his ability to act otherwise. His presence would render (5C) false, and consequently would also falsify (5). Note, however, that this sort of consideration would not count against Jones's ability to decide otherwise. And the reason here is not that a conditional analysis of

(6) Jones could have decided otherwise; that is, Jones could have decided at t2 *not* to kill Smith at t3

as

(6C) Had Jones chosen at t1 to decide at t2 *not* to kill Smith, he would have succeeded in doing so

would not make sense, in view of the obscurity of 'Jones chooses at t1 to decide not to perform a certain action'. (We certainly can conceive of circumstances in which such a locution would make sense. For example, a person S who is strongly inclined to kill another person X may, in order not to succumb to this temptation, choose to visit a hypnotist who is able to cause him to decide to act otherwise, and in such circumstances it would be true to say that S chose at t1 not to decide at t2 to kill X.) Rather, it is that the truth of (6C) is simply not a necessary condition of the truth of (6). One easy way to see this is to conceive of a Frankfurt-type scenario in which the counterfactual intervener is intent on preventing Jones from deciding not to kill Smith if and only if Jones chooses at t1 to so decide. In such circumstances, (6C) would be false, whereas (6) might still be true, since, as explained above, Jones need not, in order to exercise his power to decide *not* to kill Smith, *first* choose to decide not to do so. He can decide directly not to kill Smith, without having to go through any prior process of choosing.

The salient point that emerges is that insofar as the performance of a given action by an agent involves the realization of a certain want (volition) or intention of the agent by events that are distinct from that want or intention and that occur after the latter is formed, a Frankfurt-type counterfactual intervener can in principle prevent the occurrence of those

234 • David Widerker

events, and can consequently prevent the performance of the action. But we have not been given a good reason to think that the intervener can prevent the agent from forming that want (volition) or intention, provided of course that the agent believes that what he wants (wills) or intends to do is in his power. Putting this point in terms of freedom, we may say that a Frankfurt-type counterfactual intervener can deprive an agent of his *freedom to carry out* a given want or intention, but he cannot deprive him of his *freedom to form* it.

III.

If my argument so far is correct, there arises an important distinction between the following two principles:

(PAP′)   Where A is a complex act, a person is morally responsible for performing A only if he could have performed some other complex act instead of A;[12]

(PAV)   A person is morally responsible for performing a given act A only if he could have avoided performing it,

where the latter does not fall prey to Frankfurt's criticism. I have already defended PAV in the case where A is a decision, or the forming of an intention, etc. I wish now to defend it for the case where A is a complex action such as Jones's action of killing Smith, or Jack's action of stealing a book, etc. To see this, let us consider once more a situation in which at t2 Jones forms on his own an intention to kill Smith at t3, and carries it out. Assume also that lurking in the background there is Black, who, if he were to notice that Jones decided at t2 *not* to kill Smith, would intervene and force Jones to kill him. I wish to claim that though in the situation under consideration Jones cannot (at t1) prevent Smith's death, and cannot avoid exemplifying the property of killing Smith at t3, he nevertheless can avoid the performance of his *actual* act of killing Smith, or can bring about the non-occurrence of that act. My defense of this claim rests on the following two considerations: (a) I assume a version of action theory according to which Jones's act of killing Smith, a complex action, consists at least in part of an intention or volition by Jones to bring about Smith's death, where that intention or volition stands in some appropriate causal relation to the *event* of Jones's killing Smith.[13] Moreover, I assume that the said action (qua act-token), *essentially* contains that volition or intention.[14] (b) I then claim that by having the power to form at t1 the intention *not* to kill Smith, which Frankfurt's counterfactual intervener cannot prevent him from doing, Jones can prevent the occurrence of his intention to kill Smith (qua intention-token), and hence, given (a), can also be said to have the power to bring about the non-occurrence of his act of killing Smith (qua act-token).[15]

Note that the above defense of PAV differs importantly from Peter Van Inwagen's recent defense of the principle:

(PPP2)   A person is morally responsible for a certain state of affairs only if that state of affairs obtains, and he could have prevented it from obtaining. (1983, 171–75)

For one thing, his defense applies only to states of affairs that can be deemed consequences or results of acts, such as the state of affairs of Smith's being dead (ibid., 165). It does *not* apply to what Van Inwagen calls "act-universals" (which correspond to my act-tokens), such as Jones's act of killing Smith at t, or Jones's decision to kill Smith at t, with which PAV is concerned.[16] Second, Van Inwagen defends PPP2 assuming that in a Frankfurt-type setting an act-consequence, such as Smith's being dead, is unavoidable, whereas in my defense of PAV, I insist on the avoidability of Jones's act of killing Smith in such a setting.[17]

PAV brings out nicely the difference between acting otherwise and avoiding the performance of an act, stressing that the latter does not imply the former. It also enables the libertarian to give a simple explanation of why, in the case of Jones's unjustifiably killing Smith, we may hold Jones blameworthy for performing that act, even though he could not have done otherwise. He is blameworthy because he had a moral obligation not to perform this act and could have avoided performing it, but failed to do so. The fact that, in the circumstances, Jones could not have done otherwise, in the sense of not having the power to perform some other complex act instead of the killing, is irrelevant. His obligation was to avoid killing Smith, and not to do something else instead. To be sure, Jones's power to avoid the killing, as well as his responsibility for it, are grounded, for the libertarian, in the avoidability of and his responsibility for his *decision* to kill Smith. But this is as it should be, since, on his view, it is decisions and the like to which responsibility attaches in the first instance.

To sharpen the results of our investigation, it may be useful at this point to state exactly how the libertarian's position differs from Frankfurt's. The libertarian maintains that Frankfurt has not given a good reason to reject the following principles:

(PAPD)   A person is morally responsible for his *decision* (choice, undertaking) to do A only if he could have decided otherwise.

(PAV)   A person is morally responsible for performing a given act A only if he could have avoided performing it.

(PAV′)   Where V is a complex act-property (killing, voting, insulting, etc.), and t* is the exact time at which a person S Vs intentionally, S is morally responsible for his V-ing *intentionally* at t* only if it was within his power not to V intentionally at t*.

However, the libertarian agrees with Frankfurt that

(PAP′)   Where A is a complex act, a person is morally responsible for performing A only if he could have performed some other complex act instead of A

is false.[18]

Frankfurt's argument against PAP presents a formidable challenge to the libertarian conception of freedom and moral responsibility. In this paper, we have examined his argument and found that one central assumption of it, IRR, is unwarranted, because it does not hold for decisions, formings of intentions, etc.—mental acts that for the libertarian constitute the primary *lŏci* of moral responsibility. This being the case, I conclude that, contrary to much opinion, libertarians have nothing to fear from Frankfurt's attack on PAP.[19]

Notes

1. The dissenters include Davidson (1973, 149–50); Naylor (1984); Heinaman (1986, 275–76); and Lamb (1993, 522–23). Among those who agree with Frankfurt in his rejection of PAP, we may find, for example, Blumenfeld (1971, 340–41); Fischer (1982, 33–34); Fischer and Ravizza (1991, 258–59); Dennett (1984, chap. 6); Berofsky (1987, 31–33); Zimmerman (1988, 119–27); and Stump (1990, 255–56). For an extensive bibliography on Frankfurt's attack on PAP, see Fischer 1987.

2. Condition (i) is intended to rule out compatibilist construals of avoidability. A decision is not causally determined, as I use the expression, if prior to its occurrence there does not obtain a causally sufficient condition for it.

Some may want to strengthen the definition of libertarianism given in the text by also requiring that a free decision not be *logically* necessitated by a state of affairs (hard facts) obtaining prior to it. See, for example, Alston 1989, 164–65. For definitions of libertarianism that are equivalent or closely related to the one employed here, see Plantinga 1974, 165–66; Ginet 1990, 124; Van Inwagen 1983, 8, 13–14.

Note that this version of libertarianism differs from Thomas Reid's version of libertarianism in that it does not employ the notion of agent-causation. For a libertarian response to Frankfurt of a Reidean type, see Rowe 1991, 82–85.

3. Frankfurt's case against PAP would be considerably weaker without this assumption.

4. Thus, I shall treat an action as a dated particular consisting at least in part in an agent's exmplifying an act-property at a time. I use 'act-property' in Goldman's

sense, according to which an agent's having exemplified such a property does not entail that he performed an action, or that he acted intentionally (see Goldman 1970, 15–17). Although I adopt Goldman's use of 'act-property', I do not endorse his account of action.

5. The term 'freely' is used by Plantinga in the libertarian's sense.

6. Cf. Lamb 1993, 522.

7. Fischer (1982, 33) also tries to describe an IRR-situation with regard to decisions. I criticize his attempt in "Libertarianism and the Avoidability of Decisions" employing considerations similar to those that I have used above against Frankfurt. For Fischer's response, see his "Libertarianism and Avoidability".

8. Frankfurt seems to concede that to ensure that Jones's decision to kill Smith is unavoidable, the decision has to be caused by an earlier state of Jones's (Frankfurt 1969, n. 3). This is puzzling given that he undertakes to establish a thesis such as IRR.

9. The possibility that the inclination to make a certain decision can be used as a sign of that decision is suggested by Fischer (see Fischer 1982, 26).

10. This possible line of defense, along with the refutation that follows it, is also mentioned in my "Libertarianism and the Avoidability of Decisions."

11. I am borrowing 'simple mental action' from Ginet 1990, chap. 1.

12. Alternatively, this principle might be formulated as follows:

(PAP′) Where A is a complex act, a person S is morally responsible for performing A only if it was within S's power to perform some complex act other than A, and not to perform A.

13. For "component" conceptions of action of this type, see, for example, Searle 1983, 84–93; McCann 1974; and Costa 1987. The intention in question might be an "intention in action" in Searle's sense or a "proximal intention" in Mele's sense. See Mele 1992a, 208–9 and Mele 1992b, chap. 9–10.

14. Strictly speaking, there is a further essentialist assumption that I need to make, which is that the exact time at which an event occurs is essential to it. For an interesting defense of this assumption, see Lombard 1982.

15. Note also that a further consideration in favor of PAV is that the part of it that deals with moral blame

(PAV1) A person S is morally blameworthy for performing a given act A only if S could have avoided performing A

is entailed by the following two principles, which seem intuitively correct:

(MB) A person S is morally blameworthy for performing a given act A only if S has a moral obligation *not* to perform A.

(K) A person S has a moral obligation [not] to perform a given act A only if it was within S's power *not* to perform A.

In this connection, see Widerker 1991, 222–24, and Widerker and Katzoff 1993, 102–4.

16. In his 1978 (220–21), Van Inwagen expresses serious doubts whether his defense of PPP2 could be applied to defend what he calls "the Principle of Alternate Possibilities for act-universals," namely

(PAP2) A person S is morally responsible for a certain act-universal only if that act-universal obtains, and S could have prevented it from obtaining.

17. Note also that my defense of PAV is also not vulnerable to John Fischer's recent criticism (1982, 29–30) of

(PPP1) A person is morally responsible for a certain event-particular only if he could have prevented it.

Fischer takes the defender of PPP1 to be (i) assuming

(E)   If an event x is the product of some causes, then it is essentially the product of those causes,

and then (ii) arguing that PPP1 is not falsified by a Frankfurt-type counterexample to PAP. The alleged reason for this is that in the alternate scenario in which Jones is forced by Black or by some other factor to kill Smith, Jones's *actual* act of killing Smith does not occur, since *it* has a different causal history than Jones's act of killing Smith in that scenario. Hence, Jones's power to prevent his actual act of killing Smith (qua act-token) is not threatened. Aside from finding (E) problematic, Fischer charges the proponent of this defense of PPP1 with confusing the idea of Jones's having the power to prevent his act of killing Smith with the logical possibility of that act's not occurring. Note, however, that his criticism of the above defense of PPP1 is based on the assumption that in the alternative scenario in which Jones is forced by Black or by some other factor to kill Smith (Fischer talks about a mechanism installed in Jones's brain which does this task) Jones *never* succeeds in making the decision *not* to kill Smith. As Fischer sees it, in that scenario Jones is merely inclined towards making that decision, and is then forced by Black to decide to kill Smith nevertheless and to kill him. This assumption is not true in the case of my defense of PAV. For, as I explicitly argue, in the alternate scenario that I am envisaging, Jones *does* succeed in making that decision, and hence does succeed in forming an intention *not* to kill Smith, in which case he can properly be said to have the power to prevent his actual act of killing Smith. Now it is true that in that scenario, immediately after having formed the intention *not* to kill Smith, Jones may be forced by Black to form the contrary intention, and then to act on it. But this would be a different intention from the one he actually formed, and a different act from the one he actually performed. On this point see also note 14.

18. As for Jones's reponsibility for the event of Smith's dying, the libertarian I am representing has a choice. He may adopt Van Inwagen's view that Jones is not morally responsible for this event ("event-universal" in Van Inwagen's terms), since

(a)   no person x is responsible for the obtaining of a state of affairs that would have obtained no matter what choices or decisions x had made (Van Inwagen 1983, 171–80).

Or he may regard Jones as being indirectly or derivatively responsible for the said event by virtue of being responsible for the decision that led to it. For accounts of indirect or derivative responsibility, see Berofsky 1987, 35, and Zimmerman 1988, 55–57. Similar remarks would apply to Jones's responsibility for his exemplifying the act-property of killing Smith at t3. Ginet (unpublished manuscript) has recently argued that Van Inwagen's thesis (a) needs to be modified as follows: If a certain state of affairs would have obtained no matter what choices or decisions x had made *that x could have made,* then x is not responsible for it.

19. I would like to thank Eddy Zemach, William Alston, Charlotte Katzoff, Brian Shanley, and, most especially, Dale Gottlieb, Carl Ginet, William Rowe, and Elmar Kremer for excellent discussions and comments on earlier versions of this paper. I have also benefited from the comments of the referees for the *Philosophical Review.*

References

Adams, R. 1977. "Middle Knowledge and the Problem of Evil." *American Philosophical Quarterly* 14:109–17.

Alston, William P. 1989. *Divine and Human Language.* Ithaca: Cornell University Press.

Berofsky, B. 1987. *Freedom from Necessity.* London: Routledge and Kegan Paul.

Blumenfeld, D. 1971. "The Principle of Alternate Possibilities." *Journal of Philosophy* 67:339–45.

Costa, M. 1987. "Causal Theories of Action." *Canadian Journal of Philosophy* 17:831–54.

Davidson, D. 1973. "Freedom to Act." In *Essays on Freedom of Action,* ed. Ted Hondrich. London: Routledge and Kegan Paul.

Dennett, D. 1984. *Elbow Room: Varieties of Free Will Worth Wanting.* Cambridge: MIT Press.

Fischer, J. M. 1982. "Responsibility and Control." *Journal of Philosophy* 89: 24–40.

———. 1995. "Libertarianism and Avoidability: A Reply to Widerker," *Faith and Philosophy* 12: 119–125.

———, ed. 1987. *Moral Responsibility.* Ithaca: Cornell University Press.

Fischer, J. M., and M. Ravizza. 1991. "Responsibility and Inevitability." *Ethics* 101:258–78.

Frankfurt, H. 1969. "Alternate Possibilities and Moral Responsibility." *Journal of Philosophy* 66:829–39.

Ginet, C. 1990. *On Action.* Cambridge: Cambridge University Press.

———. Comments on Van Inwagen, "Ability and Responsibility." Unpublished manuscript.

Goldman, A. 1970. *A Theory of Human Action.* Englewood Cliffs, N.J.: Prentice Hall.

Heinaman, R. 1986. "Incompatibilism without the Principle of Alternative Possibilities." *Australasian Journal of Philosophy* 64:266–76.

Lamb, James W. 1993. "Evaluative Compatibilism and the Principle of Alternate Possibilities." *Journal of Philosophy* 90:497–516.

Lombard, L. 1982. "Events and the Essentiality of Time." *Canadian Journal of Philosophy* 12:1–17.

McCann, H. 1974. "Volition and Basic Action." *Philosophical Review* 83: 451–73.

Mele, A. 1992a. *Springs of Action.* Oxford: Oxford University Press.

———. 1992b. "Recent Work on Intentional Action." *American Philosophical Quarterly* 29:200–17.

Naylor, M. 1984. "Frankfurt on the Principle of Alternate Possibilities." *Philosophical Studies* 46:249–58.

Plantinga, A. 1974. *The Nature of Necessity.* Oxford: Oxford University Press.

Rowe, W. L. 1991. *Thomas Reid on Freedom and Morality.* Ithaca: Cornell University Press.

Searle J. 1983. *Intentionality.* Cambridge: Cambridge University Press.

Stump, E. 1990. "Intellect, Will and the Principle of Alternate Possibilities." In *Christian Theism and the Problems of Philosophy*, ed. Michael D. Beaty. Notre Dame: University of Notre Dame Press.

Van Inwagen, P. 1978. "Ability and Responsibility." *Philosophical Review* 87: 201–24. Reprinted in Fischer 1987.

———. 1983. *An Essay on Free Will.* Oxford: Oxford University Press.

Widerker, D. 1991. "Frankfurt on 'Ought Implies Can' and Alternate Possibilities." *Analysis* 51:222–24.

———. 1995. "Libertarianism and the Avoidability of Decisions," *Faith and Philosophy* 12: 113–118.

Widerker, D., and Katzoff C. 1993. Review of B. Berofsky, *Freedom from Necessity. Journal of Philosophy* 90:98–104.

Zimmerman, M. 1988. *An Essay on Moral Responsibility.* Totowa, N.J.: Rowman and Littlefield.

14

Rescuing Frankfurt-Style Cases[1]

ALFRED R. MELE AND DAVID ROBB

Almost thirty years ago, in an attempt to undermine what he termed "the principle of alternate possibilities" (*PAP*),

> *PAP* A person is morally responsible for what he has done only if he could have done otherwise (1969, 829),

Harry Frankfurt offered an ingenious thought-experiment.

The thought-experiment: Suppose someone—Black, let us say—wants Jones to perform a certain action. Black is prepared to go to considerable lengths to get his way, but he prefers to avoid showing his hand unnecessarily. So he waits until Jones is about to make up his mind what to do, and he does nothing unless it is clear to him (Black is an excellent judge of such things) that Jones is going to decide to do something *other* than what he wants him to do. If it does become clear that Jones is going to decide to do something else, Black takes effective steps to ensure that Jones decides to do, and that he does do, what he wants him to do. Whatever Jones's initial preferences and inclinations, then, Black will have his way.... [However] Black never has to show his hand because Jones, for reasons of his own, decides to perform and does perform the very action Black wants him to perform. (1969, 835–36)[1]

From *Philosophical Review* 107 (1998). Copyright 1998 Cornell University. Reprinted by permission of the publisher and the authors.

If, as Frankfurt suggests, Jones could not have done otherwise but is morally responsible for deciding and acting as he did, *PAP* is false. This objection to *PAP* has played a major role in subsequent literature on moral responsibility and freedom of choice and action. Most contributors to that literature have deemed the objection successful. Compatibilists have used it in criticizing incompatibilism about moral responsibility and about the kind of freedom that such responsibility requires,[2] and some incompatibilists have attempted to accommodate Frankfurt's moral in refined incompatibilist views.[3] However, several philosophers have argued recently that Frankfurt's example and examples like it—"Frankfurt-style" examples— are fundamentally flawed.[4]

Our aim in this paper is to show that a recent and seemingly devastating way of attacking Frankfurt-style examples fails to undermine this general style of attempted counterexample to *PAP*. We will concentrate on detailed objections raised by Robert Kane and by David Widerker (and indicate in notes how our reply to them defuses other recent objections).

I. Kane and Widerker on Frankfurt-Style Cases

For the sake of specificity, we will suppose that what Jones decided to do in Frankfurt's case was to steal Ann's car and that Jones successfully executed this decision. Bear in mind that for a traditional incompatibilist about determinism and moral responsibility, if Jones was deterministically caused to decide to steal Ann's car, then he is not morally responsible for deciding to do this. So if Frankfurt's case is to persuade a traditional incompatibilist that Jones is morally responsible for deciding to steal Ann's car, it must be a feature of the example that Jones was not deterministically caused so to decide. We assume accordingly that this is a feature of the example.

Robert Kane argues that in a scenario of this sort, "the controller [that is, Black] cannot know" in advance whether Jones will decide on his own to steal the car (1996, 142). After all, what, if anything, Jones decides on his own to do is supposed to be causally undetermined. Now, either Black intervenes or he does not. If Black intervenes and makes Jones decide to steal the car, then (other things being equal) Jones is not morally responsible for so deciding. And, Kane contends, if Black "does not intervene to predetermine the outcome and the indeterminacy remains in place until the choice [or decision] is made—so that the outcome is [a "self-forming willing" (for example, a causally undetermined decision)]—then the agent ... is ultimately responsible for it. But then it is also the case that the agent *could have done otherwise*" (142).[5] He could have done otherwise than decide to steal the car because, for example, given that Black does not intervene, and given that it is causally undetermined whether he will decide to steal the car and causally undetermined as well whether he will decide *not* to steal the car, it is causally open to Jones to make either decision. Thus, Kane contends, "the simple fact of indeterminacy right up to the moment of choice" or decision undermines Frankfurt's challenge to incompatibilists (234 n. 23).

In short, Kane confronts Frankfurt with a dilemma. Either (1) Black intervenes and makes Jones decide to steal the car, in which case (other things being equal) Jones is not morally responsible for deciding to steal the car, or (2) Black does *not* intervene, in which case, given that what Jones decides is causally undetermined, Jones could have done otherwise than decide to steal the car. In either case, *PAP* is not threatened (cf. Kane 1985, 51 n. 25; Wyma 1997).

Kane's argument resembles an argument advanced by David Widerker in a pair of papers (1995a, 1995b).[6] Widerker remarks that "the success of Frankfurt's case against PAP depends crucially upon his ability to convince us of the plausibility of" the following claim:

> IRR: There may be circumstances in which a person performs some action which although they make it impossible for him to avoid performing that action, they in no way bring it about that he performs it. (1995a, 248; cf. Ginet 1996, 409)

A Frankfurt-style case will succeed in falsifying *PAP* only if it includes circumstances of this kind; but, Widerker argues, no Frankfurt-style case includes such circumstances.

Unlike Kane, Widerker pays special attention to the idea that the Frankfurt-style counterfactual controller (Black) uses a *sign* as a basis for deciding whether to intervene (cf. Wyma, 63–67). If Black is to know when to intervene and when not to do so, it seems that he needs to be receptive to some sign of what Jones is, to use Frankfurt's expression (835), "going to decide." So suppose that Black knows that if Jones were to blush at $t1$, that would be a sign that he will do at $t2$ what Black wants him to do at $t2$—for example, decide to steal Ann's car (cf. Widerker 1995a, 249). (Like Kane and Widerker, we regard deciding to A as an action—a mental action.) Suppose further that Jones does blush at $t1$, that Black accordingly does not interfere, and that, at $t2$, Jones decides to steal Ann's car (and later executes that decision). Now, if Jones's blushing at $t1$ deterministically causes his deciding to steal the car, or is in some way associated with something at $t1$ that deterministically causes this act of deciding, the Frankfurt-style case has gone awry, for reasons we identified earlier (cf. Widerker 1995a, 250; Ginet 1996, 408–9). So suppose that there is no such deterministic causation in the scenario. In that case, Widerker contends, "it is hard to see how Jones's decision is unavoidable" (1995a, 251). Perhaps, given that Jones is blushing at *t1*, it is *probable* that he will decide to steal the car (Widerker 1995a, 250). But if what we have here is merely a probability (less than 1), then the following combination is possible: Jones blushes at *t1*, Black accordingly does not intervene, and Jones decides at *t2* not to steal the car (Widerker 1995a, 250–51).[7] Thus, in at least one intelligible sense of 'could have done otherwise', Jones could have done otherwise at *t2* than decide to steal the car, and PAP is not falsified by the case (on this reading of 'could have done otherwise').

In short, Widerker presents Frankfurt with a dilemma. Either (1') the sign Black uses is (associated with) a deterministic cause of Jones's deciding to steal the car, in which case the scenario is not "an *IRR*-situation" or (2') the sign is *not* (associated with) a deterministic cause of Jones's deciding to steal the car, in which case it is possible for Jones to have done otherwise than decide to steal the car (1995a, 251; cf. Wyma, 66–67).

II. Reply

In a more ambitious paper than ours, a variety of replies to the foregoing might be explored. One might attack the second horn of Widerker's and Kane's dilemmas. Perhaps even in the case of a causally undetermined decision, it is possible for some hypothetical being (for example, a god) to know whether an agent will decide on his own at *t* to *A*, or whether the agent would so decide at *t* if the hypothetical being were not to intervene (cf. Fischer 1995). And perhaps it is possible for some such hypothetical being to be an irresistible intervener. Alternatively, one might attack the first horn of Widerker's dilemma. It may be that cases can be described in which a Frankfurt-style counterfactual controller is sensitive to a perfectly reliable deterministic sign and, even so, some incompatibilists would be willing to grant that the agent is morally responsible for his decision (cf. Fischer 1995). Suppose, for example, that on the basis of painstaking, rational reflection, wealthy Smith judges it best to leave all her money to your favorite cause in her will, and that, given that she so judges, it is causally determined that she will decide to do this; but whether she would judge this best was causally undetermined, and if she had not judged this best, Black would have made her decide to do what she actually decided on her own to do.[8]

We have elected not to pursue these lines of reply. Instead, we offer a Frankfurt-style scenario that goes between the horns of both dilemmas. The scenario is immune to Kane's and Widerker's objections to Frankfurt-style cases.

Our scenario features an agent, Bob, who inhabits a world at which determinism is false. This is not to say that no events are deterministically caused at Bob's world. For example, a certain radioactive particle decayed in Bob's town at noon, and that event was not deterministically caused; but the particle had been recruited as a randomizing trigger for a bomb, and once the particle decayed, the bomb was deterministically caused to explode.[9]

At $t1$, Black initiates a certain deterministic process P in Bob's brain with the intention of thereby causing Bob to decide at $t2$ (an hour later, say) to steal Ann's car.[10] The process, which is screened off from Bob's consciousness, will deterministically culminate in Bob's deciding at $t2$ to steal Ann's car unless he decides on his own at $t2$ to steal it or is incapable at $t2$ of making a decision (because, for example, he is dead by $t2$).[11] (Black is unaware that it is open to Bob to decide on his own at $t2$ to steal the car; he is confident that P will cause Bob to decide as he wants Bob to decide.) The process is in no way sensitive to any "sign" of what Bob will decide.[12] As it happens, at $t2$ Bob decides on his own to steal the car, on the basis of his own indeterministic deliberation about whether to steal it, and his decision has no deterministic cause. But if he had not just then decided on his own to steal it, P would have deterministically issued, at $t2$, in his deciding to steal it. Rest assured that P in no way influences the indeterministic decision-making process that actually issues in Bob's decision.

If this scenario is coherent, then, other things being equal (for example, Bob is sane and is not a compulsive car thief), it is plausible that Bob is morally responsible for deciding to steal the car. After all, he decided on his own to do this, with no interference from P. And, assuming coherence, this is plausible even though, at $t2$, Bob could not have done otherwise than decide to steal Ann's car. Given the details of the case, any future open to Bob after the initiation of P in which he is capable at $t2$ of making a decision includes his deciding at $t2$ to steal the car. If, in this case, Bob is morally responsible for deciding to steal Ann's car, PAP is false.

The coherence of our scenario may, however, be called into question. How, one might wonder, can it happen that Bob decides on his own at $t2$ to steal Ann's car, given the presence of the deterministic process we mentioned? One can understand how, *prior to $t2$,* Bob might decide on his own to steal the car. (Notice that in that case, other things being equal, Bob could have decided otherwise at this earlier time, given that what he does then is causally undetermined (cf. Ginet 1996).) But how can it happen that Bob decides on his own at $t2$ to steal the car, and that P does not produce the decision, given what we said about P?

Consideration of the following fanciful machine will prove useful in answering this question. The machine, designed by a specialist in machine art, produces artistic widgets of different shapes and colors. The colors of the widgets produced are determined by the color of a ball bearing (bb) that hits the machine's receptor at a relevant time. The machine, M, is surrounded by several automatic bb guns, each containing bbs of various colors. The relevant aspect of M's mechanical design, for our purposes, is relatively simple. First, with one qualification, if a bb of color x hits M's receptor, and M is not already in the process of making a widget, M at once starts a process designed to result in the production of an x-colored widget. Second, because two or more bbs sometimes hit the receptor simultaneously, the artist has designed his machine in such a way that whenever this happens (while M is not busy making a widget) M at once starts a process designed to result in the production of a widget the color of the right-most bb. No other striking of M's receptor at the same time plays a role in triggering M.[13]

Bob is analogous to M in an important respect. He is physically and psychologically so constituted that if an unconscious deterministic process in his brain and an indeterministic decision-making process of his were to "coincide" at the moment of decision, he would indeterministically decide on his own and the deterministic process would have no effect on his decision. This situation is an analogue of a case in which two bbs of the *same color* simultaneously hit M's receptor (while M is not busy making a widget). Just as a blue bb's hitting the left side of the receptor at t, in a case in which another blue bb hits the receptor's right side at t, does not cause M's starting a process designed to result in the production of a blue widget, P does not cause Bob's decision to steal Ann's car.[14] Instead, Bob's indeterministic deliberative process about whether to steal the car issues in his deciding to steal it, just as the striking of the right-most bb issues in M's starting the widget-making process.

Cautious readers will wonder what would happen at $t2$ if P and Bob's indeterministic deliberative process—"process x"—were to "diverge" at $t2$. The issue may be pictured, fancifully, as follows.[15] Two different "decision nodes" in Bob's brain are directly relevant. The "lighting up" of node $N1$ represents his deciding to steal the car, and the "lighting up" of node $N2$ represents his deciding *not* to steal the car. Under normal circumstances and in the absence of preemption, a process's "hitting" a decision node in Bob "lights up" that node. If it were to be the case both that P hits $N1$ at $t2$ and that x does not hit $N1$ at $t2$, then P would light up $N1$. If both processes were to hit $N1$ at $t2$, Bob's indeterministic deliberative process, x, would light up $N1$ and P would not. The present question is this. What would happen if, at $t2$, P were to hit $N1$ and x were to hit $N2$? That is, what would happen if the two processes were to "diverge" in this way? And *why*?

We extend Bob's story as follows. Although if both processes were to hit $N1$ at $t2$, Bob's indeterministic deliberative process, x, would preempt P and light up $N1$, it is also the case that if, at $t2$, P were to hit $N1$ and x were to hit $N2$, P would prevail. In the latter case, P would light up $N1$ and the indeterministic process would not light up $N2$. Of course, readers would like a story about why it is that although x would preempt P in the former situation, P would prevail over x in the latter. Here is one story. By $t2$, P has "neutralized" $N2$ (but without affecting what goes on in x). That is why, if x were to hit $N2$ at $t2$, $N2$ would not light up.[16] More fully, by $t2$ P has neutralized all of the nodes in Bob for decisions that are contrary to a decision at $t2$ to steal Ann's car (for example, a decision at $t2$ not to steal anyone's car and a decision at $t2$ never to steal anything).[17] In convenient shorthand, by $t2$ P has neutralized $N2$ and all its "cognate decision nodes." Bear in mind that all we need is a conceptually possible scenario, and this certainly looks like one.

The following statements (among others) are true by hypothesis in our case.

(1)   Any future open to Bob after the initiation of P in which he is capable at $t2$ of making a decision—any future of "kind F"— includes his deciding at $t2$ to steal the car.

(2)   In any future of kind F, if "an indeterministic decision-making process of Bob's"—a process of "kind X"—does not issue in Bob's deciding at $t2$ to steal the car, then P deterministically is sues in his deciding at $t2$ to steal it.

(3)   In any future of kind F, if a process of kind X issues in Bob's deciding at $t2$ to steal the car, P does not issue in this.

(4)   A process of kind X does issue in Bob's deciding at $t2$ to steal the car, and P does not.

This collection of statements is both internally consistent and consistent with the other details of the case.

Review Bob's indeterministic process of deliberation about whether to steal the car (process x). It is causally undetermined whether x will issue in Bob's deciding at $t2$ to steal the car, and, indeed, whether it will issue in any decision at all. Although P does not in any way affect what happens *in x*, P has neutralized $N2$ and all its cognate nodes, thereby making it psychologically impossible for any indeterministic process in Bob to issue in any competing decision at all. It is possible that Bob's indeterministic process, x, will indeterministically issue in his deciding at $t2$ to steal the car, without P in any way contributing to this, and it is possible that P will issue in his deciding at $t2$ to steal the car (which will happen if Bob does not indeterministically decide on his own at $t2$ to steal it). But, given P's neutralizing effects, it is not possible that x or any other indeterministic process in Bob will issue in his making a decision at $t2$ that is incompatible with his deciding at $t2$ to steal the car. This is so even though P does not influence what happens in x itself. Furthermore, Bob has all along been psychologically so constituted that x would preempt P were x to hit $N1$ (the node for deciding to steal the car) at *t2*. Bob's psychological constitution is an analogue of machine *M* in that connection.

One might object that given a nomic subsumption model of causality (*NSM*), if Bob's deciding at *t2* to steal Ann's car is entailed by a correct description of some state of the world prior to *t2* and the laws of nature, that suffices for Bob's decision's being deterministically caused, appearances to the contrary notwithstanding.[18] If Bob's decision to steal the car is deterministically caused, we face a criticism that Kane and Widerker leveled against Frankfurt's own scenarios. Now, our imagined opponent may have either of two views of *NSM* in mind. We consider them in turn. (1) If *NSM* asserts that whenever *a* causes *b*, there is a law subsuming them, then the subsumption model does not entail that *P* (the deterministic process initiated by Black) or anything else caused—deterministically or otherwise—Bob's decision. Moreover, it is compatible with this version of *NSM* that *x*, Bob's indeterministic decision-making process, indeterministically caused the decision, since *x* and Bob's decision may be subsumed by a probabilistic law. (2) If *NSM* asserts that whenever there is a law subsuming *a* and *b*, *a* causes *b*, then this might seem worrisome, especially if, according to the law, *a* makes *b* inevitable. Notice that this version of *NSM* is plausible only if 'law' here means 'causal law', and a causal law that is to be problematic for us cannot be of the form "Events of *a*'s type cause events of *b*'s type unless the former are preempted." However, the law subsuming *P* and Bob's decision is in fact a law to the effect that processes of *P*'s type will deterministically cause decisions of the pertinent type unless the former are preempted, and this law does not entail that *P* or anything else deterministically caused the decision.[19]

Perhaps the intended objection is not that *P* deterministically caused the decision, but just that the decision was *determined*. If 'determined' means 'inevitable', that is fine with us. After all, the primary thrust of Frankfurt's own case is that the agent is morally responsible for his *A*-ing even though his *A*-ing is inevitable, and the point of our example is that Bob is morally responsible for deciding (at *t2*) to steal the car even though he could not have done otherwise (then) than decide to steal it.[20] However, if 'determined' means 'deterministically caused', we are entitled to ask *what* deterministically caused the decision. It was not *P*. So was it the conjunction (the mereological sum) of *P* and *x*, or of *P*, *x*, and various other things? Even supposing that a gerrymandered entity like this can be an appropriate candidate for a cause, it is difficult to see how it can have deterministically caused Bob's decision, given that *P* did *not* cause the decision and that *x* caused it only indeterministically.

Consider matters from an intuitively appealing perspective (cf. Fischer 1982, 33).[21] Subtract Black and *P* from our scenario and imagine that what happens at Bob's indeterministic world is that *x*, Bob's indeterministic decision-making process, indeterministically issues at *t2*—in some way favored by libertarians—in his deciding to steal the car. Plainly, there is no deterministic cause of Bob's decision in this case. Now add Black and *P* to the scenario in just the way we have done. At *t2*, process *x* issues in the same indeterministic way in Bob's decision: by hypothesis, Black and *P* do not influence *x*. Although at *t2* Bob cannot do otherwise than decide then to steal the car, nothing warrants the claim that his decision is deterministically caused.

Bob's case is coherent, and it apparently falsifies *PAP*. Again, other things being equal, Bob certainly seems to be morally responsible for deciding to steal Ann's car, for he decided on his own to steal it. Even so, he could not have done otherwise than decide to steal it, and he could not have done otherwise *at t2* than decide to steal it.[22] And notice that the case is what Widerker calls an "*IRR*-situation": there are "circumstances in which" Bob decides to steal Ann's car that "make it impossible for him to avoid" deciding to do this but "in no way bring it about that" he decides to do this (1995a, 248). Although process *P* makes it impossible for Bob to avoid deciding to steal Ann's car, *P* in no way brings it about that he decides to do this. Instead, Bob indeterministically decides on his own at *t2* to steal the car.

There are ways to resist our conclusion. For example, one can argue that although Bob is morally responsible for deciding *on his own* to steal the car, he is not morally responsible for deciding to steal it (Naylor 1984). (Even though Bob could not have done otherwise than decide to steal the car, he could have done otherwise than decide on his own to steal it: he could have decided to steal it because *P* made him decide this.) Alternatively, one can contend that for the proponent of *PAP*, 'he could have done otherwise' in that principle simply means 'he was not causally determined to do what he did', in which case the proponent can consistently grant that Bob is morally responsible for deciding to steal the car (Heinaman 1986, 275–76). These lines of response to Frankfurt-style scenarios have been in circulation for some time; an adequate rebuttal of them would require a paper of its own and would duplicate the efforts of others.[23] Our concern is with the more recent and potentially more damaging criticisms of Frankfurt-style scenarios by Widerker and Kane.[24] Our little story about Bob undermines those criticisms.[25]

III. A Historical Version of *PAP*

Some incompatibilists favor a historical version of *PAP* along the following lines:

PAPh: *S* is morally responsible for what he did at *t* only if (1) he could have done otherwise at *t* or (2) even though he could not have done otherwise at *t*, the psychological character on the basis of which he acted at *t* is itself partially a product of an earlier action (or actions) of his performed at a time when he could have done otherwise.[26]

If our case falsifies *PAP*, an expanded version of the case falsifies *PAPh*. What we have in mind now is what one of us elsewhere termed a *global* Frankfurt-style case—a case in which at any relevant earlier time the agent acts "on his own" but could not have done otherwise, owing to a circumstance of the sort mentioned in *IRR*.[27]

Imagine, for example, that in *any* case in which Bob makes a decision—a decision to *A*, say—a deterministic process like *P* was under way that would have resulted in his deciding to *A* if he had not indeterministically decided on his own to *A*, and imagine that the same thing is true also of all of Bob's actions that are not decisions. This global fact about Bob is quite remarkable, but it is a coincidence nonetheless. Given this fact, Bob could never have done otherwise than he did. But since he did everything on his own, the deterministic processes always having been preempted, we see no good reason to hold that the presence of those deterministic processes deprives him of moral responsibility.

It should be emphasized that we ourselves are not inclined to use our new Frankfurt-style case in either its local or its global incarnation as part of an argument for compatibilism.[28] After all, there is a significant difference between our scenarios and scenarios set in deterministic worlds: in ours, as is supposed to be the case in standard Frankfurt-style scenarios in general, the agent's decisions lack deterministic causes. In principle, a libertarian's incompatibilism might be motivated, not by the thought that determinism precludes our ever having been able to do otherwise than we did, but instead by the thought that in a deterministic world our actions (including our decisions) are ultimately causally ensured *consequences* of the laws of nature and states that obtained long before we were born.[29] Indeed, one of the responses to Frankfurt-style scenarios that we mentioned in passing—the response that in *PAP*, 'he could have done otherwise' simply means 'he was not causally determined to do what he did'—suggests that the latter thought might be the real worry for some incompatibilists.

Those who took arguments of the sort offered by Widerker and Kane to show that incompatibilists can safely dismiss all Frankfurt-style cases should start worrying again. In rescuing the Frankfurt-style scenario, we are not directly attacking incompatibilism. However, we note that it is incumbent upon libertarians and other incompatibilists to explain what about determinism is incompatible with moral responsibility (and the freedom required for such responsibility), if not that determinism is inconsistent with our having been able to do otherwise than we did.[30]

Notes

1. In reproducing this passage, we deleted a subscript after 'Jones'.
2. See, for example, Fischer 1994, chap. 7.
3. In this connection, Widerker (1995b, 113) cites Stump 1990, Stump and Kretzmann 1991, and Zagzebski 1991. He also cites a suggestion made in Fischer 1982. (Fischer is not a libertarian.)
4. See Lamb 1993; Widerker 1995a and 1995b; Kane 1996, 142–43, 191–92; Ginet 1996; Wyma 1997.
5. For a list of various kinds of "self-forming willing," see Kane 1996, 125.
6. Kane comments on Widerker's argument in his 1996 (233 n. 22).
7. Widerker seems to suggest (1995a, 251) that Lamb 1993 advances an argument of this kind. We understand Lamb differently, and one of us has replied to Lamb's argument elsewhere (Mele 1995, 101, 141–42). But if Widerker is right about Lamb, our reply to Widerker and Kane is a reply to Lamb as well. (For a detailed reply to Lamb, see Fischer and Hoffman 1994.)
8. One of us has argued elsewhere (Mele 1995, chap. 12) that a libertarian may adopt a compatibilist conception of an action-generating process that takes an agent from a deliberative judgment about what it is best to do through a corresponding intention or decision to a corresponding action and try to locate "a theoretically useful place" (212) for indeterminism in processes leading to such a judgment.
9. Even if no events are deterministically caused in the actual world, this little scenario is conceptually possible. Our concern here is with a conceptually possible agent, since *PAP* is supposed to be a conceptual truth.
10. We might just as easily have imagined that P is initiated by a freak neurochemical occurrence that no agent had a role in producing. Frankfurt himself notes that there is no need for "a human manipulator," or even a mechanical one; "natural forces involving no will or design at all" might do the trick (1969, n. 4).
11. If Bob were to decide on his own prior to $t2$ to steal the car, P would cause him to decide again at $t2$ to do this—unless, of course, at $t2$, Bob were on his own to decide again to steal the car. Notice that even in a short span of time, there are some relatively normal ways in which it might happen that a person decides twice to A. Forgetful Fred might decide at noon to call his son at 6:00, and a few minutes later, having forgotten about this, he might again decide to call his son at 6:00—or, having decided to call his daughter today to wish her a happy birthday, he might call her with birthday greetings, and then, forgetting that he called her, he might again decide to call her today to wish her a happy birthday. Cowardly Cal, having decided at noon to call for a dental appointment by the end of the business day, and having changed his mind at 12:01, might decide again at 12:02 to do this. We should mention that Ann's car is too far away for Bob to steal it by $t2$. But even if it were closer and he stole it before $t2$, he would decide at $t2$ to steal it—evidently having forgotten that he already stole it. Given the way P works, if it were to issue at $t2$ in Bob's deciding to steal Ann's car, it would erase any memories that are incompatible with its so issuing. (For stylistic reasons, we assume in this note that Bob is not dead or otherwise decisionally incapacitated at $t2$.)

12. It will become evident that a counterfactual controller's having a prior sign (Widerker) or prior knowledge (Kane) of what the agent will do is an inessential feature of Frankfurt-style cases, despite the details of Frankfurt's own case, as quoted earlier. (David Hunt independently notices this in Hunt 2000.)

13. In the interest of simplicity, we suppressed reference to another feature of the device. The rectangular receptor is too small for two bbs simultaneously to tie for the right-most position.

14. Of course, the left-most bb's striking (idle) M's receptor would have caused M's starting a process for the making of a blue widget, if no bb had simultaneously struck the receptor to that bb's right, just as P would have caused Bob to decide at $t2$ to steal the car, if Bob had not decided on his own at $t2$ to steal it. (For a general defense of the possibility of direct or "occurrent" preemption, see Ehring 1997, 47–49.)

15. The picture obviously is neuro-fictional, but it is useful nonetheless.

16. What would happen if Bob's indeterministic deliberative process were to hit $N2$ at some time tn prior to $t2$? In one version of the story, $N2$ would light up at tn—Bob would decide at tn not to steal the car—but then at $t2$, when P hits $N1$, Bob would change his mind and decide to steal it. In another version—the one we prefer, owing to its relative simplicity—P neutralizes $N2$ as soon as Black initiates P.

17. David Hunt independently makes a similar suggestion in a forthcoming article (Hunt n.d.).

18. Fischer considers an objection of this kind to standard Frankfurt-style cases (1982, 35–37). Several readers of an earlier draft urged us to address it.

19. It may be claimed that there are no "unless preempted" laws of this kind. But this requires an argument that goes well beyond a mere appeal to NSM.

20. Strictly speaking, there is no assurance that Bob's deciding at $t2$ to steal the car is *inevitable* in our scenario. It is consistent with the background details of the scenario, for example, that Bob dies just as he is about to decide to steal the car, owing to a causally undetermined lightning strike. As we put it earlier, "Given the details of the case, any future open to Bob … *in which he is capable at t2 of making a decision* includes his deciding at $t2$ to steal the car" (emphasis added). However, we deemed it best to meet head on the objection introduced in the preceding paragraph.

21. John Fischer commended this perspective to us in correspondence.

22. Again, this is consistent with its being the case that something else could have *happened* than that Bob decided to steal the car. For example, Bob might have died before $t2$.

23. For a careful critical discussion of various incompatibilist responses to Frankfurt-style cases, see Fischer 1994, chap. 7.

24. Naylor's and Heinaman's responses each make a significant concession to the Frankfurt-style argument. Naylor concedes that the agent could not have done otherwise than A. To be sure, she contends that the agent is not morally responsible for A-ing, but rather for A-ing on his own (cf. van Inwagen 1983, 181). However, that contention has been deemed an instance of biting an intolerably hard bullet even by a libertarian (Kane 1996, 41–42; see Ginet 1996, 407 for another criticism).

Heinaman concedes that the agent could not have done otherwise in the sense that he did not have open to him at the time the possibility of acting otherwise. (We have a bit more to say about his response later.) The arguments by Widerker and Kane that we have sketched make no concessions to the Frankfurt-style argument.

25. It also avoids Wyma's and Ginet's criticisms. Wyma's complaint about Frankfurt-style cases (1997, 63–67) is essentially Widerker's. Ginet contends that if an agent S cannot do otherwise than A by a time t^* in a Frankfurt-style case, then S is not morally responsible for his A-ing *by* t^*, and he argues that, even so, S may be morally responsible for A-ing at the earlier time, t, at which he in fact A-ed—a time at which S was able to do otherwise than A then (1996, 406–7). If Ginet is right, *PAP* survives the case he imagines. On his view, what S is morally responsible for, if anything, is a state of affairs that he could have avoided: namely, its being the case that he A-s at t. However, in our scenario, at $t2$, the very time at which Bob decides to steal Ann's car, he cannot do otherwise than decide to steal it, and, even so, it is plausible, for reasons that we have set out, that he is morally responsible for the decision he made at $t2$ and for his so deciding at that time.

26. Kane advances a view of this kind (1996, 39–43). Mele, who is not a libertarian, has suggested that libertarians should prefer a historical principle of this kind to *PAP* (1995, 208–9).

27. See Mele 1996, 129. Cf. Fischer 1994, 214; Mele 1995, 141; Haji 1996, 707; Kane 1996, 42–43, 143; Wyma 1997, 67.

28. Mele is officially agnostic about the main metaphysical issue that separates compatibilists from incompatibilists (1995).

29. The latter thought is featured in the incompatibilist "consequence argument." For a short version of the argument, see van Inwagen 1983, 16. For detailed versions, see, for example, Ginet 1990, chap. 5 and van Inwagen, chap. 3.

30. For a relevant suggestion, see Mele 1996. For discussion or comments, we are grateful to Laura Ekstrom, John Fischer, Carl Ginet, Bob Kane, Hugh McCann, and Tim O'Connor.

References

Ehring, Douglas. 1997. *Causation and Persistence.* Oxford: Oxford University Press.

Fischer, John. 1982. "Responsibility and Control." *Journal of Philosophy* 79: 24–40.

———. 1994. *The Metaphysics of Free Will.* Oxford: Blackwell.

———. 1995. "Libertarianism and Avoidability: A Reply to Widerker." *Faith and Philosophy* 12:119–25.

Fischer, John, and Paul Hoffman. 1994. "Alternative Possibilities: A Reply to Lamb." *Journal of Philosophy* 91:321–26.

Frankfurt, Harry. 1969. "Alternate Possibilities and Moral Responsibility." *Journal of Philosophy* 66:829–39.

Ginet, Carl. 1990. *On Action.* Cambridge: Cambridge University Press.

———. 1996. "In Defense of the Principle of Alternative Possibilities: Why I Don't Find Frankfurt's Argument Convincing." *Philosophical Perspectives* 10:403–17.

Haji, Ishtiyaque. 1996. "Moral Responsibility and the Problem of Induced Pro-Attitudes." *Dialogue* 35:703–20.

Heinaman, Robert. 1986. "Incompatibilism Without the Principle of Alternative Possibilities." *Australasian Journal of Philosophy* 64:266–76.

Hunt, David. 2000. "Moral Responsibility and Unavoidable Action." *Philosophical Studies* 97: 195–227.

Kane, Robert. 1985. *Free Will and Values*. Albany: State University of New York Press.

———. 1996. *The Significance of Free Will*. New York: Oxford University Press.

Lamb, James. 1993. "Evaluative Compatibilism and the Principle of Alternate Possibilities." *Journal of Philosophy* 90:517–27.

Mele, Alfred. 1995. *Autonomous Agents*. New York: Oxford University Press.

———. 1996. "Soft Libertarianism and Frankfurt-Style Scenarios." *Philosophical Topics* 24:123–41.

Naylor, Margery. 1984. "Frankfurt on the Principle of Alternate Possibilities." *Philosophical Studies* 46:249–58.

Stump, Eleonore. 1990. "Intellect, Will and the Principle of Alternate Possibilities." In *Christian Theism and the Problems of Philosophy*, ed. Michael Beaty, 254–85. Notre Dame: University of Notre Dame Press.

Stump, Eleonore, and Norman Kretzmann. 1991. "Prophecy, Past Truth, and Eternity." *Philosophical Perspectives* 5:395–424.

Van Inwagen, Peter. 1983. *An Essay on Free Will*. Oxford: Oxford University Press, Clarendon Press.

Widerker, David. 1995a. "Libertarianism and Frankfurt's Attack on the Principle of Alternative Possibilities." *Philosophical Review* 104:247–61.

———. 1995b. "Libertarian Freedom and the Avoidability of Decisions." *Faith and Philosophy* 12:113–18.

Wyma, Keith. 1997. "Moral Responsibility and Leeway for Action." *American Philosophical Quarterly* 34:57–70.

Zagzebski, Linda. 1991. *The Dilemma of Freedom and Foreknowledge*. Oxford: Oxford University Press.

Selected Bibliography

Books

Bok, Hilary. 1998. *Freedom and Responsibility*. Princeton: Princeton University Press.

Dennett, Daniel. 1984. *Elbow Room: The Varieties of Free Will Worth Wanting*. Cambridge, MA: M.I.T. Press.

Ekstrom, Laura Waddell. 2000. *Free Will: A Philosophical Study*. Boulder, CO: Westview Press Focus Series in Philosophy.

Fischer, John Martin. 1994. *The Metaphysics of Free Will: An Essay on Control*. Aristotelian Society Series, vol. 14. Cambridge, MA: Blackwell.

Fischer, John Martin and Ravizza, Mark. 1998. *Responsibility and Control*. Cambridge: Cambridge University Press.

Kane, Robert. 1996a. *The Significance of Free Will*. New York: Oxford University Press.

van Inwagen, Peter. 1983. *An Essay on Free Will*. Oxford: Oxford University Press.

Wolf, Susan. 1990. *Freedom Within Reason*. New York: Oxford University Press.

Anthologies

Fischer, John Martin and Ravizza, Mark, eds. 1993. *Perspectives on Moral Responsibility*. Ithaca: Cornell University Press.

O'Connor, Timothy, ed. 1995. *Agents, Causes, and Events*. New York: Oxford University Press.

Schoeman, Ferdinand, ed. 1987. *Responsibility, Character, and the Emotions: New Essays in Moral Psychology*. Cambridge: Cambridge University Press.

Watson, Gary, ed. 1982. *Free Will*. Oxford: Oxford University Press.

Articles

Austin, J. L. 1961. "Ifs and Cans," in *Philosophical Papers*. Oxford: Oxford University Press.

Alfred Ayer. 1954. "Freedom and Necessity," in *Philosophical Essays*. London: Macmillan. Reprinted in Watson, ed. 1982.

Clarke, Randolph. 1993. "Toward a Credible Agent-causal Account of Free Will," *Noûs* 27, pp. 191–203.

Davidson, Donald. 1980. "Freedom to Act," in *Essays on Actions and Events*. New York: Oxford University Press.

Dennett, Daniel. 1978. "On Giving Libertarians What They Say They Want," in *Brainstorms*. Cambridge, MA: M.I.T. Press, Bradford Books, pp. 286–99.

Dupre, John. 1996. "The Solution to the Problem of Free Will," in ed. James Tomberlin, *Philosophical Perspectives* 10, pp. 385–402.

Ekstrom, Laura Waddell. 1998. "Protecting Incompatibilist Freedom," *American Philosophical Quarterly* 35, pp. 281–291.

_____. 1998. "Freedom, Causation, and the Consequence Argument," *Synthese* 115, pp. 333–354.

_____. 1993. "A Coherence Theory of Autonomy," *Philosophy and Phenomenological Research* 53, pp. 599–616.

John Martin Fischer. 1983. "Incompatibilism," *Philosophical Studies* 43, pp. 127–137.

_____. 1982. "Responsibility and Control," *Journal of Philosophy* 79, pp. 24–40.

Frankfurt, Harry. 1992. "The Faintest Passion," *Proceedings and Addresses of the American Philosophical Association* 66, pp. 5–16.

_____. 1987. "Identification and Wholeheartedness," in Ferdinand Schoeman, ed; reprinted in Frankfurt, *The Importance of What We Care About*. Cambridge: Cambridge University Press, 1987, pp. 159–76.

_____. 1977. "Identification and Externality," in *The Identities of Persons*, ed. Amelie Rorty. Berkeley: University of California Press.

_____. 1969. "Alternate Possibilities and Moral Responsibility," *Journal of Philosophy* 66, pp. 829–839.

Ginet, Carl. 1996. "In Defense of the Principle of Alternative Possibilities: Why I Don't Find Frankfurt's Argument Convincing," in James Tomberlin, ed., *Philosophical Perspectives* 10. Cambridge: Blackwell.

Goetz, Stewart. 1997. "Libertarian Choice," *Faith and Philosophy* 14, pp. 195–211.

Heineman, Robert. 1986. "Incompatibilism Without the Principle of Alternate Possibilities," *Australasian Journal of Philosophy* 64, pp. 266–76.

Hobart, R. E. 1943. "Free-Will as Involving Determination and Inconceivable Without It," *Mind* 43, pp. 1–27.

Kane, Robert. 1996b. "Freedom, Responsibility, and Will-Setting," *Philosophical Topics* 24, pp. 67–90.

Lehrer, Keith. 1980. "Preferences, Conditionals and Freedom," in ed. Peter van Inwagen, *Time and Cause*. Dordrecht: D. Reidel, pp. 187–201.

_____. 1968. "Cans Without Ifs," *Analysis* 29, pp. 29–32.

McIntyre, Alison. 1994. "Compatibilists Could Have Done Otherwise: Responsibility and Negative Agency," *The Philosophical Review* 103, pp. 453–488.

McKay, Thomas and Johnson, David. 1996. "A Reconsideration of an Argument against Compatibilism," *Philosophical Topics* 24, pp. 113–122.

Mele, Alfred. 1996. "Soft Libertarianism and Frankfurt-Style Scenarios," *Philosophical Topics* 24, pp. 123–141.

Nagel, Thomas. 1982. "Moral Luck," in Watson, ed.

O'Connor, Timothy.1996. "Why Agent Causation?" *Philosophical Topics* 24, pp. 143–158.

_____. 1993. "Indeterminism and Free Agency: Three Recent Views," *Philosophy and Phenomenological Research* 53, pp. 499–526.

Piper, Adrian. 1985. "Two Conceptions of the Self," *Philosophical Studies* 48, pp. 173–197.

Shatz, David. 1986. "Free Will and the Structure of Motivation," *Midwest Studies in Philosophy* 10, pp. 451–82.

Slote, Michael. 1982. "Selective Necessity and the Free-Will Problem," *Journal of Philosophy* 79, pp. 5–24.

_____. 1980. "Understanding Free Will," *Journal of Philosophy* 77, pp. 136–51.

Stump, Eleonore. 1996. "Persons: Identification and Freedom," *Philosophical Topics* 24, pp. 183–214.

_____. 1990. "Intellect, Will, and Alternate Possibilities," in *Christian Theism and the Problems of Philosophy*, ed. Michael D. Beaty. Notre Dame, IN: University of Notre Dame Press, pp. 254–85.

_____. 1988. "Sanctification, Hardening of the Heart, and Frankfurt's Concept of Free Will," *Journal of Philosophy* 85, pp. 395–412.

van Inwagen, Peter. 1980. "The Incompatibility of Responsibility and Determinism," *Bowling Green Studies in Applied Philosophy* 2, pp. 30–7.

_____. 1978. "Ability and Responsibility," *The Philosophical Review* 87, pp. 201–224.

Warfield, Ted and Finch, Alicia. 1998. "The *Mind* Argument and Libertarianism," *Mind* 107, pp. 516–528.

Watson, Gary. 1987. "Free Action and Free Will," *Mind* 46, pp. 145–172.

Wiggins, David. 1973. "Towards a Reasonable Libertarianism," *in Essays on Freedom of Action*, ed. Ted Honderich. London: Routledge and Kegan Paul, pp. 31–62.

Wolf, Susan. 1987. "Sanity and the Metaphysics of Responsibility," in Schoeman ed., pp. 46–62.

_____. 1981. "The Importance of Free Will," *Mind* 90, pp. 386–405. Reprinted in Fischer and Ravizza. eds., 1993.

_____. 1980. "Asymmetrical Freedom," *Journal of Philosophy* 77, pp. 151–166.

Contributors

ELIZABETH ANSCOMBE is Professor of Philosophy at the University of Cambridge.

MICHAEL E. BRATMAN is Howard H. and Jessie T. Watkins University Professor of Philosophy at Stanford University.

RODERICK M. CHISHOLM was Professor of Philosophy and Andrew W. Mellon Professor of Humanities at Brown University.

LAURA WADDELL EKSTROM is Associate Professor of Philosophy at The College of William and Mary.

JOHN MARTIN FISCHER is Professor of Philosophy at the University of California, Riverside.

HARRY FRANKFURT is Professor of Philosophy at Princeton University.

ROBERT KANE is University Teaching Professor of Philosophy at the University of Texas, Austin.

DAVID LEWIS is Professor of Philosophy at Princeton University.

ALFRED R. MELE is Professor of Philosophy at Florida State University.

DAVID ROBB is Assistant Professor of Philosophy at Davidson College.

SIR PETER STRAWSON is Professor Emeritus at the University of Oxford.

PETER VAN INWAGEN is John Cardinal O'Hara Professor of Philosophy at the University of Notre Dame.

GARY WATSON is Professor of Philosophy at the University of California, Riverside.

DAVID WIDERKER is Professor of Jewish and General Philosophy at Bar Ilan University.

SUSAN WOLF is Duane Peterson Professor of Ethics at The Johns Hopkins University.

Index